i

THE CURE FOR BURNOUT

THE
CURE FOR
BURNOUT

How to
Find Balance
and Reclaim Your Life

EMILY BALLESTEROS

THE DIAL PRESS

NEW YORK

Published in the United States by The Dial Press, an imprint of Random House,
a division of Penguin Random House LLC, New York.

THE DIAL PRESS is a registered trademark and the colophon is a trademark
of Penguin Random House LLC.

LIBRARY OF CONGRESS CATALOGING-IN-PUBLICATION DATA
Names: Ballesteros, Emily, author.
Title: The cure for burnout : how to find balance and reclaim your life / Emily Ballesteros.
Description: First edition. | New York : Dial Press, [2024]
Identifiers: LCCN 2023035847 (print) | LCCN 2023035848 (ebook) |
ISBN 9780593596319 (hardcover) | ISBN 9780593596326 (ebook)
Subjects: LCSH: Burn out (Psychology) | Work-life balance. | Quality of life.
Classification: LCC BF482 .B35 2024 (print) | LCC BF482 (ebook) |
DDC 158.7/23—dc23/eng/20231129
LC record available at https://lccn.loc.gov/2023035847
LC ebook record available at https://lccn.loc.gov/2023035848

Printed in the United States of America on acid-free paper

randomhousebooks.com

2 4 6 8 9 7 5 3 1

First Edition

For my parents,

who met every unconventional turn in my career
with unwavering support.

CONTENTS

The Breakdown Before the Breakthrough

On a negative twenty-degree day, in the Top Ramen aisle of a downtown Chicago Walgreens, I finally swallowed my pride and called my parents. With silent tears and snot running into my scarf, I told them that I couldn't do it anymore. For two years, my life felt like a never-ending to-do list. From dawn until dusk, I sprinted from responsibility to responsibility, never feeling like I was doing enough. (You know things are bad when you start looking *forward* to your debilitating migraines. Waking up with strobing vision and the sensation that someone was stabbing me in the eye gave me an alarming sense of relief—at least while I was lying on my cold bathroom floor trying not to throw up from the pain, I would get a short break from my all-consuming schedule.) Sobbing in a drugstore, getting the side-eye from other Chicagoans just trying to grab some snacks in peace, was a personal low. I was in a very bad place. I wanted to quit my job, drop out of grad school, leave the frozen hellscape known as the Midwest, and just . . . "disappear." "Just for a little while," I told my parents.

RED FLAGS. RED FLAGS EVERYWHERE.

In case you don't know, saying you want to "disappear" is a major red flag.

I had been running on fumes for two years. How could I be so early in my career and so incredibly worn out? Certainly, these were not the fun, freedom-filled twenties everyone raved about. Each morning, when my alarm sounded at six A.M., the first thing I'd feel was a heavy dread in my chest, quickly followed by racing thoughts about everything I needed to do that day. I would peel myself out of bed, throw on one of my wrinkled work outfits, and walk a mile through Chicago's often-freezing temperatures to the train. Eyes vacant, zombie-like, with a giant pit in my stomach, I'd put one frozen foot in front of the other.

I would spend my hour-and-a-half commute to work each day catching up on reading for my graduate program and smearing makeup on the bags under my eyes. Professionally, I conducted myself like your run-of-the-mill people-pleaser: with complete disregard for my own limits. I didn't believe I had the authority to set boundaries, so I'd say yes to every request that came my way, regardless of who was asking and what they were asking for. I would find myself in meetings at all hours of the day, on committees I didn't even know our company had, taking on tasks nobody else wanted, all to demonstrate that I was reliable at any cost. I wanted to prove myself, advance in my career as fast as possible, and, perhaps most important—I wanted everyone to *like* me. As a result, I prioritized performance over everything else—my health, my relationships, my personal life and interests. And I was one hell of a performer, but it came at a price.

At the end of my reverse commute back to the city each night, I would *sprint* (in snow boots—not recommended) to my 6 P.M. class. With shin splints, bone-deep exhaustion, and disbelief that the day wasn't over yet, I would use my last two brain cells to take notes. After class, I'd make the mile walk home, eat a Top Ramen, do my homework, doomscroll on my phone, and fall into a fitful sleep already anxious about what awaited me in the morning.

Ideally, Saturday and Sunday would have been my time to rest. But instead of recuperating, each weekend I let my guilt (and other people's demands) take the wheel. Friends with good intentions and bad timing invited me to social gatherings across town. I didn't know how to say no without feeling like I was letting them down, so I said yes and just hoped I'd find another time to rest. (Spoiler alert: I usually didn't.) As much as I valued my friendships, *any* invitation felt like a burden, simply because I was desperate to be at home catching up on sleep instead. Forget going to the gym, enjoying my youth, or reading for pleasure; I was just grateful if I made it through the week. For years, regardless of whether it was a good day or a bad day, it was a *busy* day.

Contrary, though, to this dread that I felt in my day-to-day life, from the outside it appeared that I was doing pretty well for myself. I had a job in my field of interest (corporate training and development) and was earning my master's degree in industrial-organizational psychology. In the name of achievement, I had stuffed my schedule to the brim, and it had awarded me a life that looked great on paper. I felt like a duck: calm on the surface and paddling my feet like hell underwater to stay afloat. But the thing I've come to understand is: **It doesn't matter what your life *looks* like; it matters what it *feels* like.** And mine felt like crap.

HOW I STUMBLED INTO THE BURNOUT SPOTLIGHT

On that winter day in Chicago, my parents (who very much believe in tough love) told me that I was strong, this was temporary, and I needed to keep going. Now, obviously I would have liked to hear them say, "Don't worry about it, just drop out and we'll support you financially forever," but what they gave me was the shake back to reality I needed in order to recognize that I—and I alone—had to pull myself out of my downward spiral. No one was going to do it for me. I believed them when they said I could do it . . . but I was also struggling to keep my head above water. I was willing to keep going, but I knew I couldn't keep going the same way I had been. I could no longer be a bystander when it came to my burnout. Reading an article here and there about work stress or fatigue was not making my situation better. I needed a solution, so I resolved to create it myself. I wiped away my tears, told my parents I loved them, and marched home with my ramen. I knew this was the start of something new, but that night, I just needed to eat my noodles curled up under a blanket and get some sleep.

After researching my symptoms (everything from "having nightmares about work" to "crying in conference rooms"), it turned out that this prolonged mental and physical exhaustion was burnout, and I checked every box: I was lethargic, stressed 24-7, and disengaged from the things that normally brought me joy. I had been worn down before (during finals season, in a busy period at work, while dealing with personal tragedies), but it was never this hopeless exhaustion with seemingly no end in sight. I'll dive into the cultural and scientific background on burnout later—as well as the constellation of factors that contribute to it—but suffice to say that at the time, my burnout simply felt like one hard day after another.

At first, it was difficult to take my burnout seriously because everyone around me seemed to be experiencing it, too. And not only was it prevalent, it was . . . *trendy*. Sit down at any bar and within ten minutes, you'll hear people trying to one-up each other about how overworked and exhausted they are: "I haven't taken a lunch in years." "I'd be lucky to get out of the office by seven P.M." "If I took a vacation, the department would fall apart." Too many people are normalizing their suffering.

In the weeks that followed my desperate phone call, I began asking my network, especially the people whom I admired, how they managed their busy lives and avoided long-term exhaustion. In return, I got blank stares, uncomfortable laughs, or unconvincing platitudes. Because I worked in professional development, I felt confident that *someone, somewhere* had to have created a simple, easy-to-enact solution for this problem. I searched online spaces and came upon only outdated websites. I scoured social media, found abysmal results, and developed an unhealthy resentment toward recommendations to meditate or try yoga. (I won't yuck someone else's yum, but these two practices really don't resonate with me. Which is my nice way of saying they fill me with rage.)

The resources I did find were out of touch with the modern demands of the virtual workforce (like, say, the suggestion to "leave work at work," with no clear plan for how to cauterize work from life in a time when our work is literally in our home and on the phone that's attached to our hand) and riddled with obvious advice ("get enough sleep"), or they recommended that I cut something out. Quit the job. Pause the degree. Be ruthless about saying no to new opportunities. But the problem was: I *wanted* to keep doing everything I was doing. I *liked* my colleagues and my job; I wanted this degree and was interested in the material. Independently, each element was fulfilling enough not to give up. But combined, it was too much for anyone to complete comfortably. At the end of each day, **I didn't wish for a different life with different goals; I just wished it *wasn't so hard*. I wanted to keep doing what I was doing without feeling like it was taking *everything* from me.**

When I'm faced with a problem, my first step is almost always to do some reconnaissance. So, to start, I spoke with scores of other burned-out individuals about their struggles and what kind of solutions they were looking for. After conducting extensive interviews and diving into research about burnout management, patterns and solutions began to emerge. The same topics kept coming up—mindset, personal care, time management, boundaries, stress management—as areas that either helped prevent burnout or made people more vulnerable to it. With these subjects in mind, I took on the role of my own guinea pig. I hadn't yet removed anything from my plate when I set out to create resources for burnout management, and so my schedule got yet another degree busier. What better time to see if implementing solutions around these topics could actually make a difference in my life?

In short: They did. By applying the array of solutions you'll find in this book, I saw a dramatic improvement in my quality of life and work, *despite* the fact that I had technically added more to my plate. (So did my parents, who, to their great relief, stopped receiving tearful phone calls from aisle nine.) First, I did a sincere evaluation of my capacity and cut nonessentials wherever I could. I set necessary personal and professional boundaries. I improved my stress management—and by that I mean started doing consistent stress management for the first time in my life. And I actually created a structure for personal care that was realistic. We all know that these topics are valuable independently, but I had never seen them packaged together as a holistic method. I had also never practiced them together. Over the course of a few months, I became less frazzled and more focused. I felt less guilty about things I said no to and thoroughly enjoyed the things I said yes to. I felt like I was in control of my own life again. My migraine episodes lessened. It didn't happen overnight—and it took serious effort and some ruthless decision-making—but it was worth every difficult change and conversation. And it all begged the question: Could other people see positive results from this combination of tools as well?

I had a gut feeling they could. To test my theory, I began building a one-on-one coaching program. A one-on-one approach tends to be the most reliable way to test a methodology, ensure results, and get direct feedback. My own experience with burnout—and the tools I utilized to combat it—served as an invaluable foundation. You don't know what will *really* work unless you've been in the trenches. Once clients going through my program were seeing consistent results, it was time to spread the good word about burnout management through my social media platforms.

And boy, did it feel timely. Soon after I began sharing burnout content online, Covid-19 swept the world. One of the many adverse effects of the pandemic was record-high employee stress in 2020, hitting 38 percent globally. In 2021 and 2022 it spiked even higher. With 44 percent of workers reporting *daily* workplace stress, it's no surprise that interest in a cure for burnout skyrocketed during these years and has continued to rise.

My full client waitlist, overflowing inbox, and increased social media following were evidence of this growing problem. At the height of the pandemic, my platform on TikTok grew from a couple thousand followers to a hundred thousand within the span of one month. There was so much demand for my coaching that I could no longer justify delivering the information in a one-on-one format. In order to reach as many people as possible, I created a burnout management training session that I could offer to larger groups. Today, I have had the privilege of facilitating this training for organizations like Pepsi, Nickelodeon, Thermo Fisher, PayPal, and many more. In these sessions, some of the most accomplished, high-powered people you could imagine still ask questions like, "How do I tell someone I'm not available after seven P.M.?" Because the thing is: Burnout does not discriminate. It can find anyone, in any industry, in any position, and force them to compromise on their quality of life in the name of performance.

BURNOUT? IN TODAY'S WORLD? GROUNDBREAKING.

The Covid-19 pandemic made burnout an epidemic. People all over the world had to contend with global unpredictability, impractical working conditions, social isolation, and disheartening news on every media platform. Employees began to question being stressed about their inboxes when people were dying. They resented the mundanity of their responsibilities at work in the face of worldwide tragedy. This combination of stressors resulted in extremely poor mental health nationwide. The World Health Organization reported a 25 percent increase in anxiety and depression worldwide in the first year of the pandemic as a result of Covid-19.

Everyone, all at once, had to bootstrap together a new life with an undetermined end date. Parents struggled to balance their day jobs without childcare or school. Living with roommates whose work-from-home schedules clashed with your own made every day a little bit harder. Students were pulled out of school and their dreams of going to college were crushed, slowly, one delay at a time. In a million unique ways, people's suffering went from short-term stress management to long-term burnout. By the end of 2021, nearly two-thirds of professionals reported experiencing burnout.

The term *burnout* is no longer reserved for healthcare workers pulling twenty-four-hour shifts, consultants working one-hundred-hour weeks, and accountants during tax season. Now more than ever, it lurks just under the surface for nearly everyone. The definitions of burnout from every resource I've come across—whether it's a book addressing the topic or the World Health Organization*—don't seem to describe

---

* The World Health Organization, in the eleventh revision of the International Classification of Diseases (ICD-11), defines burnout as a syndrome that results from chronic workplace stress that has not been successfully managed. It is characterized by three main symptoms: 1) feelings of energy depletion or exhaustion,

what it really looks like in today's post-pandemic world, in which your work life and your personal life are harder than ever to separate. We now live in a world where many people describe their situation as "living at work" rather than "working from home."

That's why I define burnout as *a state of exhaustion, stress, and misalignment (with the direction your life is heading in) for an extended period of time.* The misalignment piece is significant because you can live a very traditionally successful life that does absolutely *nothing* to fulfill you and, as a result, find yourself displaying signs of burnout.

Rarely is burnout the result of *one* thing that you can point your finger at and correct. **Burnout is death by a thousand paper cuts. It is the small ways in which we compromise on our quality of life over time, resulting in exhaustion and unhappiness.** It's spending every morning in a stressed rush, "catching up on work" late at night and over the weekend, feeling guilty for being too tired after work to start that project you've been meaning to do, isolating yourself socially because you are always drained. These small habits can lead to some big problems.

Burnout has been linked to many health conditions, including sleep disorders, depression, musculoskeletal pain (wrist, neck, and back pain), cardiovascular disease, unhealthy changes in the brain, diabetes, and a weakened immune system. That's because burnout puts the body and mind under constant stress, exposing it daily to hormones such as cortisol, which is healthy in short bursts but raises blood pressure and blood sugar *and* causes inflammation when the faucet isn't turned off. We *know* that there are physical repercussions for ignoring burnout, and yet, we persist.

---

2) increased mental distance, or feelings of negativism or cynicism related to one's job, and 3) reduced professional efficacy. The WHO also states that burnout is applied only to an occupational context and not other life areas. The organization's definition, while important, doesn't account for the overlap between work and personal life, does not take into account roles such as unpaid caregiving, and does not address a lack of a sense of purpose, or misalignment, which can feature prominently in some people's experience of burnout.

In the short term, prioritizing work feels advantageous. If we want to get ahead, we feel like we need to be willing to sacrifice balance until we "earn our stripes." But there is strong evidence that maintaining work-life balance results in higher productivity, engagement, retention, and worker satisfaction. A career is a marathon, not a sprint. And burnout is not just a trendy by-product of today's professional demands or a flip way to say, "I'm exhausted." It's a hugely consequential condition that deprives us of many of our fundamental human needs.

Research shows that healthy relationships have a positive impact on our quality of life. Having social support—whether it's your ride-or-die friend on speed dial, a co-worker you consider a friend, or your mom, whom you phone every day like I do—has been found to alleviate burnout and increase personal satisfaction. But here's the irony: The things proven to inoculate us against burnout—like quality time with friends or watching your favorite team while having a cold beverage with buddies—are the very things that burnout steals from us. It's wickedly sneaky. Unfortunately, the correlation between exhaustion and isolation means that those struggling with exhaustion and burnout are very likely to isolate further instead of seeking social support.

Resolving burnout requires spare time and energy to do the things that will help alleviate it, but of course, time and energy are precisely what a burned-out individual doesn't have. Naturally, alongside the rise of burnout we see a decrease in personal leisure. We can't put all of ourselves into our responsibilities and then act befuddled when we look up to find all the good things in our lives are gone. Spending our time and energy on goals that result in deprioritizing health, relationships, and leisure *will* catch up to us—and it will do so with a vengeance.

FIRST, GET HONEST WITH YOURSELF

Do you find yourself thinking, *There's not enough time in the day?* Do you neglect the things that once brought you joy to make room for tasks? Maybe you've been working through lunch and in the evening, or staying up too late because it's the only time nobody is asking anything of you. Or if you're like I was, you can't stop saying yes to every-thing as a default—and then drowning with a smile on your face so nobody thinks you're incapable.

You might have disassociated (switched into mental autopilot, found yourself "just going through the motions") months ago to sur-vive this reality, only to realize you've slipped into deeper burnout wa-ters. Maybe you find that you have anxiety about work every morning, on weekends, and on vacation. When anyone asks something of you, you're tempted to cry out, "Isn't it obvious I'm busy?!" Forget "quiet quitting"—you constantly feel like you're a day away from rage-quitting. Sometimes you even find yourself daydreaming about run-ning away from your life altogether. (I hear Alaska is beautiful this time of year.) Perhaps, if things have gotten very dark, you fantasize about disappearing . . . just for a little bit.

Maybe you struggle to turn down opportunities, everything on your plate feels essential, or you've been "in a busy season" for as long as you can remember. Maybe you guilt yourself into doing things for others even when you don't have capacity, and confrontation is your worst nightmare. Or maybe you feel "stuck," are struggling to show up for long-standing commitments, and don't feel particularly engaged by the things on your plate.

Regardless of the form your burnout takes, we're going to find a way for you to combat it. Because—and I'm not being dramatic—*the qual-ity of your entire life depends on it.* Tangibly, burnout will consume your calendar, sabotage your relationships, and harm your physical health. Intangibly, it will steal the best years of your life while you have your head down in survival mode. It will destroy your mental health and cause exhaustion and helplessness akin to depression.

Imagine how you'd feel if you *didn't* put so much pressure on your-self to do everything and please everyone; if you had spare time and energy to do the things you love; and if you didn't feel guilty when you took a break or enjoyed leisure. How much more pleasant, comfort-able, and fulfilling would your life be if you didn't constantly feel ex-hausted, stressed, or disconnected?

Breaking habits that lead to burnout is *hard,* I know. (*Seriously,* I know.) But spending years of your life burned out is harder. Working yourself into the ground and not having boundaries has likely gotten you pretty far—the world we live in loves a hard worker, regardless of what it costs that person. **Our world has no limits on what it will demand of you, so you must have limits on what you will give.**

WHAT YOU ARE NOT CHANGING YOU ARE CHOOSING

Everything we do, from the second we wake up to the moment we close our eyes at night, is a choice: if you grab your phone first thing in the morning, whether you think about work after you leave the office, how you allow yourself to be treated—*everything!* Some of it is trivial, some of it serves you, and some of it is killing you.

This book will feel like I'm (lovingly) shaking your shoulders and asking you, "When you look back at your life, what will you wish you did differently?" The answer will probably not be working more, participating in a dozen committees, or spending time in relationships that make you feel like crap more often than they make you feel supported. I will then outline the steps you can take to make your life as calm, fulfilling, and manageable as possible. Many of the tools we discuss will be illustrated by clients' powerful stories.*

In order to manage yourself in a way that mitigates your current burnout, prevents burnout in the future, and reinforces balance, you'll learn to identify the signals that indicate you are experiencing burnout. We'll explore the intricacies of modern burnout and how differentiating between the three types can help you quickly identify the changes you should make. And you'll become very familiar with the five pillars of burnout management: mindset, personal care, time management, boundaries, and stress management. Different stressors in your life will require different combinations of the pillars, but mastering these five areas will allow you to confidently protect yourself and your quality of life in the face of various stressors going forward.

---

* Names of my clients have been changed but the spirit of their stories remains.

The suggestions I make can be tailored to your specific stressors. If you often find yourself thinking, *My workload is unreasonable,* I'm excited for you to learn about boundaries and time management. If you tell everyone, "I work with really difficult people," let's talk about mindset and stress management. If you start each week thinking, *I don't feel rested at all,* allow me to introduce you to personal care and time management.

My methodology will help you create the life you want *now* and help you fight off the numerous burnout threats that you'll confront throughout your lifetime. Because burnout is an ongoing problem, you're going to have an ongoing relationship with this material. Different seasons of life will cause you to lean on different areas of burnout management. Make notes as you go along, dog-ear your favorite tools—please don't be precious about this book. Make yourself at home in these pages so that the advice that resonates is as easy to access as possible in the future.

Your circumstances and disposition are unique. Everyone will have slightly different starting points and experiences using these tools. The important thing is to at least give everything a try. If you hate something, you never have to do it again. I promise.

If it ever feels like you're looking directly into the sun reading this book, it's because I *was* you. I know what it feels like for your life to be so far out of your control that you don't even know where to start fixing it—especially when you're getting nothing but praise for how things look from the outside, and you feel too tired to make changes from within.

Being the way you are has gotten you the life you currently have. **If you want a different life, you're going to have to be a different version of yourself.** You're going to have to do things differently. You already know what your life looks like if you keep doing what you've been doing and, given the fact that you are reading this, I'm going to assume you think there is some opportunity for growth. **You can make a couple hard changes, or you can live a hard life.** I'm here to support you through the former. If I did it, you can, too.

Everyone deserves to live a life they enjoy waking up to. At the very least, everyone deserves a life they don't *dread* waking up to.

THE CURE FOR BURNOUT

PART I

MODERN BURNOUT

CHAPTER ONE

Identifying Burnout in a World on Fire

When Stress Becomes Burnout

Have you ever had the overwhelming sense that driving into the nearest field and screaming at the top of your lungs would be therapeutic? Have you ever pulled into your driveway, sat in your car, and stared blankly out the window, not wanting to go inside to whatever responsibilities await you? Have you ever had such a bad day you started doing mental math to calculate whether you could get away with quitting your job? Whether it's because of overwhelming professional, social, or personal responsibilities, the bottom line is you're running on fumes. You're just pushing through with the little to no gas left in your tank. **Burnout is living your life on fumes *for an extended period of time.***

More commonly, this sense of "running on fumes" is the experience of mismanaged, prolonged stress. We know that a little stress is good for us: It keeps us alert and engaged. But significant stress for a long or indefinite period does not suit our physiology, and when we must endure it for too long, it transforms into something much more sinister: burnout. When our bodies are relentlessly combating stress hormones, getting irregular sleep, and experiencing daily fatigue, we have no op-

portunity to replenish our reserves. And it's not just a physical depletion; it's also psychological—we start to view our circumstances and
future more negatively. Whereas short-term stress is perceived as a challenge that we can overcome with extra effort, burnout feels endless and
insurmountable: We become resigned and hopeless, fearing things will
never change.

WE ARE PRODUCTS OF OUR ENVIRONMENT

You don't need me to tell you that global causes of stress—the impacts
of Covid-19, inflation, political turmoil, and "hustle culture," just to
name a few—are on the rise. While most of us have long been accustomed to some stress, more of us than ever are reporting high amounts
of it in recent years. Increased, prolonged stress means an increase in
burnout.

As the pandemic bore on and showed no signs of abating, and as
burnout continued to increase, the dam broke. People reached a breaking point and were forced to reassess *what* they were working—and
burning out—for. As if we had a collective near-death experience, everyone reevaluated what they were spending their precious time on. The
reminder of our finite time brought with it a renewed indignation and
motivation *not* to waste it doing things that did not serve or fulfill us.

This widespread burnout reared its head in movements like the
Great Resignation (the mass exodus of workers from the workforce),
the Great Reshuffling (folks who quit and "shuffled" into different jobs
instead of leaving the workforce altogether), and quiet quitting (the
conscious decision to no longer go "above and beyond" basic job duties). These global trends, driven by employee dissatisfaction, illustrate
millions of professionals' desire for change. We are ready to work for a
living rather than live to work.

For anyone who missed it: The 2021 Great Resignation was a period during which a record number of U.S. employees quit their jobs,
hitting a twenty-year high of 4.5 million in November of 2022. And
this was not a case of people simply retiring early. The main reasons

workers left their jobs included low pay, working too many hours, lacking opportunities for advancement, and feeling disrespected by their manager or company. Those who changed jobs were more likely to take jobs that offered higher pay, more room for advancement, and a better work-life balance. Additionally, the increased flexibility in the shift to remote work made many people question the need to work as rigidly as they had been. Many workers left their roles in favor of remote positions that offered more freedom than they previously had in the office.

For the first time in modern history, the nine-to-five structure was questioned by employees who had successfully achieved the same work on a different schedule and in a different setting than before. When people's jobs were stripped of the office, culture, and distracting hustle and bustle, many felt their roles left something to be desired.

"GET YOUR F*CKING ASS UP AND WORK. IT SEEMS LIKE NOBODY WANTS TO WORK THESE DAYS."
—KIM KARDASHIAN

The quiet quitting trend—popularized by social media throughout 2022 and 2023—is further evidence that professionals have been disillusioned. While "going the extra mile" or "going above and beyond" is virtuous, many employees who felt they'd been doing so for years realized that they had merely been "rewarded" with a lot of drain and personal sacrifice (and, in many cases, being asked to take on the work of a colleague who wasn't doing their job as well). A "promotion" in duties but not in title or pay has become upsettingly common. It's no wonder workers have essentially gone on strike, mounting to a mass refusal to "pick up the slack" and "be a team player" to their detriment. Indignation about these unfair and untenable expectations, and the realization that many others were feeling the same resentment, gave the quiet quitting campaign the fuel it needed to catch fire.

Of course, not everyone is fist-pumping in support of these movements. Often, the response to these "do less" trends is the assumption that "nobody wants to work hard anymore." Even when the recommendation to scale back is for the purpose of reducing burnout or boosting mental health, many people still hesitate to acknowledge they're burned out for fear that it will sound like they "don't have what it takes." To anyone who has internalized that belief: It is in your best interest to mentally decouple work ethic and burnout right now. Burnout is not a result of a lack of effort, determination, or grit. **To perceive burnout as a personal failing instead of the result of persistent stress is incorrect.**

- "Burned Out"
- "Resilient"
- "Hardworking"
- "Ambitious"

There are universal factors that lead to burnout (such as feeling overworked, being in stressful relationships, or experiencing prolonged fatigue), and these are helpful to be aware of. However, equally important for managing burnout is knowing how *you* tend to respond to those factors. To help you catch and correct burnout in your unique circumstances, I'm going to teach you what to look for in yourself.

I SPY WITH MY LITTLE EYE SOMEONE REWATCHING THEIR COMFORT SHOW

So how can you recognize if you are experiencing burnout? Over time, perpetual stress causes symptoms that get our attention. Brain fog, shortness of temper, feelings of hopelessness, physical fatigue—this is our body tapping us on the shoulder to let us know we need to take notice because something isn't quite right. Some folks misdiagnose their burnout as anxiety or depression because they share symptoms: feeling fatigued, overwhelmed, detached, and hopeless. While these maladies can look and feel similar, one of the main differences is that burnout is largely circumstantial—it's directly connected to your conditions, and most often to your work. When those conditions are changed, your burnout can be alleviated. Conversely, anxiety and depression usually cannot be fully abated through a change in circumstance. Someone with depression is probably going to feel depressed even if they scale back their workload, get enough rest, or book an emergency vacation.

There are both internal and external indicators that you're slipping into burnout. Internal indicators are signs you might notice in yourself; external indicators are signs others might be able to notice in you. Familiarizing yourself with both will help you spot and address burnout in yourself or others in the future.

INTERNAL INDICATORS: EXPERIENCES YOU MIGHT HAVE AS A RESULT OF BURNOUT

- Emotional exhaustion (feeling emotionally unavailable as a result of expending excessive amounts of energy)
- Cynicism or pessimism
- Detachment or disassociation
- Feeling drained before beginning your tasks/day
- Anxiety before and about work (Sunday Scaries, but every day)
- Loss of motivation
- Impaired concentration and attention
- Feeling ineffective

EXTERNAL INDICATORS: OBSERVABLE BEHAVIORS YOU MIGHT HAVE AS A RESULT OF BURNOUT

- Physical exhaustion
- Insomnia
- Forgetfulness
- Isolation
- Escapism (using distractions such as media or hobbies to escape reality)

- Increased irritability
- Lowered immunity
- Procrastination
- Change in food/drug/alcohol use
- Persistent physical pain

These are the signs of burnout as we feel or display them. We tend to slide into old habits, so your indicators of burnout are probably familiar to you. But you likely also show some signs that are less clinical and more personal. What do you know you do when you're feeling fried? Perhaps your go-to self-soothing tool when things get rough is rewatching a comfort show, snacking on your favorite junk food, ignoring people's texts and calls, amping up your online shopping or food ordering, staying up later, or isolating socially. If you spend a lot of time with a partner, family member, or friend, ask them what they observe about you when you're starting to get burned out. I'll offer you tools to fight burnout throughout this book, but they're no use if you can't spot when you actually need them.

When I start slipping into burnout, my credit card is the first to know. I begin ordering most meals and buying things I don't need as a means of getting feel-good dopamine. Essentially, I become a short-term reward glutton. I sleep until my third alarm, skip my workouts, escape into my hobbies, and stay up way too late. If I'm in a really, really bad spot, I sit down in the shower. My husband knows that if I'm sitting down in the shower, it's a Code Red situation.

By contrast, when I feel like my life is within my control and I am not burned out, I operate from a place of long-term reward. I wake up early so that I'm not rushing before the day has started, I look forward to my workout, I go to sleep at a reasonable time, and I can enjoy my hobbies as a supplement to my daily responsibilities, rather than as an addictive escape from them. (I also remain vertical in the shower.)

Recognizing these less clinical signs of burnout has brought many clients to my door. You don't need to wait until you're in the hospital, being prescribed antianxiety medication, or having panic attacks (I say from personal experience) to take action. Whatever your signs of burnout, they are valid (right now) and today is a reasonable time to make a change.

COPING WITH CHAOS

A woman named Jessica scheduled a call with me after her partner gently pointed out that she probably shouldn't be receiving online purchases in the mail *every day*. Jessica's demanding job was leaving her exhausted, so, in an attempt to self-soothe and get a little "pick-me-up," she had fallen down the retail therapy rabbit hole. Buying things online brought her joy and gave her something to look forward to during an otherwise stressful week. She felt she deserved to treat herself with the money she earned from her demanding job.

Jessica almost didn't call me because she didn't think online shopping qualified as a sign of burnout. Why shouldn't she be able to buy herself nice things with her own money? But it wasn't the *things* that were concerning; it was the timing of when she was buying them. Her online purchase history tended to spike during her busy seasons at work. I explained that indicators of burnout can start out as commonly recognized physical and mental symptoms (exhaustion, anxiety, insomnia), but they can also manifest as more personal, less obvious signals (online shopping, neglecting hobbies, indulging in comforts). In fact, several of my burned-out clients have struggled with a shopping addiction, for good reason: Compulsive shopping, like overusing a substance such as alcohol or drugs, taps into our reward circuitry and gives us a hit of pleasurable dopamine, which is tempting when you're constantly feeling on-edge and depleted.

Jessica was going through the classic burnout cycle.

She would work herself to the bone, begin to display her personal burnout signs, reach a breaking point and make a change (usually by setting some boundaries at work), and then, once she felt calmer, she'd begin to accumulate more work again.

She repeated this cycle over, and over, and over, as if she were aller-

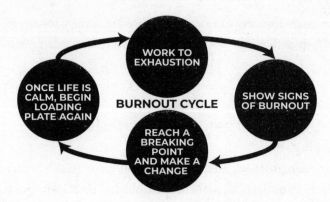

gic to peace. It's said that insanity is doing the same thing repeatedly and expecting a different result. Jessica knew this working pattern burned her out, but for one reason or another, she justified slipping back into it. "Things will calm down after I finish this project," she'd tell herself. "End-of-year reviews are coming up." "If I don't do this then my team will have to, and I don't want them to burn out." "What if this opportunity doesn't come around again? I need to take it."

Sound familiar? Justifying burnout with thoughts of this nature is not uncommon for members of the A. B. C. (Always Burned-out Club). As soon as there is a new demand, more room on their plate, or a chance to prove themselves, A. B. C. members throw themselves back into the fire.

KNOW THYSELF

We each have unique patterns of burnout. In order to get a better visual of what yours might be and how you can interrupt them, let's take a look at the three major components:

- Conditions or behaviors that lead to burnout
- Signs that you are burning out
- Your response to the conditions or behaviors that are leading to burnout

What does this look like in Jessica's case? Upon further examination, we found that the **behaviors** that lead her to burn out were not saying no when she was at capacity, and struggling to put work down (simply put, compulsively checking her email after work hours and on weekends).

The **signs** that indicated to her that she was burning out were comfort shopping, near-constant anxiety (when she was normally a calm and happy person), and withdrawing socially.

To determine Jessica's **response** to her burnout, we looked at her upcoming workload and identified items that could be simplified, delegated, or paused for the time being. She committed to saying no to any nonessential work through the rest of the quarter so she could get her feet under her again. She also communicated to her team that she had gotten in the bad habit of being online at all times and, going forward, she would be available only during business hours (which, frankly, probably came as a relief to them as well). This clarification of expectations helped reduce Jessica's anxiety about being available and doing work around the clock. In turn, her decreased anxiety reduced the behaviors she was using to cope with that anxiety (online shopping and withdrawing socially).

Our goal is always to get to the root of burnout, not just correct the *signs* of it. Jessica could have stopped online shopping and started spending time with friends again, but that wouldn't have resolved her burnout. Our *signs* of burnout aren't the fundamental problem; they're *clues* that we are coping with a problem.

Consider the conditions and behaviors that trigger this cycle for you:

What *conditions* tend to trigger burnout? Certain seasons of work? Certain types of projects or deadlines? When you spend excess time with certain stressful people? This is a fancy way of figuring out "Is the problem something I can address?" In Jessica's case, she knew *she* was responsible for most of the behaviors that were leading her to burnout—which meant she had the power to change those behaviors herself.

What *behaviors* tend to lead you toward burnout? Perhaps you aren't setting boundaries at work or with demanding people in your life, or maybe you're engaging with circumstances that have historically caused you stress or you're putting undue pressure on yourself.

What are the *signs* that you're slipping into burnout? Maybe you took on extra work because you didn't know how to say no (behavior) and the *sign* that you should have said no is that you now have to skip lunch for the next week to finish your work on time.

How might you *respond* to disrupt your burnout behavior? For example, you might memorize a go-to phrase for turning down work you don't have time for in the future: "Can I check my calendar and get back to you on whether I have capacity for that?" followed by "Unfortunately I don't have the bandwidth to support this without compromising elsewhere at this time," or "I can help with that, but the soonest I'll be able to get it back to you is tomorrow morning. Does that work for you?"

UNLIKE BEYONCÉ, YOU DID NOT WAKE UP LIKE THIS

Most of us find ourselves burned out somewhat accidentally. It happens gradually. You know how they say that if you drop a frog in boiling water, it will jump out, but if you leave a frog in a pot of tepid water and then bring it to a boil, it won't notice that it's being boiled alive? Burnout is much the same. If you take someone from a balanced workplace and drop them into extremely stressful circumstances that require unhealthy behavior to endure, the burnout will immediately get their attention. But if you slide into burnout gradually, you may not realize the unhealthy habits you've picked up along the way. Before you know it, your conditions are bad enough that you don't even register the alarm bells that would be sounding for someone else.

It's up to you to know your baseline (in other words, the water temperature that is livable for you) and maintain it. Your baseline is how you behave when you're balanced. It's your homeostasis. During a calm, manageable season, how do you spend your time? Your baseline should be sustainable enough that you could show up for one hundred days in a row without experiencing burnout.

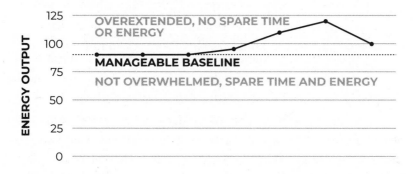

The problem for many of us is that we ignore behaviors and signs of burnout until they are "bad enough." We might register that we're tired, busy, and in low spirits, but until things really start to break down around us (or inside of us), we discount the symptoms. We justify operating far beyond a manageable baseline as we push through one more project, or until we earn that next raise or promotion. We tell ourselves it's a temporary phase and assume that we have enough fuel to keep going until we hit the jackpot. Or we might even claim, "This is just how I am," believing that this state of chaos is our point of equilibrium or our personal lot in life—which usually isn't true, but it's easy to believe it is.

For the most part, **we are the way we are because it has worked for us before.** The habits you repeat are probably habits that once served you. When I was burned out, I know I tuned out the warning bells because I could barely hear them over the cheers. I was doing so well that I thought my burnout was just the price I had to pay for success. It was worth it to me for a very long time to brush off my signs of burnout . . . until it wasn't anymore. Burnout starts slowly until one day you make the leap from unhappy to dangerously unwell.

What ended up finally convincing Jessica to establish a more reasonable baseline at work was realizing that, when she started making and maintaining healthy changes, nothing bad happened. She could hold the boundaries that kept her from burning out, her performance didn't plummet, and her colleagues didn't hate her. Did it take some experimentation? Of course. Figuring out when she could take breaks and for how long, finding ways to redirect people who still sought her attention outside of working hours, quantifying the work on her plate so she had more awareness of her time management—all these changes required that she start somewhere and then refine the solution until it was right for her and her circumstances. But was getting her time and energy back outside of work worth a little discomfort? Absolutely.

Jessica was struggling with burnout by volume, one of the three types of burnout. Each type of burnout has its own set of stressors, signs, and solutions. Had she been struggling with another type, we would have examined her burnout cycle using the same method, but with a different strategy for managing it. Although some of the tools I share can be adapted for any kind of burnout, a personalized approach is the most effective one, and that starts with diagnosing your particular type of burnout.

CHAPTER TWO

The Three Types of Burnout

(and Yes, You *Can* Go Three for Three)

The first client I worked with who made me realize there was more than one type of burnout was Lisa. "How's your workload?" I asked. "Fine!" she said. She got each day's work done in eight hours. "How are you feeling at work?" "I enjoy my work," she responded. "So, what would you say is causing your burnout?" "Well . . . other people," she said. She explained that despite her workload being reasonable, she felt drained by the people in her everyday life. Her manager was volatile, so Lisa felt like she was walking on eggshells, always reading the room to gauge how she would need to maneuver around him. Her desk was in a high-traffic area and she had a friendly smile, which meant that nearly every person who passed by interrupted her to chat. Finally, she acknowledged that she seemed to attract needy people and frequently received unexpected visits and emotional calls from friends or family in the middle of the day. As a people-pleaser who didn't know how to turn anyone away without immense guilt, Lisa suffered in silence.

While we're used to volume of work being the main culprit for burnout, Lisa is not alone in experiencing *social burnout* as a result of unmanageable demands from other people. Rather than expending resources like time and energy on professional responsibilities, she was squandering them on difficult relationships in her life. Her normally happy demeanor was becoming resentful and withdrawn; she was emotionally fatigued, growing increasingly anxious, and having trouble sleeping. To cope with these stressors, Lisa resorted to turning her phone off in the evenings and claiming she was working late so that she could have a couple hours of quiet without getting calls, texts, or emails from anyone. At work, she found every excuse to avoid her unpredictable manager and resorted to wearing her headphones constantly so she could feign a phone call if someone tried to stop by whom she didn't have the energy to chat with. (Nothing makes people as desperately creative as burnout. Just ask a mom with multiple kids who wants five minutes to herself.) This people-related burnout was different from the professional burnout I saw most often, but it was burnout nonetheless.

Eventually, after I had dozens of calls with clients like Lisa, three major categories of burnout rose to the surface:

BURNOUT BY VOLUME	SOCIAL BURNOUT	BURNOUT BY BOREDOM
Burnout as a result of a high volume of responsibilities, a compact schedule, and very little downtime	Burnout as a result of interpersonal demands that exceed your available social resources	Burnout as a result of chronic disengagement and disinterest in the items in your life

Burnout by volume applies to people with much more to do than they can possibly get done. It is often described as trying to "drink from a fire hose." As we saw with Jessica, burnout can be self-inflicted, but often those who suffer from burnout by volume have jobs that can easily become overwhelming. **Social burnout** afflicts people, like Lisa, whose battery is consistently low because they aren't sticking to their social limits. These folks become the person everyone confides in, vents to, or asks for favors because they are pleasant and reliable. **Burnout by boredom** besets people who feel uninspired by and disengaged from their life for an extended period. Remember that idea of misalignment I talked about? This sense of meaninglessness is a common feature of burnout by boredom.

You can suffer from more than one type of burnout at a time—about 50 percent of my clients struggle with a combination of burnout by volume and social burnout—and you can recover from one while still grappling with the other. Recognizing these three types of burnout allows for a more comprehensive understanding of what exactly might be causing you distress so that you can get to the root of the problem. Once these different faces of burnout are clear to you, you will be better equipped to assess your needs, bottlenecks, and blind spots as you alleviate your burnout.

BURNOUT BY VOLUME: DRINKING FROM A FIRE HOSE

Mandy accepted that she was burned out when she bought one of those phone holders that you wear around your neck. She was officially so busy that she could be bothered neither to put her phone down nor to keep it in her pocket. Why put it away when she would just as quickly need to take it out? She was working on a PR team managing her clients' media, and her agency behaved as though every project was a matter of life or death.

Everything Mandy's team did was on their clients' timeline (clients who often didn't differentiate weekends from weekdays). Their work was public facing, so mistakes were out of the question and every detail was scrutinized. Each waking hour—and let's be honest, a lot of sleeping hours, too—Mandy was flooded with correspondence from impatient people who were paying a hefty fee for her company's services. Accompanying these demands was an internal sense that she was always behind. Like in the Greek myth of Hydra, she would cut off the head of one task and two more would grow back in its place. Mandy conceded that she knew the work wasn't terribly important in the grand scheme of life, but the day-to-day pressure and expectations had driven her to take antianxiety medication.

Mandy was suffering burnout by volume—the feeling of being crushed by the weight of your to-do list and feeling like your life is out of your control, exacerbated by the fact that you neglect your needs in the process and become increasingly fatigued.

The same picture could be painted of a stay-at-home parent drowning under the mental and emotional load that comes with childcare, or of a medical student with thirty hours of lectures to memorize by tomorrow. Burnout by volume is easy to succumb to in our busy world, and nobody teaches us how to claw our way out of it.

Whenever I find myself slipping into burnout by volume, racing thoughts plague me at all hours, including the middle of the night. Bleary-eyed, I'll roll over a dozen times to grab my phone from the nightstand and add another item to my list titled "shit to do tomorrow." This is a list that I keep in my notes app and add to between the hours of 11 P.M. and 6 A.M. when I definitely should be asleep. It isn't enough to be sprinting from one task to another during the day; the feeling of having too much to do without enough time to do it causes me to sleep fitfully, wake up in a panic, and convince myself that I can't leave my phone behind for a twenty-minute walk because *what if something important comes up?* It's not always the busy days that get you; often it's the inability to detach from responsibilities during the time that is meant to be your leisure or recharge time.

Burnout by volume is the result of having too many items on the docket for an extended time. It is, as Greg McKeown, author of *Essentialism,* would say, "doing more today than you can recover from tomorrow" over, and over, and over again. Whether you're working on a huge project at work, it's finals week, or you committed to too many extracurriculars, you're running your tank to empty on a regular basis and mucking up your machinery's ability to bounce back from the wear and tear. With the schedule that burnout by volume comes with, there is little room for human error. Feeling like we can't run five minutes over, make mistakes, or catch our breath exacerbates our sense that life is a high-stakes emergency and to maintain order, we must take ourselves very seriously.

Taking ourselves seriously often looks like seeking control so that things go as planned. While some control can be a good thing—we need agency and freedom to chart our course—wanting total control all the time is a recipe for disappointment and stress. **The more you believe that life is an *experience* and not a *performance,* the less stress and disappointment you'll feel.** For as long as you feel like life is a performance, you'll wonder what the imaginary audience is thinking, you'll curse yourself over every misstep, and you'll make decisions based on what things *look* like rather than what they *feel* like. If you are only ever performing, odds are that your experience is suffering as a result.

Volume victims

Burnout by volume plagues people who ask, "How much can I do?" instead of "How much can I do well?" or "How much can I do while still retaining time to do what makes me feel taken care of every day?" If we haven't collapsed, had a health scare, or been sat down and reprimanded for our behavior, we keep going. Why is this? How have we advanced in so many areas as a society, yet it seems like no amount of human effort is enough to keep all the balls in the air? Shouldn't it be easier to live our lives by now?

If you've ever wondered how we haven't managed to make universal things easier (as I know I do every time I participate in the hot mess that is tax season in America), you aren't alone. In 1930, economist John Maynard Keynes wrote an essay titled "Economic Possibilities for Our Grandchildren," in which he projected that industrial, technological, and social advancement would result in his grandchildren working no more than fifteen hours per week. Obviously . . . that is not the case. Work responsibilities have not decreased, and social obligations have increased. A 2018 Pew Research Center survey revealed that 55 percent of people without children (or with adult children) are "too busy to enjoy their lives." For parents with younger children, that figure jumped to 75 percent. In addition to feeling too busy to enjoy our own lives, the degree of guilt we feel about not "doing it all" has been exacerbated by a culture of sharing our success on social media. **Not only do we live our lives, we perform them publicly.** Even when we feel proud of ourselves after a productive day, we pick up our phones and see someone doing something we didn't and then we feel bad about that instead.

We are creatures of habit. Most people who experience burnout encounter it more than once in their lives due to repeatedly finding themselves in circumstances that exacerbate burnout (gravitating toward stressful jobs, tough industries, and difficult people) or reverting to habits that have burned them out before (people pleasing, prioritizing achieving over recovery, and agreeing to things out of guilt). Those who are prone to burnout by volume typically have a bad habit of being pulled into these things despite past evidence that doing so drains them.

For these reasons, those who suffer from burnout by volume end up benefiting most from the burnout management pillars of mindset, time management, boundaries, and stress management. They need to evaluate the patterns that are leading them to burnout by volume, get honest about what is on their plate, create boundaries to maintain balance when their plate is overflowing again, and manage the stress of having a high *or* low volume of work. Just as there are growing pains, there are also shrinking pains when you reduce the load you've become accustomed to. Going from a heavy workload and high stress to a lighter workload and calm can be just as unsettling.

Reprioritizing achievement

How do you know if you tend to burn yourself out by volume? Here are some common indicators:

- Most of the time you describe yourself as busy
- Other people would describe you as busy
- When people ask things of you and your already compact schedule, you feel resentful
- You feel like you have very little room for error in your days and mistakes feel more costly because of limited spare time to fix them
- You often find yourself thinking *there is not enough time in the day*
- You frequently feel you would benefit from an assistant or having two more of yourself
- You feel anxiety about starting the workweek because you know when it starts the stresses will be back-to-back until the next weekend

- You feel guilt and fear when you don't "take every opportunity"
- You tell yourself, *This is just a busy season,* even though you've consistently had busy seasons for the past few years

As you continue to burn yourself out with these patterns, I guarantee you will hear nothing but praise. Just when you think about quitting out of exhaustion, someone will deliver a well-timed "We don't know what we would do without you." For someone who prioritizes achievement, it can be very difficult to make behavioral changes that seem like they may cut off the achievement and praise tap. I assure you, the well does not run dry. Assuming you're a hard worker, opportunities will continue to present themselves, and your ability to prioritize thoughtfully will keep you afloat.

Prioritizing achievement is likely your default. If you want to prioritize something else like peace or freedom, you need to fully commit to it even when (not if, *when*) it looks and feels different or uncomfortable. I once worked with an incredible woman who wanted to take her lunch breaks but worried a manager would find her less ambitious if she did so. It can feel like there are a dozen factors at play in a situation like this, but it truly came down to *Would you rather take your lunch or have Gerald's approval?* In other words, would you rather bolster how you're perceived or bolster your work-life balance?

Presenting the options in this cut-and-dried fashion helped her make the decision going forward that she needed to prioritize lunch over Gerald's approval. Although it was difficult, she acknowledged that the positive impact a lunch break had on her mood, performance, and overall sense of balance outweighed the occasional nod of approval from Gerald. It's not easy, but you make the shift to new priorities one choice at a time.

Most people have a Gerald in the workplace—someone from whom you want—borderline *need*—a blessing to feel like you're doing a good job. Do you trust that you do good work during the hours you spend at work and that the work speaks for itself? Why does it feel like the projects that demand you to overextend yourself (working before the "workday" starts, during lunch, late at night, or on weekends) are the ones that speak the loudest? I understand that the people going "above and beyond" often seem like the people who care the most, are the hardest working, and are the ones on whom you can rely. But if you are receiving these asks *all the time,* then those aren't special cases; that's a new job description.

One decision at a time, you can reshape the high achiever in you who is convinced that performance is *the* most important thing, even if it costs you everything else. Let's look at some ways you might begin to reduce burnout by volume. What steps can you take that will slow you down without compromising everything you've worked so hard for?

1. **Create clarity.** What do you want to be prioritizing three years from now? Based on that answer, what should you be focusing on now—*today*? When you are clear on what direction you want to aim for, you can cut out many detours along the way. Loading yourself with tasks that don't align with your goals is like accepting payment in Monopoly money when you do not plan on playing Monopoly in the future. You want payment that you can actually cash in later because you plan to stay in that arena. Take a critical look at the things on your plate and decide what stays and what goes based on the direction you would like your life to take.

2. **Get comfortable with boundaries.** This work cannot be done without being able to draw the line with nonessentials. Fortunately for you, there is an entire chapter on boundaries ahead in which you will learn how to determine your limits, set them, and not feel a knot of guilt in your stomach for doing so.

3. **Show yourself tough love.** You are the one driving this vehicle! You are responsible for not just trimming the fat in your schedule and setting boundaries, but also for not telling yourself you're falling behind by not saying yes to everything. The person in your driver's seat has learned to drive this way; it will take some time and adjustment to get yourself in the habit of thinking about and doing things differently.

4. Know that the well will not run dry. **Stop thinking of success, opportunities, and achievement as scarce resources that will disappear if you don't snap them up as quickly as possible.** When you believe that there are ample opportunities for success, you can make more thoughtful decisions about what you agree to, put less pressure on yourself to be everything all at once, and stop comparing yourself to others who are in different phases of their own success.

SOCIAL BURNOUT: BEING EVERYTHING FOR EVERYONE

Maybe this sounds familiar: You've had a long day at work and are finally settling into the couch to decompress when an incoming call flashes on your phone. You stare at it, debating whether it's an emergency or you'll just be sucked into forty minutes of pretending to be chipper, thereby draining the last 5 percent of energy you have for the day. If you don't answer, you feel guilty; if you do answer, you feel resentful. This situation is emblematic of people's primary struggle with social burnout. They choose personal drain and resentment over setting clear expectations or prioritizing their needs.

Social burnout occurs because relationships are an exchange—an exchange in which we give away limited resources (time, energy, attention) that are rather difficult to defend. As Lisa learned, seemingly small social demands here and there can cumulatively drain you. And as a "people person," she was devastated that she couldn't be exactly what everyone wanted, manage everyone else's experiences, and simultaneously keep herself afloat. While there is plenty of research showing that socializing can be energizing and beneficial—humans are social creatures, after all—it still demands energy from us. Some research shows that even if we feel great about interacting in the moment, a couple of hours later mental fatigue can set in, in part because of the effort it takes to focus our attention on others.

If relationships have always been paramount to you and you suddenly have to reprioritize them, it can feel like a personal failing and

threat to your social health. However, if you know that you are struggling to manage social demands, you need to be honest with yourself
and others. It is not a reflection of how much you care, but instead a
matter of being human with limited resources. For the time being, acknowledge that you're being stretched thin and that you must be more
selective about the distribution of your relationship resources.

Social burnout is very common in people pleasers who feel guilty
saying no even when they have nothing else to give. It is also common
in individuals who feel responsible for the feelings and experience of
others (such as peacemakers, highly sensitive people, or those who are
very empathetic), as well as those who have an intense fear of being
disliked. **While burnout by volume weighs on your calendar, social
burnout weighs on your spirit.**

Working against yourself

Often, our fear of hurting others—or of being disliked for expressing
our needs—is fed by an overactive imagination. One of the most common and damaging ways we work against ourselves is by storytelling.
Have you ever thought something like, *If I don't agree to go to that gathering, they're going to think I don't care about them. I bet they'll stop invit-
ing me to things if I say no*? **Storytelling** is our tendency to predict how
an interaction might pan out or how a person might respond before
we've even tried to have the conversation. In an effort to not rock the
boat, storytelling is a way we rehearse difficulties before actually experiencing them. Conjuring a story—typically a stressful one—decreases
the chance that we will handle something the way we should out of fear
of what *might* go wrong.

Perhaps you have a friend or family member who disregards your
expressed availability. They tend to call you at their convenience and then
get upset when you aren't free. You know you need to have a conversation
to clarify expectations with them, but you avoid it because you envision
them getting defensive or feeling hurt, and you don't want to make them
feel bad or ruin the relationship. This practice of storytelling stops you
from taking a simple action on your own behalf, like texting them, "Hey

:) I don't want you to think I'm ignoring you, so I just wanted to remind you that I can't answer calls before 7 P.M. Monday to Friday or on Sundays. Love you! Looking forward to speaking on Saturday!" You could do yourself a disservice by storytelling, or you could do something that might feel harder: Assume the best. Assume they'll read the text and understand. (And even if you do have evidence to the contrary from prior experience, you *can't* spend your life babying people; it's unrealistic.)

When we story-tell, we tend to make catastrophizing assumptions ("She'll stop talking to me!" "He'll be so hurt that he'll question his value to me as a friend!" "She's going to talk crap about me with our mutual friends, and then they'll hate me!"). We allow these worst-case-scenario suspicions to stand in for reality without a guarantee that they will be the result. We can waste our entire lives trying not to step on nonexistent toes.

Lisa was convinced that if she set any social boundaries, she would jeopardize her relationships. She hesitated to stop dancing around her volatile manager's attitude or set clear expectations with friends and family because she felt responsible for their emotions. Put another way: She didn't consider that these are fully grown adults who are reasonable and resilient enough to manage their own experiences. Instead, she believed that it was *her* duty to cushion the blow between them and the world, that she was more valuable when she behaved as a buffer between people and reality. This created an outsize sense of self that led her to overestimate the need for her intervention and underestimate the agency of those around her.

You are not responsible for everyone

We learn from a very young age that people who are accommodating are well-liked. Many people grew up in environments that took it one step further and were taught, through words or actions, that if they were not a communal basket of resources for those around them, then love and connection would be restricted. Over time, putting other people's needs before your own can make your day-to-day experience—and eventually, your life—feel draining and out of your control.

The realization that finally got Lisa to stop trying to control her manager's moody outbursts at work and to set clearer expectations with her friends and family was that *her quality of life could not depend on other people's needs and feelings.* Believing she was responsible for other people's needs and feelings was making her feel like a victim in her own life. There isn't a magical day when people will stop needing and feeling things and when you become comfortable prioritizing yourself. You have to give yourself permission—*right now!*—to set reasonable limits that protect and preserve you. You must develop confidence that you, more than anyone else, know your needs and will stand up for them *despite* what other people say. You need to set a limit on how much you can give, trust that it's a reasonable amount, and then decide how you might reinforce that limit going forward.

How can you tell you're suffering from social burnout? Let's look at some common indicators:

- Being known as the "reliable," "selfless" friend, family member, or colleague
- Always having things you need to do that you wouldn't be doing if someone didn't ask
- Guilting yourself into doing things before you've even tried to say no
- Justifying decisions by thinking, *I'd want someone to do this for me so I should say yes,* even though you have a history of not asking for things in return
- When people invite you to things and your first response is an internal *Ugh*
- Dreaming about having no social obligations and disappearing for a while

If these signs feel familiar to you, you're in luck! The chapters in this book on mindset, personal care, and boundaries will be particularly beneficial. These areas of burnout management will help you to trust that *you* are your priority; they will help you to identify exactly *what* you need; and finally, they will help you to protect those needs. You'd be surprised by how often social burnout prevents us from taking care of ourselves (or maybe you wouldn't, because you know this struggle all too well).

I have spent many weekends without groceries on hand and opting out of my Sunday food-shopping trip because someone invited me to something. I'd hesitantly RSVP yes, all the while knowing I'd pay the price later when I had to eat cereal for dinner that week. There is a time to prioritize social asks, but it is not when you're already experiencing burnout and your body's basic needs aren't being met. Because ironically, our basic needs are often the first thing to go when we get busy.

Who has time to cook a meal when a deadline is approaching? Why would I sleep when 10 P.M. is the only time I have to mindlessly scroll on my phone and feel a little joy? Why would I skip my friend's birthday party just because it happens to be on the only day off I've had in a month? When people experience social burnout, they usually deprioritize their own needs. In a recent study from Finland, women with the highest levels of burnout were also the least likely to consume healthy, nutrient-rich foods. (I mean . . . there's a reason nobody's "comfort food" is salad.) And research finds that people who show signs of burnout get less and poorer sleep (and in a cruel twist, poor sleep, of course, leads to higher risk of burnout).

Prioritizing your social calendar when basic survival needs are unmet is putting the cart before the horse, and it *will* exacerbate your burnout. Maslow's hierarchy of needs reinforces that social needs are secondary to physiological needs.

We've all heard airline flight attendants tell us to put on our own

oxygen mask before helping others. Social burnout is common in people who sincerely struggle to justify prioritizing themselves, especially when it comes at the cost of accommodating others.

FOMO: A busy death

Social burnout isn't common only in those who show up out of guilt; it is also common in those who experience FOMO (fear of missing out). As a member of what my mom calls the FOBI (fear of being included) club, people who *want* to go to and be a part of everything amaze me. FOMO has gained steam as a cute way to describe yourself, when in reality the effect of the internal pressure to be everywhere can be quite damaging.

Believe it or not, scientists have studied FOMO and identified two parts to it: First, there's that feeling of exclusion, the sense that everyone is doing something fun without you. You may also feel ostracized (even if you're not actually being rejected). The second part of FOMO is the compulsion to do whatever you can to maintain those relationships so that you no longer feel left out. You may forgo sleep to attend a concert with friends or binge-watch a show after a marathon day at work because everyone at the office is talking about it.

If this is you, don't be too hard on yourself—evolution has stacked the deck against you: Neuroscientists have found that humans are actually hardwired to be part of the "in group" because it ensures safety and survival (strength in numbers and all that). So, when you feel out of step with your peer group, feelings of rejection arise as a signal to preserve those ties.

The problem is that in our wired world, it's easy to feel FOMO with every click and scroll, and it's taking a toll. If you believe that by not going to that one brunch with friends or that one networking event you will be disproportionately left out or miss professional opportunities, you might perceive social stakes as higher than they really are. Remind yourself of all the times you haven't gone to things before and nothing bad happened. Don't let a vague sense of FOMO bulldoze your need for personal time.

Get pickier

Ideally, you know yourself well enough to understand which types of socializing mean the most to you so that you can be selective with your time and energy. Do you prefer one-on-one or small group coffee dates to giant parties where you barely get to talk to anyone anyway? Do you get more out of an in-person networking event than virtual ones? Do you show up with more joy in your heart to family gatherings when you go only once a month instead of every weekend? You know yourself! You can sense when those internal lights start flashing red, signaling you don't want to do something. You've likely just gotten very good at overriding them or explaining them away.

After you recognize your preferences, get comfortable expressing what you are available for. I think we've all anxiously passed around a text or email draft before hitting send to ensure it reads the way we intend it to. Being able to clearly express yourself is one of the most valuable skills you can have. It helps you set expectations in relationships so there isn't tension, and it ensures that you don't waste time due to shyness or miscommunication. While it might seem like communicating your true needs can jeopardize relationships, it is more likely to salvage them. Here's a conversation-starter that has saved many of my friendships during cycles of burnout:

> As a preface, I'm telling you this because I love you and don't want to be distant without explanation. I'm going through a busy season and the best I can show up in this relationship is a 4 out of 10 for the foreseeable future. I can't promise I'll answer texts or calls—though I will try my best—and I can probably only get together once every few months. This is just all I have left in my tank by the time I've taken care of everything else. I'm hoping to have my feet under me again by _____, but until then, can you accept my 4 out of 10?

Social burnout is often a result of feeling like you need to show up at a 10/10 in all your relationships all the time. Odds are, you've already built a strong rapport with those individuals, and they will understand if you need to pull back in busy seasons. If they don't . . . let's just say you'll *love* the chapter on boundaries. We are not victims of the relationships in our lives. *We* decide how we show up in them, and there is no better time to be clear on *how* you can show up than when you are experiencing social burnout.

Here are a couple of ways you might begin to reduce your social burnout:

1. **Start asking, "If this could go any way I wanted, how would it go?"** What would your relationships look like? What would you prioritize? What would you stop doing? If you grew up being told or believing that your desired experience comes second to everyone else's, this change will take practice. We're getting you back in the driver's seat, even if that means having a scary moment when you realize you need to change how you're showing up in relationships. There will be some adjustments for everyone involved, but the right people will be happy to give you the space to screw your head back on, and they will be thrilled to be reunited with you when you emerge from the other side.

2. **Assess your calendar.** If you're thinking, *I'm definitely socially exhausted, but I don't know how to start cutting things out—it feels like everything is mandatory,* then take a good, hard look at your calendar. Highlight all the things that drain you the most and get clarity about why those interactions sap your energy. Is it the person themselves? The duration? The long drive? The frequency? The topics that come up when you're together? Then start making the adjustments necessary to get closer to an endurable experience.

    Bonus: Also highlight the social items on your calendar that refill you the most. Unpack what makes those so pleasant. The company? The location? The activity? The clearer you are about what fills your social battery instead of depleting it, the better off you will be when prioritizing social commitments going forward.

3. **Stop punishing yourself because you can make the best out of things.** I hate when people say, "You always have fun once you're there," as an argument for getting you to do something or go somewhere. Having fun once I'm doing something is a reflection of my ability to make the best of my circumstances, not confirmation that I needed to be there in the first place.

BURNOUT BY BOREDOM: MORE THAN "DISENGAGED"

"You've had a lot of appointments lately" was my manager's polite way of pointing out that I had been using every possible excuse to ditch work for a couple of hours for the past few weeks. And he was right: I was scheduling any doctor and dentist appointment I could think of just to shake up my schedule a bit. As a rule follower who wanted to be perceived as hardworking and dedicated, this was odd behavior for me. But the mere thought of sitting at my desk and completing mundane tasks had become painful. Inspirational speaker Iyanla Vanzant famously said, "When the time comes for you to make a change or to grow, the universe will make you so uncomfortable you eventually have no choice." I had begun having the creeping feeling that I had outgrown my role, and slowly but surely, the walls felt like they were closing in. I was officially becoming uncomfortable enough that change was necessary.

Our brains need novelty and variety to remain engaged. From the moment we're born, we learn best about the world from new, unfamiliar stimuli. In a 2015 study from Johns Hopkins, babies were more likely to remember attributes of an object that surprised and bewildered them compared to an object that behaved in a way they expected. One reason we gravitate time and again toward things that are fresh and surprising: A part of our brain called the hippocampus releases a hit of feel-good dopamine when we are confronted with new things. (This is another reason it can be so hard to put your phone down at night. By design, social media is like a dopamine slot machine. What will you see if you keep scrolling? Something funny? A product you've been curious about? News you've been following? People you like? Dopamine is a silent but pushy motivator.)

Not only do novelty and variety benefit us, but their absence hinders us. Studies have shown that repetition leads to lower levels of task engagement and critical thinking. This is one of the reasons burnout by boredom plagued so many people during the pandemic, when our schedules offered very little novelty or variety—we could no longer pop out for coffee with a colleague or break up the workday with a visit to the gym. Even those who did enjoy their day-to-day work found themselves wondering what was missing.

We need to feel engaged in what we're doing, or we risk switching to autopilot as a means of enduring the repetitiveness of our lives. "Autopilot" is the sense of "just going through the motions." Have you ever driven home and once you arrived, you realized you didn't remember the drive at all? You've done that drive a hundred times; you likely went on mental autopilot and just went through the motions. Conversely, when you drive a new route, you are alert, looking around, ensuring you're following the directions correctly. Novelty and variety force us to pay attention. When we aren't paying attention, we miss out on much of our lives. Some repetition and predictability allow us to feel a sense of security, but too much predictability results in disengagement and can lead to malaise and discontent.

Interpreting boredom

Burnout by boredom is this experience of being mentally checked out, disengaged, and uninspired for an extended period of time. It can look different for everyone, but here are some common indicators it has found you:

- Feeling detached from your day-to-day life

- Not remembering the last time you did something "fun"

- Feeling envy or confusion when you see other people who are engaged and excited about their life

- Feeling frustration and resentment toward responsibilities when you wake up in the morning

- Having trouble getting started with your day

- Knowing you're unhappy in your work, studies, or role but missing the energy to make changes

- Lacking confidence in yourself and the direction of your life

- Never feeling like you're "doing enough"

There are times in life when you must see hard or boring commitments through. School generally takes a set amount of time. Gaining years of experience in certain industries takes as long as it takes. So long as those experiences ultimately align with your goals, it still makes sense to engage in them. Plus, the promise of a big change at the finish line can help you wade through the tediousness.

However, if these tasks or experiences are largely unpleasant or disengaging *and* they are misaligned with your long-term goals . . . you might need to evaluate their standing. If your job is killing your spirit, if your hobby isn't bringing you the same joy or relaxation it once did, it might be time to shake things up. Throughout this book, I'll delve into different ways to make your current circumstances work, as well as how to know when it's time to walk away from something that isn't serving you anymore. Keep in mind: This is not to say that you should quit something the moment it bores you. Rather, always be aware of when you can introduce novelty or variety to a repeated activity.

An object at rest stays at rest

Often, burnout by boredom is difficult to combat because of weeks or months (or years!) of inertia. Boredom in short bursts can actually be helpful—it tells us we'd rather be doing something else, so (ideally) we change things up and get busy with a more stimulating pursuit. But when we're burned out because of chronic disengagement, we may not have the momentum to get ourselves going again. It's like trying to go from a walk to a sprint, whereas having momentum feels like going from a jog to a sprint.

A devastating but true sentiment I've heard from many managers is: "If you want something done, give it to a busy person." Research shows that busy people are more motivated to complete tasks and actually do them more quickly than their less scheduled counterparts, possibly because busy people have so many competing deadlines that they're more motivated to whip through them so they don't fall behind. When you're already busy, throwing one more thing into the mix somehow feels less difficult than if you have an entire day off and need to muster the energy to go to the post office. The post office is just one thing, yet somehow the resistance is so much stronger when it's the only thing forcing you to get off the couch.

The most beneficial pillars of burnout management for those suffering from burnout by boredom are mindset, personal care (which you'll learn also includes lifestyle design to help set goals and create momentum), and time management. Keeping yourself invested is critical as you reestablish how you will spend your time and energy.

Positive challenge vs. negative challenge

It is in our best interest to remain positively challenged so that we are forced to sit up straight and care about what is on the horizon. This is why it's so important to set goals by asking ourselves, *What am I moving toward?* Positive challenge is a balanced combination of growth outside of our comfort zone and building toward the things we want. It's adopting a "growth mindset"—believing that we will improve through effort—and being motivated by something that brings us personal satisfaction and enjoyment (versus being motivated by fear of punishment). By contrast, negative challenge is doing things outside of our comfort zone that make us unjustly uncomfortable and don't align with anything we're hoping to move toward. Where positive challenge offers value, negative challenge drains us.

In their book *First, Break All the Rules,* an analysis of a Gallup survey of eighty thousand managers, authors Marcus Buckingham and

Curt Coffman deduce that a significant factor in employee satisfaction is getting to develop in areas that interest the employee. Revolutionary, I know. No job is perfect, and you won't always get to work in the golden zone of positive challenge, but it is essential to think about positive challenge as you assess your circumstances.

In my own case, several years ago, I had a great manager who could sense that I had outgrown my current role. His recommendation was that I specialize in something so that I could grow with the company. But I knew the available opportunities for specialization weren't aligned with my interests. I began to think about leaving for something new. Coincidentally, a former classmate was leaving her training and development position and offered to tell her manager that I was interested in her role. I applied, interviewed, got the position, and leaped into the new job.

In my new role, I suddenly found myself the small fish in a big pond as opposed to the big fish in a small pond—and I loved it. I had an intimidating amount of room to grow, but I could feel myself fully engaging and evolving because I was working outside of my comfort zone and growing into my interests.

If it sounds like you are experiencing burnout by boredom, I encourage you to:

1. **Track how you spend every hour of your day for two days.** Highlight items in green that engage you and that align with long-term goals. Highlight items in red that drain you, take without giving back, and do not align with long-term goals.

    *Note that sometimes red begets green. The long-term goal of being a pharmacist, for example, requires many red days of schooling despite being a green long-term goal. This is when constant reminders that the red is temporary, worth it to you, and ultimately aligns with your interests are essential.

2. **Decide what you want the next few months to look like and how they could more actively engage you.** Can you pause or minimize the time you are currently spending in the red and replace it with one of the green items? Can you begin working toward a replacement for a red item? Get creative about how

you might change your day-to-day engagement with red or green items.

3. If you're willing to be extreme with it, **toss out the way you currently do things and start from square one.** For a month, wake up at a new time, buy only groceries you haven't bought before, do all your work at different times than you normally do it, find a new hobby, watch a new show, walk a new route, read different types of books. Wake your brain up. Remove the repetitive factors in your life that you have control over and shake it up just to see where you land after the dust settles. Even if this is only an exercise in breaking up your routine, it might help you learn something about yourself or appreciate your original routine a little bit more.

With your newfound awareness of the three types of burnout, you are more likely to notice when you're tempted to overcommit, people please, or disengage—the unholy trinity of burnout. From here, you can begin to unpack what beliefs and attitudes might be driving you to these types of behaviors. It's time to dive into the first pillar of burnout management: mindset.

PART II

THE FIVE PILLARS OF
BURNOUT MANAGEMENT

CHAPTER THREE

Mindset

Is It Me? Am I the Drama?

Mandy logged on for our first meeting five minutes early and with a notepad ready, so I wasn't surprised when she later described herself as a "control freak." She had grown up putting pressure on herself to get good grades, she worked her way through college, and she started her own business in her twenties. On paper, she had achieved everything she had hoped to achieve in her career. Her six-figure income was stable, she found her work fulfilling, and she had the traditional indicators of success she had always hoped for (the house, the car, the large social media following). Despite these things, she felt incredibly burned out. She worked around the clock, always thinking about her business, never allowing herself to rest. From the outside she had her life together, but behind the scenes she was running herself into the ground. Mandy's problem was that even though she knew she was doing well, she retained the fear of failure and workaholism that had gotten her this far. She believed that her success was the result of overworking, and believing this meant that regardless of the success she had, she wouldn't feel comfortable scaling back on work for fear of losing it all.

Many individuals who see results from unsustainable amounts of output struggle to reduce output even after they've established themselves enough to take their foot off the gas. Mandy had internalized beliefs and habits that would take time to unlearn in order to show up differently in her life, to be able to release the stress that was no longer serving her and instead was taking her closer to the edge of burnout.

Expecting a lot of herself and working extremely hard to meet her goals had afforded her a comfortable lifestyle thus far, so it was understandable that she felt anxious about changing her behavior.

Mandy was burning out by volume even though her life had the potential to be calm and manageable. She was uncomfortable feeling satisfied unless *everything* she could think of was done. Satisfaction felt like complacency to her. It quickly became clear to me that Mandy's burnout was not a matter of time management, boundaries, or stress management—it was a matter of mindset.

You are always balancing two experiences: internal and external.

EXTERNAL EXPERIENCE
Visible, tangible experience

INTERNAL EXPERIENCE

Mental, emotional experience

Your internal experience is not visible; it's your thoughts and feelings, and how you are managing those thoughts and feelings. Your external experience *is* visible; it's how you manage the tangible items in your life. So if you get nervous before speaking in a meeting, your internal experience might be reminding yourself to breathe or reassuring yourself, and your external experience is your organized outline and delivery. All others see are the external, tangible elements; however, you are also managing your internal experience.

While Mandy had efficient external systems in place for managing her workload and personal responsibilities, she still always felt strained when she thought about what she had to get done. Nothing she did felt like enough—there was always more untapped potential, more projects to get ahead on, more people she could help. Despite hitting all her tangible targets as a business owner, she managed her thoughts and feelings as if she were constantly falling behind. Someone with access to her inner monologue and emotions might confuse her for someone whose life was a disaster and who needed to overwork or risk losing her business. As we've established, that was not the case.

Many people who are burned out have a strong handle on their external experience; they can fit everything they need into their day, they don't have outstanding items to do, and they prioritize well—from the outside, they look like they "have their shit together." But their management of their internal experience is another thing entirely. We all know that it's possible to "have your shit together" on the outside and feel like we are completely out of control on the inside—being flooded with racing, critical thoughts; ruminating on mistakes; imposing an unrelenting string of expectations on ourselves. We can't as easily gauge someone's internal experience from the outside. When friends of mine have done speaking engagements, they have walked off the stage and groaned, "That went horribly!" even though the audience thought they did a fantastic job. Externally, they made clear presentations and answered all the questions thoroughly and tactfully. Internally, they'd be berating themselves for all the things that they didn't say perfectly. It didn't matter how much anyone praised them; how satisfied and peaceful they felt at the end of the day depended more on their internal experience than on external perception of their experience.

Mindset can be described as many things—thoughts, attitude, learned responses—but when it comes to burnout management, **your mindset is how you manage your internal experience.** Thinking about how you talk to, motivate, and manage yourself can help you identify whether you could use a mindset tune-up. If you drive yourself with criticism and the belief that you are never doing enough, adopting a gentler and more upbeat inner voice will make the difference between enjoying or dreading the same external experience.

Let's say two people—we'll call them Katie and Erin—go to a spa and have identical treatments. Katie spends the day focused on enjoying the experience. She thinks to herself *This is so nice. I'm glad I'm doing something for myself. My body will thank me for this,* and she leaves feeling refreshed and relaxed. Erin spends her time at the spa ruminating about all the other things she "should" be doing, feeling guilty for taking time to herself, and in general not being present. Erin leaves feeling just as tense as when she arrived. Externally, Katie and Erin had identical experiences. Internally, they had entirely different experiences because of how they managed themselves.

Your mindset is the lens through which you see the world. If that lens causes you to judge yourself, live in fear of what others think, ruminate on stressors constantly, hold yourself to unattainable standards, or never be content, you will be more likely to burn out, and to burn out more often. Thankfully, our brain's neuroplasticity—its ability to change the neurons and neuronal connections in response to stimuli (people, places, experiences, substances)—allows us to rewire our thoughts, beliefs, and behaviors. Just as you learned your current style of internal management, you can master a new mode of operating, one that is kinder and more hopeful. We can learn to be more optimistic, even if we weren't exactly born with a glass-half-full outlook, says Hilary Tindle, MD, author of *Up: How Positive Outlook Can Transform Our Health and Aging*. That change in attitude, however, takes *practice*. Our brain's habit-forming machinery is equal opportunity—it can lay down tracks for positive thoughts and behaviors or take us down a darker path. But with intention, we can train our brain to be hungry for things that are good for us, notes Tindle. Every time you choose an optimistic thought or a self-compassionate response, you are hardwiring your brain for happiness. The payoff for building happier habits? Not only do optimistic individuals have lower rates of burnout; they also have lower levels of stress hormones, better immune functioning, and reduced threats of diabetes and stroke. The impact of your mindset is not contained to your mind; it seeps into your body, as well.

Most people's internal experience is a hodgepodge of the ways their parents and early influences (such as teachers, relatives, and coaches) spoke to them, whom they spend the most time around now, their individual demeanor (inheritable traits such as extroversion or conscientiousness and other personality characteristics that are particular to you), their belief system, and the messages they receive from the broader culture. These factors are often talked about as nature and nurture. You are born with your general demeanor. Experts think anywhere from one-quarter to one-half of our outlook is genetic, but the way we manage ourselves internally is largely learned and within our control. Think about the ways you talk to yourself when you make a mistake, the ways you think about challenges, the ways you support yourself during a long day. All of these are learned behaviors that make up your internal experience.

If you struggle with conceptualizing your mindset this way, instead imagine that your thoughts are another person who is strapped to your hip 24-7. How do you feel about that person?

Are they critical of and rude to you?

Are they kind, understanding, and supportive?

Are they embarrassed by you?

Do they believe in you and encourage you to take risks?

Do they instill fear in you?

Do they give you the push you need to be your best self?

If the person strapped to your hip (that is, your mindset) is a bully who is hard on you every time you make a mistake, then that is going to influence how you approach various challenges in your life. Because your mindset is internal, you often overlook how acutely it influences burnout. It is easier to try to control strategies that feel more tangible, like time management or personal care. Unfortunately, your practices around personal care are meaningless if your inner voice is sabotaging any good they are doing. Your mindset has the power to compromise any external efforts you might make, which is why it is paramount to correct it first. Your goal is to get into the habit of listening to the thoughts that create your internal experience and shift them to better support yourself.

Let's say you forget to do something at work. Your initial, instinctual reaction that has been ingrained in you is self-reproach. You feel embarrassed and think: *Damn it! How could I let this happen? People are going to think I'm incompetent.* We have all experienced this type of shame when we feel like we should have known better. This kind of self-berating can hijack our nervous system and trigger a release of stress hormones, putting us in a state of anxiety. But a negative response doesn't change the thing that happened; it just makes us feel worse on our path to recovering from it. Not only that, but when we do try to course-correct, we may not be as mentally sharp: Research by Sian Leah Beilock has found that we perform more poorly in exercises like math and memory tasks when our anxiety is in the driver's seat.

Instead, try to replace that initial response with a reminder that the stakes are probably not as high as they feel in the moment: *Not a big deal, I'll just correct it. I'm going to be working the rest of my life; making mistakes is inevitable.* A calm, reasonable response results in the exact same outcome as a punishing one—fixing the mistake—but it does so without the fire hose of criticism and stress. Gentler, kinder self-talk also moves us into a more optimistic headspace that gives us more room to correct the error and achieve the given goal.

Whether we learned to be hard on ourselves in childhood, in an unforgiving academic environment, or in an overly demanding industry or organization, we can unlearn the critical way of thinking and adopt a different approach. And while we're working on it: Let's not beat ourselves up for expecting a lot of ourselves. **Being the way we are has gotten us this far, but it is *not* going to work if we wish to go further.**

THE THREE BURNOUT MINDSETS

One of the primary reasons I am prone to burnout is because I am a high achiever. My high-achieving tendencies have long sabotaged me. While being high achieving is generally praised, it can be a very unforgiving mindset. Before I adopted a kinder mindset, I was my harshest critic: I always worried that I was being lazy (I have since learned that truly lazy people don't worry about whether they're being lazy) and falling short of my potential. As a result, I accumulated a good amount of success fairly quickly and sacrificed all my peace in the process.

The three mindsets that most commonly lead to burnout are a high-achieving mindset, a people-pleasing mindset, and a self-victimizing mindset. Each of these mentalities tends to lead people toward behaviors that will burn them out over time. Broadly speaking, those with a high-achieving mindset overload themselves for the sake of "achievement," those with people-pleasing mindsets struggle to justify and set boundaries, and a those with a self-victimizing mindset feel helpless to their circumstances. You can struggle with more than one of these at a time (fantastic, I know), though you will manage each in different ways. Familiarize yourself with each of these mindsets so that you can recognize the burnout-inducing beliefs that you may have internalized.

Those with a **high-achieving mindset** generally believe that their worth is dependent on their accomplishments. They tend to feel most valuable when they are performing well and are on track to achieving traditional success (praise, money, an impressive job title, a big house, social status, power, influence). These individuals have the potential to burn themselves out because their internal drivers are turned up to maximum. They compare themselves to the top 10 percent of people they know and hold themselves to extremely high standards for where they "should be" in their lives. People with high-achieving mindsets might have grown up in households that valued performance and ambition as indicators of worthiness of love and connection. The honor roll meant ice cream, but no honor roll meant a lecture. High achievers tend to be system- and planning-oriented and can find team-based, collaborative learning challenging. As a result of believing they should strive for more, better, always, their behaviors can tend toward unsustainable output and dissatisfaction with where they are, despite technically doing well.

Though a high-achieving mindset tends to accelerate a person's burnout, their intrinsic motivation to excel no matter the challenge is admirable at face value. People who prioritize achievement often become our most knowledgeable doctors, Olympic athletes, and innovators. The problem arises when this mindset causes compromise in other areas of life—areas that need to be nurtured and grow as much as professional life.

Every day, I talk to successful individuals (who many people would kill to trade places with) who say things like, "I don't know who I am outside of my work." They stay at their desk until sundown, are constantly praised for their contributions, and appear content to the people who work with them. But then, the truth comes out: "I never see my kids," "I never see my partner," "I'm not happy with my health," "I remember when I used to go play pick-up basketball at the gym after work, I was so much happier then," "I don't have any hobbies," "Even if I worked less, I don't know what I would do with my time." When we see high achievers in action we assume they have everything. In reality, they often have *one* thing. **If the cost of achievement is everything else in your life, then the cost is too high.** To my fellow high achievers: If being calm, feeling personal satisfaction, and resting without guilt sound appealing to you, then you will have to let some of the high-achieving tendencies go.

The most beneficial—and difficult—shift a high achiever can make is identifying and prioritizing values outside of achievement. Knowing what offers you satisfaction and boosts your self-esteem *outside of your work* reduces a high achiever's tendency to form their identity around their work and accomplishments. What gives you satisfaction does *not* need to be "productive" or garner praise from anyone else. You don't need to choose a performative hobby that doesn't add value or bring joy to your life. I used to force myself to finish every book I started even if I dreaded reading it. This behavior, in retrospect, was a colossal waste of my time. (I mean . . . have you ever read *Crime and Punishment*? The punishment is that it's five hundred pages long.) I stopped reading for optics or out of some strange sense of duty and started reading for pleasure (I think I've read every hockey romance on the market by now, which has gained me zero social capital but brought me immense joy). By including reading in my life in a way that wasn't necessarily "productive" or praise garnering, I actually got to enjoy it.

If you were simply *experiencing* your life for yourself instead of performing it for other people, what would you do more of? Maybe you'd like to spend more quality time with people you love, pursue interests or hobbies that aren't related to professional or personal development, or maybe you'd just want the freedom to do whatever it is you feel like in the moment instead of living so rigidly. Try it, one small change at a time—put aside that book you aren't enjoying, sign up for that art class you've been eyeing, or take the day off work to do nothing in particular. Consider how things *feel*, instead of how they look.

Having a **people-pleasing mindset** is common in individuals who learned from an early age that when they are available and accommodating, they receive love and connection, and when they are not managing the experiences of those around them, they could be ostracized or feel unsafe. As adults, people pleasers often find themselves in relationships that affirm for them *the more giving and the less confrontational I am, the more people will like me.* This is not always a negative trait—in fact, we are built with some degree of social conformity so that we can get along in group settings. We exhibit this cooperative behavior from the time we are toddlers. But the trouble comes when we lose sight of our own needs. A people-pleasing mindset insists upon making others happy over respecting ourselves and our limits. Facing disappointment in ourselves feels more bearable than disappointing others, so we burn out trying not to let anyone else down, no matter the tradeoff (like lost sleep, downtime, or opportunities we would like to take). In fact, disagreeing with someone can be so unpleasant for people pleasers that fMRI brain imaging scans can actually detect neural changes that reflect the resulting mental stress and discomfort. Prioritizing others' needs isn't just inconvenient for people pleasers—the tension caused by not being truthful about their own experience can result in a physical stress response and difficulty regulating emotions following the incident. People pleasing hurts you not just socially but physically.

Women in particular often struggle to speak up for their needs, out of fear that they will seem "difficult," whether it's saying they don't care for a particular restaurant their partner likes or telling someone at work they don't think their idea will work or that they don't actually have time to (or want to) run the company's internship program. Women are raised to be docile, warm, and accommodating, and to anticipate others' needs before daring to have their own. This type of socializing is detrimental for many reasons, not the least of which is that it normalizes a people-pleasing mindset for women. Things are slowly improving with each generation, but old habits die hard.

In her book *Untamed,* Glennon Doyle writes, "Every time you're given a choice between disappointing someone else and disappointing yourself, your duty is to disappoint that someone else. Your job throughout your entire life, is to disappoint as many people as it takes to avoid disappointing yourself." This advice can feel scary and in direct opposition to people pleasers' instincts. But you *must* believe that your relationships can survive having thoughts, opinions, and boundaries of your own. Those with people-pleasing mindsets tend to struggle to break their people-pleasing habits because they haven't gotten enough practice *not* people pleasing and seeing that, most of the time, everything turns out fine. **We gain confidence through evidence and experience.**

To gain confidence that we can tone down the people pleasing, we need to have positive experiences *not* people pleasing. If every time you have prioritized yourself over others in the past, you've been met with anger or disappointment, then you've learned that not people pleasing = anger and disappointment. **You can't heal in the environment that made you sick.** The people who *taught* you people pleasing probably aren't going to be the people who love it when you stop people pleasing. To combat the belief that prioritizing yourself results in negative social consequences, identify some *different, reasonable* people with whom to practice *not* people pleasing.

Take, for example, my client Trish, a teacher whose people-pleasing nature made her wonderful at her job but vulnerable to imbalanced relationships. She had a friend, Molly, who could be described as codependent on a good day, and a stage-10 clinger and expert guilter on a bad day. Trish engaged with this friendship out of habit and guilt. Molly *needed* her, and each time Trish set boundaries, Molly felt strongly rejected and let Trish know how upsetting it was. To practice not people pleasing in a less volatile environment, Trish decided to tell a handful of her more even-keeled friends that she wasn't available for their call time or their coffee date to see how they responded. It was important for Trish to experience setting boundaries and getting reasonable responses. In every case, her other friends were accommodating and understanding. Her confidence in *not* people pleasing grew with each *No problem, let's reschedule!* that came through. Now, sure that she had no reason to feel guilty, she began using the same boundaries with Molly, her needier friend. Molly wasn't happy about it, but Trish was. The guilt she felt lessened, and over time, they grew apart as their push and pull of resources became mutually unsatisfying.

When you stop people pleasing, you quickly realize that being a person with an opinion or needs doesn't diminish your morality; it's just part of being human. Most people understand the need to prioritize themselves sometimes. And the people who would prefer that you act like a doormat will definitely let you know, so you'll be able to brace for interactions with them or, better yet, avoid them altogether.

If you've had a people-pleasing mentality all your life, your first step is to start asking yourself, *What do I **really** think? How do I **really** feel? What would **I** like the outcome of this situation to be?* Start speaking up for your needs.

Perhaps your brother-in-law asks you to pick up his kids from school, a detour that would require you to reschedule the doctor's appointment you've already had to move twice. This is a people pleaser's nightmare. Your internal voice is screaming, *It takes a village! He would do it for you; you need to help him!* But the self-preserving part of you is saying, *This is a last-minute request and reasonable people know that sometimes last-minute requests can't be accommodated. You need to uphold your own commitments.* Your needs do not always come second to other people's needs. Of course, there will be times when you decide that your needs can or should come second. The important thing to notice is how quickly and how often you dismiss your original plan as soon as someone else asks for something. At a certain point, this behavior goes from selfless to reckless, because you are not taking care of yourself.

. . .

The last burnout mindset is a **self-victimizing mindset.** A self-victimizing mindset is a combination of feeling helplessness for an extended time and being skeptical about finding long-term satisfaction. When things haven't gone your way repeatedly in the past, you may lose hope about current and future endeavors and feel as if you have no power to change anything. You may also have a tendency to view external factors as barriers and believe that bad luck is inevitable. To see whether you have this mentality, ask yourself *When someone makes a suggestion, is my instinct to poke holes in the solution rather than embrace it?*

Let's say a friend of yours insists that they want to have date nights with their husband but every suggestion you make about how to squeeze it in is met with resistance. "Why don't you get a babysitter?" *It's expensive and I don't trust anyone with my kids.* "Could you just wait until they go to sleep, order food, and have a picnic in the house?" *They might wake up and that barely even counts as a date.* "You could ask family to watch them one morning and go have coffee or breakfast together." *I don't want to burden anyone, I guess this is just my reality now.* Do you hear how insistent this person is that they are a victim to their circumstances? Their responses were valid in their own way, but instead of coming up with additional solutions, they focused only on the problems.

Listening to our thoughts and acknowledging when we might be erroneously projecting helplessness is the first step toward correcting this behavior. It is not uncommon for people with a self-victimizing mindset to seem like they *want* to be unhappy and like they're *seeking out* problems because they are so skeptical about happiness. But a self-victimizing mindset is a learned pattern just like anything else, and it isn't a reason to beat yourself up. Rather, it's a reason to be honest with yourself about whether you have genuinely exhausted every option. Nothing is ever so doomed that we can't be resourceful or creative about how we handle it. When something "bad" happens—you get stuck in traffic or your colleague gets the promotion you wanted—your first response should not be *of course this happened to me.* Very few things are actually about us or require an emotional response from us. Often, we just happen to be there when bad things happen. We are not a victim in the situation; we are just *in* the situation.

People with a self-victimizing mindset often burn out because they are fielding disproportionate negative emotions in response to any inconvenience, and the fallout can be physically and emotionally harmful. Someone being rude at a store is just someone being rude at a store, not an indictment of your character. Someone rushing off the phone with you is just someone in a hurry, not someone who hates talking to you. Someone who doesn't acknowledge all the hard work you did is just someone who wasn't thoughtful enough to note it, not someone who is hell-bent on undermining you. Again, these situations are not necessarily happening *because of* you; you just happen to be on the receiving end. You can either have a miserable day rehashing the stressor and believing that it was personal, or you can depersonalize it and turn your attention back to other things.

You need to adopt a solution-oriented mindset, not a problem-oriented one. Or, as my dad would say, "Have a can-do attitude, not a can't-do attitude." Having a "can-do" attitude—a positive, thoughtful approach to problem-solving—doesn't just result in a better outcome, it results in a better experience for you. You can tell whether someone has a can-do attitude or a can't-do attitude within thirty seconds of speaking with them. A can-do, solution-oriented person says things like, "Let me see what I can do" or "What are our options? Let's explore them." They are resourceful, persistent, and optimistic. A can't-do, problem-oriented person will likely lead with the problem and dwell on it: "See, the problem with that is . . ." or a final "That's not going to work" without pivoting to trying something new, something that might in fact work. They poke holes in solutions before they start, giving you the impression that they don't even want things to progress.

This isn't to say that you shouldn't acknowledge the reality of serious problems or show blind positivity all the time. Life is hard. Disappointments abound. Inequities exist. Not everything works out the way we want it to even when we put in the effort. But . . . in the face of most day-to-day challenges, you get to *choose* how you respond, and when you choose with a can-do attitude, you are allowing for the best possible outcome given the situation. Again, a self-victimizing mindset is just a pattern people have learned to follow because it seemingly benefits them on some level—adopting a self-victimizing mindset might make a person feel safe because if it doesn't work out, they won't be disappointed, since their expectations are so low. Now, for those of you who are calling me some colorful things at this point, this victim mindset section is not a personal attack—it's a chance to reflect on whether this might sound familiar and, if so, to decide what changes you can make going forward to prevent feeling like a victim.

Whether you're burning out as a result of having a high-achieving, people-pleasing, or self-victimizing mindset, you can change your mindset and your reality. You can rewire your default responses. You only get one life. Nobody is coming to fix it for you. What do you want to change?

MINDSET INFLUENCES

In addition to the three mindsets that most often lead to burnout, there are several mindset influences that can compromise you on your journey to balance. The things that affect your mindset are typically learned from others or are patterns you fell into and haven't broken out of. Learning these influences will help you recognize when they might be guiding you toward burnout and how you can make more thoughtful choices going forward.

Conforming to culture

I was confused speaking to my client Charles, who worked as an information technology consultant in New York. "It sounds like you're comfortable with your workload," I said, "so, why is it that you stay at the office late?" Shaking his head, he responded, "Everyone stays late. If I leave on time, they'll think I'm not working as hard." "Shouldn't it reflect well that you're efficient enough to complete your work on time?" I asked. With a sad chuckle he confirmed, "Surprisingly, no." It was time to unpack how Charles's company culture was impacting his mindset and causing burnout.

Company culture—the identity, values, expectations, and traditions that determine "the way things are done"—is a potent driver of employee behavior. Charles had come to me with an interest in time management, but after a few conversations, it was clear that the tendencies leading him to burnout were rooted in his mindset. He was working long hours to fit into the company's unbalanced culture, and those long hours came at the cost of his work-life balance. No matter how much he boosted his productivity during his working hours, he still didn't feel comfortable leaving the office on time. Every evening when 5 P.M. rolled around, it became a silent competition to see who dared to go home first. When the first person rose, there was a collective moment of judgment, and then a sigh of relief that someone had broken the seal, sacrificing themselves so that other people could begin to trickle out. On good days, the seal was broken at 5:15 P.M. by someone who usually announced they *had* to leave to pick their kid up or go to an appointment—like it was a shame they had a life outside of their cubicle. He recalled one silent standoff that lasted until nine P.M. during a busy season. And nine P.M. was when the *first* person left.

Charles didn't want to compromise his reputation and standing at work by leaving on time. But—and we'll discuss this more in depth in the boundaries chapter—often the things we worry about compromising are already being threatened in another way. Charles's mental health and his future at this company were already being compromised by his burnout.

His options were either to accept that he needed to start leaving on time, perception be damned, or to allow himself to grow frustrated enough to leave the company entirely. He resolved to be the first person to leave every day and become known for it. He shifted his mindset and instead of thinking about it as embarrassing or shameful, he thought about all the gratitude others would probably feel that they would have "permission" to go home sooner on a regular basis. And in fact, he eventually did receive verbal appreciation from some colleagues for doing this. Unfortunately, he also received the poorest performance review he had gotten thus far the next time quarterly reviews came around. He knew he was still performing well and this was just an attempt on his manager's part to curb his new habit. But being the perfect employee no longer mattered to him more than the quality of his life. The performance review didn't impact his pay, so he kept leaving work at five P.M. He was so much less resentful and mentally fatigued after committing to being the guy who leaves on time. He lasted in his role for another year before letting me know that he was excited to move to another company that had reached out to him—one he had time to speak with because he was no longer spending so many futile hours at work. The most important question he had asked at the end of his interview with the new company? "What time do people typically leave the office?"

Company culture is determined by people. It only takes a couple of bad eggs in positions of power with toxic messaging to influence an entire organization. If you work in a setting with a harmful culture, comments like these may sound familiar:

"We notice who stays late . . ."

"That's just the industry standard. Make it happen."

"When you took this job, I thought you understood that it would re-quire some sacrifices . . ."

Statements like these essentially convey that the employee with the fewest boundaries wins. It's not even clear *what* they win. Sure, sometimes it's a promotion (and let's be honest, not nearly often enough to justify the sacrifices). But most of the time, it is just a slightly higher mark on a performance review, praise that does not have that much impact on the scope of your career, or an imaginary gold star of validation that feels gratifying but disappears just as quickly as it came, leaving you hungry for more.

The company's employees feed into this social game, with everyone holding each other accountable through nuanced social pressures like giving people side-eye when they take their full lunch break or use their vacation days. This pressure, in turn, creates a culture of critique, distrust, and prioritization of work over life. When one employee submits to this pressure, there is typically a desire to enforce this culture for others as well. This is how detrimental behaviors and attitudes spread to infect an entire group and make them fearful of prioritizing themselves over their work.

When a company culture anoints work as *the* top priority, it is easy to forget that **a job is just an exchange of service for money.** At the end of the day, you are providing a service worth X amount. People aren't working out of the kindness of their hearts; we all have to pay for the roof over our head and food in our fridge. Our relationships with work have just evolved to the point that it's easy to forget the fact that it's an exchange. It feels like a little ecosystem, a mini-world we belong to with its own rules, relationships, and culture.

Company culture wasn't seen as important until around the 1980s, when research began to reveal that culture has a powerful impact on an organization's outcomes and success. At the time, "culture" often meant a reduction in smoking, blatant discrimination, and sexual harassment at work. But throughout the 2000s, company culture expanded to encompass everything from rethinking office layout, to promoting egalitarianism and diversity, to improving employee benefits.

It makes sense that we have an intimate relationship with our work, organization, and colleagues. We spend nearly a third of our lives at work, so it would be impossible not to form a symbiotic relationship with it. However, the evolution of work culture over the last decade—higher expectations, increased hours, the bleeding of work into our homes and personal devices—has prompted us to forget that at the end of the day, we work because we signed a contract to do A, B, and C for X amount of money. **Expectations become unclear when our contract says one thing and the culture says another.**

A contract might specify that forty hours of work on Monday through Friday from the hours of 9 A.M. to 5 P.M. is what is expected of you. When everyone shows up an hour early, leaves an hour late, and works through lunch, sticking to what you contractually agreed to can feel like paddling upstream. It can also feel slightly shameful. Your reasonable attempts to maintain a work-life balance might even be called out by a manager. So instead of fighting the culture, employees follow the current and find themselves further downriver from what they signed on for.

In the United States, the lack of laws protecting employees only reinforces this blurring of lines between our work and our personal life. For a developed nation that prides itself on industry, we have rather weak laws protecting the people that make those industries run. In 2021, Portugal passed a labor law making it illegal for employers to contact employees outside of working hours. In Britain, a new working mother can take up to fifty-two weeks off, thirty-nine of which are paid at about 90 percent. Australians are entitled to a minimum of four weeks of PTO. Comparatively, the United States offers no mandated paid leave for new mothers, no mandatory paid time off for employees, and in many industries no protection for employees with employers who don't respect boundaries. Ideally, we work for organizations that are striving to compete with the best, not meeting the bare minimum and telling us that we're ungrateful to want more. If we don't currently have that dream employer, we instead need alternative methods for protecting ourselves from job-related burnout.

To combat the negative aspects of company culture, find ways to remember that your job is an exchange of service for money. At the end of the day, you fulfill a business need. Should you leave your role (and to be blunt, in the case that you literally die), your job opening would be posted within the month. That isn't to say you don't do important work or that your colleagues don't value you, but it's a *business*, and it will figure out how to run without you. Some companies love people who lose sight of this transactional relationship. They use phrases like "we're a family" and "you've got to earn your place in this industry" to justify asking for more than the exchange you agreed to at the outset. We buy into and normalize this culture because we see others doing so and because we may even believe it—it feels *good* to belong to something that we admire and that aligns with our career goals (and if we're lucky, maybe even our values). It's not a bad thing to love your job and want to give 100 percent. But it is *your* responsibility—not your boss's or your team's—to make thoughtful decisions about the relationship you want to have with your work.

Often, we don't realize that we've been coaxed into our current beliefs and behaviors. Think back to your mindset and expectations when you started your current job. If you were suddenly thrust into your situation today, would you be alarmed? Would you note a couple of things that don't seem quite right or fair? Maybe those expectations or interactions don't regularly catch your attention because they just seem "normal" at this point. But culture and shared beliefs needn't be loud and public in order to exert influence over a person's mindset; sometimes they creep in, silently and subtly.

It is easy for learned thoughts, beliefs, and behaviors to feel like the status quo, so we have to stay sharp enough to notice when something seems normal but *isn't* and empowered enough to know that we *can* do something about it.

Limiting beliefs: Coloring inside the nonexistent lines

Limiting beliefs are exactly what they sound like: beliefs that limit us. They are often arbitrary lines we have drawn in the sand that we live by. We typically hold these beliefs because they have been reinforced frequently enough that we perceive them as truth. How many times have people told you their opinions as though they're facts?

Finding a new job will be extremely difficult, says the person in a completely different field with a completely different network who hasn't applied to a job in ten years.

You need to stay with this company for at least a year, says the person who doesn't have to show up for that job every day.

If you set boundaries at work, they'll think you don't work hard, says the person who constantly works overtime, complains nonstop, and generally seems to be miserable.

Quite frankly, many people are talking out of their ass. **Nobody knows your life like you do, nobody knows your limits better than you do, and nobody's truth is truer than yours just because they say it with more conviction.**

We tend to internalize repeated messages—from friends, colleagues, media—as truth, especially if those messages are reinforced by our natural fear of taking the path of more resistance. If you want to stand a fighting chance against burnout, you are going to need to reexamine some of your beliefs to ensure they aren't keeping you where you are.

The tendency to live our lives conforming to our beliefs even when they are no longer true (or never were!) has been illustrated in a variety of experiments. Researchers have found that sometimes we can develop a learned helplessness—we adapt to an initial set of conditions and, even when those conditions change, we continue to act as if the original conditions were still in place. Here's a common example that demonstrates this phenomenon: A researcher places fleas in a jar. The fleas jump out almost immediately. The researcher then places a lid on the jar, and the fleas continue to jump up and hit the lid. Once the researcher removes the lid, the fleas continue to jump, but only to the height of the lid that's no longer there. Although the lid is gone, the fleas continue to limit themselves to the height of where it once was.

I don't mean to imply that we don't have more agency than some fleas in a jar, but we do have a tendency to filter our present and future through our past. On the one hand, that's smart, right? If you learn that eating too much cheese gives you a stomachache, you don't eat as much the next time you're presented with it. (Or maybe you do. Your relationship with cheese is your business.) Our aversion to strong unpleasant feelings is not just practical; it supports our biological desire to avoid pain. Studies find that adverse feelings and memories remain in our long-term memory longer than neutral or positive events. The problem comes when our past experiences engender beliefs that might no longer be valid or applicable. You need to hit the lid of every jar you encounter to make sure you aren't carrying past limitations into a reality in which they do not exist.

Many burned-out people with whom I have worked feel guilty being unavailable after working hours, not always because it is an expectation in their current roles, but often because it was an expectation in past roles. They keep their phones or laptops nearby during dinner in case they get any messages. They check their emails before they've even gotten out of bed in the morning. They learned these behaviors to adapt to old expectations but couldn't shake them even when the expectations changed. It took acknowledging and breaking these limiting beliefs to feel comfortable with new behaviors that reduced their burnout.

In your own life, what limits may have existed for you previously that you carry forward unnecessarily? Most of them sound like *I can't ___ because of ___*. Or *I'm not ___ enough to ___*. Or *I have to ___*. *I can't move out of state . . . I'm not experienced enough to start my own business . . . I have to have at least X amount of money saved before I can quit my job.* Politely, *says who?* Who is writing the rules in your life? Acknowledging where your limits came from can help you dismiss many of them.

Too many of us don't question our limits from one season to another. We believe that something someone said to us five years ago is true today, even though *we* are not the same as we were five years ago (and they very well may have been wrong about it in the first place!). I challenge you to question everything as you begin to disassemble the mental cage of beliefs that is keeping you from making changes. You are not as helpless as your most helpless situation. **If you assume the future based on the past, you will never outgrow yourself.**

Maybe you have tried jumping out of the jar and hit the lid. It's reasonable to feel the exhaustion and defeat associated with burnout when you feel stuck for long enough. When we feel trapped, our lives can begin to feel out of our control. In order to get back into control we have to take a hard look at how we're managing ourselves and what we might need to do differently. If what you're doing isn't working, do something different. Nothing changes if nothing changes.

All-or-nothing mentality

I used to *hate* spin classes. Why? The instructors act like we're training for the Tour de freakin' France, and I experienced unbridled anger every time they told me to turn the resistance up when I was already dying. One day in class I got so mad that I just *didn't* follow their instructions. To the tune of swear words in my head, I increased the resistance knob only to a point that challenged me but didn't leave me miserable. Because I had an all-or-nothing mentality, this felt like cheating. I almost didn't count that class as a workout because I didn't do what I'd been instructed to do at 100 percent, despite the fact that I was still dripping sweat. My all-or-nothing mentality made me believe that because I didn't do it perfectly, somehow my efforts were void. To feel a sense of accomplishment, I had to look at myself in the mirror afterward and acknowledge that my results were approximately the same, while my experience was a hundred times better. By pushing as hard as I could— and not a resistance notch higher—without becoming enraged, I actually enjoyed my workouts again and wasn't leaving angrier than I arrived.

When I realized that I was struggling with an all-or-nothing mentality, I noticed how this mindset was seeping into other areas of my life. As the saying goes, "How you do one thing is how you do everything," and boy, was that true for me. Whether in my personal, social, or professional life, I felt like I had to give 100 percent or it didn't count—homemade food instead of store-bought food, a personalized gift instead of a gift card, staying for the entire team happy hour when I could have gotten away with leaving after twenty minutes. I had convinced myself that anything less than 100 percent said something terrible about me. When I came to this realization, I took a step back and asked myself, *In what situations am I overextending myself in order to hit 100 percent instead of just choosing to engage at, say, 90 percent or 70 percent and getting approximately the same results?* Have you ever had the experience of drafting and redrafting an email a dozen times only for the person to respond, *"OK. —Sent from iPhone"?*

You realize that you could have saved yourself a lot of time and overthinking if you had just sent the initial draft of that email. Have you ever made a recipe for the first time, measuring everything exactly right, and then by the tenth time you make that recipe you're just eyeballing ingredients? You're following it 90 percent correctly and trusting that the other 10 percent won't make or break the recipe. We can give our energy in moderation. You don't need to pour your heart and soul into everything; you can just do it well enough. Constantly expecting 100 percent from yourself is what leads to burnout. **We can reduce**

our chances of long-term exhaustion by doing things reasonably instead of perfectly.

After years of reducing my 100 percent to a reasonable 80 percent, this approach is now muscle memory to me. In fact, when someone asked at a training session I recently conducted, "Can you come in again and teach a training on [another topic]?" rather than panicking and committing either way, I replied, "I would be happy to consult with your training team on the topic but unfortunately I won't be able to create it myself." In response, the person who made the request actually said, "Wow, that was a great boundary." What that team saw in action was the benefit of not having an all-or-nothing mentality— I knew that there were many options between agreeing to their exact ask and saying no altogether, so I just had to find what it was that would meet their need without overextending myself—and I had a boundary phrase at the ready (you'll get more of those in the boundaries chapter).

When people are asked to do something or be somewhere, they often think they either have to show up at 100 percent or 0 percent. What they don't realize is that occupying that middle area sometimes reaps the most benefits relative to effort. Just because something isn't perfect doesn't mean it isn't good. Many people with high-achieving mindsets believe that "a job worth doing is worth doing well." Instead, I encourage you to tell yourself that "done is better than perfect." **Just because something doesn't look like you thought it would doesn't mean that it wasn't worth doing.**

In what areas might you be overburdened because you have an all-or-nothing mentality instead of exercising moderation? It won't slow your career down to scale your work ethic back to 80 percent. In fact, your 80 percent probably rivals other people's 100 percent if you're used to pushing yourself above and beyond. You don't have to see friends every time they ask; you can just see them once a month. You don't have to abandon carbs and work out daily; you can just drink enough water and get enough sleep. You don't have to deep clean the entire house every day; you can just clean the most important areas so that it feels tidy. You don't have to commit to the day-long family gathering; you can have a high-quality, hour-long visit and then get back to what you need to do.

Give yourself permission to do things well enough. There are so many areas in your life that could be satisfied with just 30 percent. Seriously. If you bring store-bought cookies instead of homemade cookies and frosting, are you a less valued member of your holiday book club meeting? No. Are you a less valuable team member because you agree to take meeting minutes once a week but don't want to take on the duty 100 percent of the time? No, that is reasonable!

Find ways to make things more reasonable so that you aren't constantly overwhelmed. As you adopt this "good enough" mentality, everything will feel less daunting. Give yourself permission to shift with the amount of energy you have. Different seasons of your life will demand you give yourself to different values, goals, and interests. Let's talk about how you can identify where you might want to give more or less.

Seasonal values: We're allowed to change? Yes!

Paul, a software engineer living in San Francisco, was frustrated because his values had changed and his job hadn't. He didn't say it in those words, but after unpacking the source of his dissatisfaction, I realized that his problem was a misalignment between his priorities and what his job offered him. When he began his job at a start-up, he wanted status and money. He was achieving those goals in spades. It was worth it to him to work twelve-hour days because he got to tell everyone he worked at a start-up, and he was making a salary he was proud of. Now, five years, *serious* burnout, and about $10,000 worth of Uber Eats later, his priorities were freedom, connection, and calm. He craved freedom to do what he wished with his own time, energy to connect with people again, and a calm life instead of needing to put out fires constantly. What worked for him then was not working for him now. His values had changed, but his job had not.

"Seasonal values" are values you hold, priorities you set, or goals you establish for the season you're in. By recognizing the season you're in, you can better prioritize. Think about your seasonal values as a kind of filter through which you run things in your life. Does what you're prioritizing align with your current values? *Not* outdated values you held a few years ago. *Not* values your parents impressed upon you. *Not* the values of the culture you live in. Your *current* values.

In Paul's case, he needed to accept that this job no longer lined up with his values and what would make him happy. When we fight to include things in our lives that don't align with us, we compromise our inner peace. If you want to be living somewhere calm but instead you live in a busy downtown, if you want to have a few close friendships but you instead have a large group of distant friends, you will not feel satisfied. Sounds obvious, right? I'm sure at one point you valued living downtown or having a large group of friends, but those things suited a past season of your life and they don't suit you *now*.

Margaret was the first client I worked with who was a stay-at-home mom. Her children were finally all school-age, and she was figuring out how to show up in her life after constantly managing at least one child at home for the past eight years. Her primary value while having the kids in the house was "to remain sane." Now, with hours back in her day and mental energy to spare, her values were able to shift to "doing nice things" and "making memories." In this season, she wanted to put energy into planning lovely things that she and her family could enjoy: having a water balloon fight in the backyard after school; taking a nice, long, uninterrupted bath in the middle of the day; putting a tablecloth down and plopping spaghetti directly on the table so the kids could eat it like animals. Things that, in her previous season of life, were not a priority because they would have compromised her previous value of "remaining sane" (I have it on good authority that cleaning spaghetti off the dining room floor does not yield sanity).

People typically burn out when they try to "do it all" because they overestimate how many values they can hold at a time. When you emerge from your busy season, you can go to trivia night with your friends at the bar downtown. If you've been collapsing onto your bed each night for a month, now is not the time to try to relearn how to play guitar. In Margaret's case, she was able to prioritize doing nice things now that she was out of her season of survival mode. So many things in the world change seasonally—climate, produce, trends—so why do people behave as though our values, priorities, and goals are stagnant?

What might you be trying to fit into this season that is honestly not a priority right now? Write down your current values in pencil, then rewrite them during the next season of your life. One of the biggest mistakes we make is planning with too much permanence. This misconception gives a stiff, fearful edge to a life that could otherwise be fun and have room for exploration and error.

It is difficult to admit that our values from a previous period in our lives have changed. When you recognize a shift in priorities, you have to reassure yourself that you aren't throwing an old goal or dream away; you're just prioritizing something else you want or need more right now. Will it be upsetting to put that goal to knit your new niece a blanket on the back burner? Probably! Nobody wants to feel like they're giving something up, regardless of whether it's because they don't have time or energy for it right now. I know it's hard, but you have to look out for yourself so that you can show up better for your current priorities.

Are your values and priorities in this season of life growth, money, connection, influence, creativity, or rest? How does changing your priorities change how you behave in your daily life? I like to do a "seasonal value audit" quarterly. What am I focusing on in the next three months? What might need to be paused for the next three months so that I can focus on those things comfortably? A good gut-check is asking, **Could a stranger look at how I spend the hours of my day and see what I prioritize?**

I used to force as many responsibilities into my day as I could manage to fit. All my tasks were created equal and all my time was fair game. I had a warped sense of what a good life looked like thanks to the highlight reel of social media, and I was prioritizing all sorts of crap that I didn't really care about. *I should be making nice meals each night,* I would tell myself. It turns out I'm just as happy with Costco and Trader Joe's frozen meals. *I should be going on a long walk each day.* I actually feel just as refreshed if I just step outside for a while. *I should have more hobbies.* I've since accepted that one hobby is enough for me as long as it makes me happy.

Without clarity around what you value most, you can find yourself enduring one of the worst combinations out there: being busy *and* unsatisfied. Pay attention to what takes up your time and energy every day and make changes so that your time reflects your values. You can *always* revert to your old priorities; don't feel bad if this isn't the season for them. What is meaningful for you right now? How can you prioritize that, so you don't end up busy and unsatisfied?

Squashing the busyness bug

I worked with April, a director of human resources at a large international organization, for more than a year. I got to see her during her calm months and during her busiest months. At one point, she was preparing a huge annual report to present to her organization, managing her team, doing her own high-stress job, experiencing a busy season in her own small business, moving houses, and planning her sister's bachelorette party. If anyone were to be plopped in her shoes, I have no doubt they'd be screaming into a pillow within the hour. She was experiencing something I call "The Suck." AKA, when your life is so objectively hard or overwhelming for one reason or another that things, quite frankly, just suck. There's no sugarcoating it, it's objectively unpleasant, people grimace when you describe your situation to them . . . it sucks.

When you're in The Suck, each day is so bad that all you have to rest on is the "bragging right" and acknowledgment from others that you're enduring The Suck. "I worked one hundred hours this week," "I don't even have five minutes between meetings today," "I haven't been getting home until nine p.m.," "I haven't gone to the bathroom for six hours!" Like *The Devil Wears Prada*, it's the glamorization of living a borderline unbearable life.

Most people find themselves in The Suck by accident, but others choose it. The natural next question is, "Who would choose that?!" It becomes a choice when you can see The Suck on the horizon and you don't make any changes to avoid it. You know better; you know you should be scaling back and setting boundaries so you don't end up there again, but you don't. For some reason, we think that there is virtue in finding ourselves in this position, and that's a mindset everyone—yes, you—should outgrow.

There's a story I love about a businessman who went on vacation, met a local on the beach relaxing, and asked the local why he doesn't work to make something of himself. The local says, "Why?" And the vacationer responds, "So that you can work really hard, build something, and then retire on a beach and relax." I used to be the guy on vacation. I thought that work was virtuous and rest was a reward. What do you mean you indulge in rest without working tirelessly for it like the rest of us? Hearing this story gave me perspective: I don't need to achieve a certain amount of success before I can be at peace. I don't have to build an empire to deserve to relax on a beach.

Until that point, constantly having demands on my time made me feel like I was valuable. Nowadays, being busy all the time is a form of status signaling—*you're so busy because you're so important!* And tragically, in today's world, it has been found that the less leisure time you have, the more ambitious and competent you seem to others. In order to change what I considered valuable, I needed to reframe my beliefs about what made me feel like I'd "made it." Instead of equating busyness with success, I committed to believing freedom and peace were more valuable.

This was, of course, deeply uncomfortable for me as a high achiever, particularly when my friends hit milestones more often than I did. Previously, I would have envied them for doing more and achieving more because I equated worth with action; the more you do the more worthy you are. I was uncomfortable doing less until I believed that **my worth is not determined by how much I do.**

With this mental shift, I scaled back my obligations and set boundaries I would need to protect the free time I'd gained. I no longer had the desire to be the person sprinting from one responsibility to the next. Freedom and peace were my goals—not busyness and praise. Now, when I do exactly what I want with my time and someone who *is* enduring The Suck says, "Oh, I could never do that. It must be nice to . . ." I just respond with, "It *is* nice! That's why I do it." Rather than get defensive because we hold different values, I continue to enjoy what I enjoy.

Valuing freedom over busyness and status requires prioritizing *your* peace over society's praise. The world we live in will never cheer as loudly for you for taking a nap as they will for getting a promotion. That doesn't mean the nap isn't more personally fulfilling for you. **For as long as your internal validation depends on external validation, peace will feel out of reach.** I want you to be sure about who you are and what you value without external feedback.

WORK IS WHAT YOU DO, NOT WHO YOU ARE

We all went to school with a kid who took school so seriously that when they didn't get an A they had a mental breakdown, felt extremely disappointed in themselves, and believed they were a failure. We (hopefully) all agree that in the grand scheme of life, the grade is not a big deal, and it doesn't mean they are a failure or did anything wrong.

Now, how come after making a mistake at work we don't reassure ourselves the same way? Why do we show others so much grace and put so much pressure on ourselves? Think about a time a colleague made a mistake and your first instinct was to minimize the incident. You supported them through the panic and made sure they didn't take the incident to heart. Why do you assume others wouldn't feel the same about mistakes you make? Why wouldn't they give you the same benefit of the doubt?

Many people believe their work is a direct reflection of who they are, when in reality our work is a reflection of a myriad of factors. The outcome of a project is informed by expertise, the scope, input from other colleagues, your effort, and probably some sheer luck. Too many of us look at a project outcome and feel it is a direct reflection of us and we should take any mistake or shortcoming personally.

Our society needs a mass depersonalization of work. Even if our work feels like a calling or vocation, it is still too much pressure to put on ourselves to perceive our work as a reflection of who we are and to disregard the numerous other factors at play. We tend to derive our value and identity from our work, which makes us feel bad about ourselves when we have a bad day at work. For this reason, having an identity outside of work can contribute to our sense of balance.

Without work, what is left?

Areas of identity are distinct, unique areas of your life that construct who you are as a person. Typically, our knee-jerk response to "What do you do?" is to describe our jobs. But besides what you do for a living, what else do you do? **Who are you and what gives your life meaning outside of work?** Sure, your career and professional goals are one area, but what are your hobbies, interests, or personal passion projects? What does your day-to-day life consist of? What roles do you play in your relationships? All of these make up who you are as a person. This paints a much richer picture than just what you do to earn a paycheck.

If work consumes 90 percent of your time, then yeah, a bad day at work is going to feel like your whole life sucks. Let's assume work is only 50 percent of your life (or 50 percent of your waking day, presuming you sleep eight hours, work eight hours, and have the remaining eight hours for leisure). The rest of your day consists of rich relationships (the number one contributor to happiness and health according to the Harvard Study of Adult Development), hobbies you love (leisure activities—whatever leisure floats your boat—are scientifically shown to boost your happiness quotient), a home you're at peace in, and personal goals you're working toward. If this is the case, then a bad day at work is no more consequential than a day you were bummed you didn't have time to engage with your hobby. It's like when people are totally consumed by a relationship and then devastated when the relationship ends. If 90 percent of your life revolved around that relationship, then it takes much longer to refill that now-empty space. If you go through a breakup but maintained a lot of your independent areas of identity, it still absolutely sucks, but you are more likely to have healthy alternatives to lean on and pick yourself up faster.

Who are you outside of your work? What are your identity pillars? The more stock you put in those things, the less weight work will hold in your life.

WHY SO SERIOUS?

I was walking around downtown Sacramento a decade ago when I saw a sign in a boutique that said *This is supposed to be fun.* I stopped in my tracks and stood in front of the sign, my mouth agape. This is supposed to be fun? When was someone going to tell me?! I did a quick inventory of my life and felt disheartened: Why wasn't I having any fun? At what age do we go from seeking fun to just surviving?

What was preventing me from letting my life be fun was my mindset. My attitude was intense, do-everything-like-someone-is-watching. I was always aware of how I was perceived, I planned everything ferociously, I treated most things like they were high-stakes emergencies. As a result of taking myself so seriously, I was constantly robbing myself of enjoyment. You know that person speed walking around Disneyland with a perfectly organized map and agenda, who is so focused on doing it right that they aren't enjoying it? That was me, trying to do life as productively and perfectly as possible.

I was predisposed to burnout not just because I was high-achieving and people pleasing, but because I did things like my life depended on them. Now, after years of reminding myself that life is not that serious and that this is indeed supposed to be fun, I can operate with a much lighter spirit, recover from mistakes quicker (with less angst) and with greater amusement. In fact, science has found that the emotion of amusement (yes, it's an actual emotion) boosts our ability to learn, tamps down negative feelings, and helps us tap into our affiliative system, which is our body's natural self-soothing mechanism.

I know I'm not alone in this struggle because after seeing that poster, I found a label maker, and I printed a sticker that said "This is supposed to be fun" that I kept on my laptop. Over the years, I was approached by countless people who said that they really needed to see that sticker.

So many of us are walking around clutching life with a closed fist to try to control it. Instead, try loosening your grip and experiencing it with an open palm.

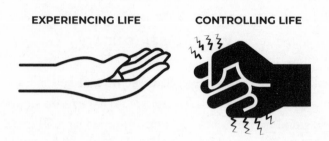

Often, we alone are responsible for turning what could have been a small stressor into a big stressor because of how seriously we are taking ourselves and the hurdles we encounter. Very few things are really worth expending that much energy on.

When we take ourselves too seriously, we miss out on so much. We take fewer risks, hesitate to try new things, and anticipate disproportionate punishment or judgment for failure or imperfection. **We live less life when we take it too seriously.** There is not one right way to do things and you are not always being perceived and judged. You don't want to look back when you're eighty and think, "I deprived myself of so much joy for nothing."

Burnout wears many faces. You will experience these mindsets at various times in different ways. The more familiar you are with them, the easier they'll become to recognize. It took you many years to adopt your default mindsets; it's going to take time to catch and correct them until you have new default mindsets. The least helpful thing you can do is beat yourself up. The most helpful thing you can do is *try*.

A change in internal management will work wonders, but it is made even stronger when you can reinforce it with external management. Much of this book is about external management in a work setting, but first I want to discuss external management in your *personal* life. It's time to destroy and rebuild your definition of personal care.

CHAPTER FOUR

Personal Care

Rebranding "Self-Care"

Ella was so overwhelmed that she was in tears during our initial call. She had a full-time job, two kids, an endless personal to-do list, and a husband she didn't feel she could share the load with, not wanting to burden him. After work, she would manage the moving pieces that came with parenthood and, in the evenings, she'd quickly shift to taking care of household tasks. Dishes, laundry, cleaning out the fridge, yard work—there were always more tasks she could add to her list. When it was suggested that something like cleaning out the fridge wasn't entirely necessary on a Monday night, she would reject the suggestion. Ella simply could not justify rest unless everything was done.

She was physically, mentally, and emotionally exhausted. When she wasn't actively doing something, she was *anticipating* everything she needed to do. Emotionally, she felt like an exposed nerve—one "you-need-to-relax" away from an outburst she would regret shortly thereafter. She prioritized doing everything for everyone over taking the rest that she needed, and it was catching up to her. In this day and age, there is always more to do: more to clean, more to work toward, more to improve. As you can imagine, Ella's pattern of not justifying personal care until everything on her to-do list was done—coupled with the unrealistic length of her to-do list—was a great way to never, ever rest.

When I first spoke with Ella, she dropped her head in her hands and admitted, "I've never been good at resting." She explained that for as long as she could remember, she had been a go, go, go person. Throughout her childhood, she learned that rest—doing something that brings you peace or joy—came last. It was something to be earned, and too much of it was overly indulgent. In adulthood Ella struggled to justify sitting still and prioritizing personal care regularly. When she did get a break, she would worry she wasn't spending it as well as possible, both out of a lack of knowledge about what made her feel truly rested and a desire to "maximize" her rest. If you have ever wondered how you could "rest more productively," you can likely relate to her plight.

Before we could identify what would help rejuvenate her and incorporate personal care into her schedule, Ella needed to overcome something many of us struggle with: resting guilt. **Resting guilt** is a sense of unease, anxiety, and in some cases, shame—the painful feeling of not living up to our own or others' expectations—when resting or when confronted with downtime. This feeling, compounded with the Zeigarnik effect—our brain's tendency to recall things we have *not* completed more often than things we *have* completed—can increase restlessness. While guilt can be beneficial in certain situations (it alerts us when we may have harmed someone and we need to make amends), the problem is that many of us are consumed by it when it is unwarranted.

Many experiences can lead you to have a strained relationship with rest. You may have grown up in a house where rest was seen as laziness; maybe you had to jump up to look busy when someone entered the room or you would get criticized. Maybe you believe that if you aren't constantly making yourself useful in a relationship, you could lose love or connection. Maybe you think that you don't *deserve* to rest until every last possible thing is done. Or maybe you believe that while you're resting, someone else out there is working hard, and if you don't push yourself past your limits, you won't make it as far as they will.

Ella needed to understand it as an essential practice to be incorporated regularly, not an indulgence to be ashamed of. Only then could she reevaluate how she was spending her time and energy so that she could prioritize personal care. She had a handle on her work life and her personal life; she was just constantly overloading herself at the cost of serenity. By calling out this bad habit and managing herself and her responsibilities differently, she was able to scale back on unnecessary work to create room for personal care.

Your perception of rest determines your relationship with it. If you perceive rest as an inconvenience, indulgence, or task to check off, you will likely never be able to relax. Prioritizing rest, if it's not what you're accustomed to doing, will feel uncomfortable at first. Some people have even told me it feels "irresponsible." They aren't familiar with having time and energy to use as they please. It's like someone who is used to being strapped for cash suddenly having a disposable income: All of a sudden, they have a resource they've always perceived as hard to come by and they are worried about spending it right. Just as that person would need to reestablish their relationship with money, Ella was now reestablishing her relationship with time and getting comfortable spending it.

Once Ella had come to accept that rest was as productive a use of her time as anything else, she started to read books for pleasure for twenty minutes a night. That was all she could sit still for. She began dividing her work more equitably with her husband and cutting down on personal to-do items that didn't *need* to be done after a long day. When nothing bad happened after taking this time to herself, she increased her nightly reading to an hour. She slowly got comfortable with spending time resting instead of sprinting from one project to the next. It took a change in mindset, intentional choices, and a whole lot of trial and error for Ella to reclaim and redirect her time and energy. The last time we spoke, she told me she had managed to get through all of *Game of Thrones* with her husband and was loving "getting to be a person again."

I could relate to Ella's resistance to rest—I've battled resting guilt since childhood. I grew up with some sort of activity on my calendar every single evening of the week. Rarely did my family have a "lazy day" (a day where we did nothing) and when we did, it was literally labeled a "lazy day" because we had them so rarely. It was an anomaly for us to do nothing, whereas other people grow up in households where it's an anomaly *to* do something. This skewed my perception of how much I should be taking on in a day. But of course, my parents raised me this way as a result of how they were raised.

My dad and his seven siblings are first-generation immigrants who grew up working alongside my grandpa selling tortillas and bread each morning before school and on weekends in Sacramento, California. They would go door-to-door with 10-cent bread, 25-cent bundles of tortillas, and a deeper understanding of how to run a business than most university graduates had. As a result, their work ethic is unmatched—and their ability to sit down and do nothing is pretty much nonexistent.

All my cousins (and I'd guess most people who have an immigrant parent) would agree: As the child of an immigrant, you inherit a sense of intergenerational restlessness. You are aware that people worked *extremely* hard to get you what you have today. Only being a generation removed from backbreaking labor makes it difficult to turn around and take a mental health day from your "cushy office job." Even those who aren't first- or second-generation may have a long-standing familial belief that being a "hard worker" is the most virtuous thing you can be, no matter the cost. The "you need to make something of yourself" speech knows no cultural boundaries or language barriers.

It is with this understanding that I want to reiterate that *everyone still needs to rest*. This guilt-driven restlessness—whether learned or inherited—will rob you of the rest you need regardless of past, present, or future circumstances. You need rest, the people who came before you needed it, and the people who come after you will need it, too.

FIGHTING FOR YOUR TIME

Think of personal care as the equivalent of getting gas on a road trip: There is never a convenient time to stop. You have to get off the freeway, sacrifice time that could be used to get closer to your destination, and spend some hard-earned money. We stop for gas because if we didn't, the car would quite literally stop running. People, however, are more resilient than cars—we can run on empty for a while, and we punish ourselves with this resilience by pushing ourselves too far.

The personal care pillar mandates that we go out of our way, stop to refuel, and sacrifice the time we could spend "productively" on something else. We're conditioned to continue answering emails, complete chores around the house, and do what others ask of us, even when our bodies tell us we're tired. It's hard to put work down before you get to inbox zero, to justify a messy house, or to tell people, "No, I can't make it to your housewarming party" for no reason other than you would rather spend that time recovering.

We used to be better at personal care. Or at least, we didn't have to be as intentional about dedicating time to it, because life was slower. I grew up in the 90s, which means I am of the last generation not to grow up with smartphones. I spent most weeknights playing in the cul-de-sac with the other kids in my neighborhood. All the parents on the block brought lawn chairs out and talked while we rode our bikes and made up games. The only phones were landlines, computers were not yet ubiquitous, and television was not a library of choices. We weren't always available, we weren't trying to keep up virtual lives on social media, and entertainment was less consuming because we had fewer choices. Sounds quaint, doesn't it?

Nowadays, unscheduled downtime is as rare as the rotary phone. Over the last decade, Americans who worked full-time in the workplace have watched their leisure time drop as their working hours have increased. The reasons for this decrease in leisure run the gamut from equating busyness with success to competitiveness with the neighbors, but the result is the same: We are one restless culture. People are taking up meditation left and right because if we aren't intentional about stepping away, we'll never get a moment of goddamn peace and quiet. We are surrounded by noise—texts, podcasts, YouTube, Slacks, social media, unlimited TV streaming—that seems to demand our attention at all times. It's easy to have a complex about rest and prioritizing leisure when there is seemingly *so* much to do.

Collectively, we think that if we slow down we will fall behind. But **rest and leisure are not the enemy of progress.** In fact, it has been proven many times over that steady periods of recovery improve productivity, whether it's a weekend without logging into your work email, a lunch break, or a fifteen-minute power nap. Research shows that people who take naps are better at remembering new things than people who don't: Naps essentially clear your brain's inbox, allowing you to process new experiences. Even closing your eyes can boost memory performance by nearly 43 percent compared to not taking a restful break. Taking a walk outside or even just looking at nature photos are also proven ways to help concentration.

Engaging in enjoyable leisure activities helps our psychological and physical well-being, which helps us better deal with our responsibilities. A study in the journal *Psychosomatic Medicine* of nearly fourteen hundred women found that those who spent more time doing enjoyable, restorative activities—hobbies, sports, socializing, spending time in nature—had lower cortisol levels (cortisol is the main stress hormone), lower blood pressure, lower body mass, and greater life satisfaction. Leisure has also been found to help prevent prolonged fatigue, the kind that goes on for weeks and can lead to illness and even disability. Routinely scheduling some leisure activities puts a stop to the grinding depletion and gives a green light to restoration. Whether it's simply resting, socializing, or doing something fun and creative, these activities trigger the natural ways your body and mind bounce back, from releasing feel-good dopamine to calming down the nervous system and hijacking the stress response. Best of all, the benefits of these mini-vacations persist for hours. So the stress relief you get from a morning walk in the park or grabbing a midday matcha with a friend will spill over into your afternoon and evening.

The perks are especially strong, research finds, if you are fully immersed in the activity (translation: Try not to scroll on social media while you're on a call with your sister, think about work while out with friends, or chew over that horrible date you went on while in your yoga class). Leisure breaks also interrupt mental worry and rumination over a stressful event (you know, that challenging conversation with a passive-aggressive co-worker that you play on repeat in your head), giving you a chance to mentally recharge. Bottom line: It is to your benefit to reserve time and energy for activities that bring you joy, and you should feel good (and not guilty) about engaging in them. So, forget the notion that downtime is a waste—it's essential to refuel your tank.

ARE WE BEHIND, OR DOES THE
GOALPOST KEEP MOVING?

Given all these benefits, why is it so hard for us to relax? Well, our resistance to rest is perpetuated by "hustle culture." Hustle culture encourages us to work past our limits. It teaches us that we should always
be striving and overextending ourselves or it reflects poorly on our
character and work ethic.

Like most people, I subscribed to hustle culture for many years.
Where did it get me? Therapy. Recently, even *Forbes* called hustle culture toxic and dangerous. The creators of "30 Under 30" know the
damage of hustle culture and celebrate it simultaneously. (No offense to
Forbes intended. I would still be happy to be considered for your list
exaggerated wink.)

We are conditioned to believe that being an overextended martyr is
better than being a "selfish" or "lazy" person who says no to people and
opportunities. When we admit to being overwhelmed or try to cut
back, we often receive responses like *everyone is tired, suck it up; be grateful you have this opportunity;* and *it could be worse.* This messaging may
be well intended, but all of it—resting guilt, hustle culture, forced
gratitude—asks us to neglect ourselves rather than listen to what our
bodies and minds are asking for: rest.

If you are guilty of disqualifying your need for recovery and having
thoughts like *Who am I to complain about ___ when others have it
worse,* then I want you to keep this in mind: Everyone's difficult is difficult, and pain is not a competition. Don't disqualify your needs and
experience. You don't have to convince anyone but yourself that your
needs are important. (And sometimes, you are the hardest person to
convince.)

Your new mantra about rest should be: *Rest is not a luxury; it is a
necessity. I prioritize myself and my quality of life. I am at the center of my
life—if I don't take care of myself, it will show in everything that I do.*

If you feel like the world will stop spinning if too many people believe that they deserve to rest, know that, in the past, society has had an

abundance of leisure . . . and things went fine! In fact, Charles Darwin reported working only about four hours per day. Do you know how many hours we would milk out of a guy like Darwin nowadays? He would be a professor, write books and articles, host a podcast, and probably have his own YouTube channel. How many greats have we burned out in modern history because we didn't give them the proper space to breathe?

Prior to the industrial revolution, work was done seasonally, based on demand—a stark contrast to the constant work we have today, particularly in the United States, where we have a higher share of people working forty-nine or more hours per week than most countries in Europe and South America, according to the International Labour Organization. Not only do we twenty-first-century workers have fewer holidays and less time off, but people don't even take the paid time off they are allotted. In 2018, an estimated 768 *million* vacation days in the United States went unused. Most people are uncomfortable taking rest, even when rest is not only owed, but given.

All this said, it's important to note that not everyone is afforded equal resources and time with which to rest. The wage gap in our country puts many of us at a disadvantage. On balance, women—and especially Black and brown women—must work more hours to achieve the same financial equity as their male, white counterparts. In 2020, women working full-time earned 83 cents for every dollar a man earned; Hispanic women earned just 57 cents for every dollar white men earned, and Black women earned 64 cents. In *2020*! There has always been an imbalance of opportunities for success and rest, resulting in a difference in the experience of rest for all groups. Feeling like you need to work twice as hard to get half as far doesn't set the stage for prioritizing rest. Arguably, the groups who are working twice as hard are the ones with the greatest need for rest—and the ones who experience too much pressure *not* to rest. If you don't rest now, your body will *make* you rest later (and probably at an inconvenient time for longer than you would like).

Because rest is no longer built into the calendar for us, we must build it in for ourselves. Having a sense of predictability and control—

in any area of our life including personal care—has been linked to better health, greater life satisfaction, and fewer depressive symptoms. It is not enough to do personal care as damage control; we need to be in the habit of proactively creating **predictable rest** for ourselves.

PREDICTABLE POCKETS OF REST

Recall a time when you were doing some kind of physical activity, either in a workout class, on a sports team, or even back in phys ed class. To this day, when I receive an instruction to, for example, run for two minutes, my immediate question is, *Well, what comes next? Will I get to rest afterward? Or will the next interval be even harder?* That will determine how hard I push for those two minutes.

This instinct for self-preservation in the face of unknown demands doesn't stop at workouts. In my work and personal life, I work harder when I know that in the near future I will have a pocket of rest to recover. Our need to pace ourselves and conserve energy so we don't reach a dangerously low level of resources is innate.

A successful entrepreneur I once coached credits much of her success and day-to-day peace to her afternoon latte break. Rain or shine, amid a dozen deadlines or back-to-back meetings, she takes ten minutes to drink a latte in the afternoon. This is her predictable pocket of rest. Every other minute of her day is booked, but this nonnegotiable downtime is her chance to give something to herself. Anticipating this physical and mental break combats the potential for being overwhelmed when times get hard. She can instead focus on the light at the end of the tunnel, know she has recovery coming, and forge on.

Many of us understandably don't know how to approach resting and taking care of ourselves. "Self-care" is ambiguous and wide-ranging enough that it can be difficult to know where exactly to start. To help make it easier, I've created an easy-to-implement method for personal care called the personal care pyramid—a simple outline for a complex concept.

Before I had this model, the way I practiced personal care was chaotic, inconsistent, and usually chocolate-flavored. Once I understood the elements of personal care and how simple it was to include them, I actually felt a surprising surge of anger. You're telling me it could have been this straightforward the whole time? I didn't have to patch up my stress meltdowns with whatever self-soothing tactic I could muster in the moment? Do you know how many weighted blankets I own because I didn't figure this out sooner?!

Using the personal care pyramid, you can practice sustainable personal care that supports your needs, helps you recover from burnout, and brings you joy—all without feeling overwhelmed.

THE PERSONAL CARE PYRAMID

The personal care pyramid is made up of three components: nonnegotiables, three-dimensional personal care, and lifestyle design.

Lifestyle Design
Business, Health, Personal, Social, Lifestyle

Three-Dimensional Personal Care
Maintenance, Rest, Refill

Nonnegotiables
Essentials

PERSONAL CARE PYRAMID

We will examine one level of personal care at a time. Each level will build on the previous one, until you're comfortable incorporating rituals from the entire pyramid into your life.

Nonnegotiables

Forget everything you know; we're starting from scratch. The first layer of personal care we need to institute before we get to any fancy bells and whistles is nonnegotiables. Nonnegotiables are day-to-day personal care essentials.

These are not things you'd *like* to do in a perfect world; they're things that *must* be present in order for you to feel taken care of and to perform your best every day. A few common nonnegotiables are drinking coffee, getting a minimum amount of sleep, eating food at certain intervals, having alone time, keeping a clean space, getting movement, and spending time outside. Of course, you won't literally cease to function without these things, but they feel like a lifeline. What do you *need* in order to be functional? You probably know the top two to four items that *really* make the difference in your day. Are you a different person if you don't get seven hours of sleep? Does being hangry change the entire trajectory of your day?

Coffee is one of my nonnegotiables. If it's one of yours, too, then you understand what I mean when I say that if I wake up in the morning and there is no coffee in the house, I will walk three miles uphill in the snow to get to the nearest coffee shop. If I don't have it, I am a notably worse person to be around and everything else in my day is harder. I feel the same way about going more than two days without doing some kind of movement and having at least an hour of alone time to decompress each night. I can get away with less than eight hours of sleep, I don't get hangry, and I don't mind if my space isn't spotless. Those are bonuses for me, not nonnegotiables. I know that even if I have back-to-back meetings and a challenging project to work through, so long as I have coffee, movement, and alone time sprinkled into my day, I will feel like I have both feet on the ground and control over my life. Nonnegotiables are not about having a laundry list of things to do; they're about knowing what makes you tick so that regardless of what life throws at you, your base needs are covered.

What do you do if your work schedule doesn't allow you to do the same things around the same times every day? Maybe you work in a field like healthcare, disaster management, or event planning that doesn't offer that kind of predictability. In that case, think of your non-negotiables as flexible touchstones. It does not matter where they fit into your day so long as you know what they are and get them at some point. These items are the gasoline you need to keep the car running.

Once you identify your nonnegotiables, how can you make them happen daily? What obstacles might you need to plan for? What can you set up in advance to reduce your daily effort?

For example, I have coffee (and the protein powder I add to my coffee) automatically ordered on a subscription so that I don't have to order them when they run out. Is it such a burden to order them when I need more? No, but it makes me feel at ease when they just arrive at my door, and I don't have to scramble to find replacements for a couple of days between shipments. I also reinforce my need for movement by booking workout classes in advance. If I don't attend, I am charged a fee. This penalty has gotten me to drag my tired ass to more classes than I care to admit, and I always feel better after hauling myself to the gym (unfortunately).

How do we make our goals inevitable? With preparation that drives us toward what we want, rather than relying too heavily on hazy concepts like "motivation," "discipline," and "willpower." We don't always need to muscle our way through hard things; instead, we can make them easier and pave the road with some thoughtful preparation. As fitness expert Autumn Calabrese says, "Being prepared isn't half the battle, it *is* the battle." If we prepare well, we significantly increase our chances of meeting our goals.

Identify your nonnegotiables and be honest with yourself about the preparation you might need to do to make them happen. If you need alone time at night, maybe you need to have a conversation with your partner about that expectation instead of just trying to sneak away. If you need to take regular walks but live somewhere it snows for five months of the year, move a walking pad in front of the TV. If you need to keep a clean desk, institute a "closing shift" after work every day where you clean off your desk and prepare it for the next day. Consider your needs and then prepare for them as well as possible.

Three-dimensional personal care

After you establish your nonnegotiables, you can work on three-dimensional personal care. Many people still think of personal care as anything that you do for yourself, but that is not a sufficient way of practicing personal care. Often, this approach results in an uncoordinated series of "little treats," like retail therapy, the classic bubble bath and glass of wine, or ordering your favorite takeout (you wouldn't know it from my Uber Eats order history during my busy seasons, but I assure you, takeout is not a sustainable form of self-care). These are temporary comforts that will wear off as soon as your meal is finished, the item arrives in the mail, or the last bubble pops. In order to ensure you are practicing personal care effectively, think about it as three categories: **maintenance, rest, and refill.**

Three-Dimensional Personal Care
Maintenance, Rest, Refill

Maintenance

Maintenance items are responsibilities or tasks that contribute to taking care of yourself. They keep you functioning at the most basic level: cleaning your space, personal hygiene, grocery shopping, doing chores, paying your bills, doctor appointments, getting gas. Pretty much everything that falls into maintenance is what we refer to as "adulting"—not particularly fun, but essential to feeling taken care of in today's world.

Rest

Think of rest as the genuinely relaxing, soothing activities that bring you peace: going on a walk, low-energy hobbies like reading or painting, taking a nap, watching a show or movie, playing a video game, or listening to a podcast. These pastimes don't demand much energy of you and allow you to recharge. During these relaxing moments, your brain may switch into a mode known as the "default mode network," a state of wakeful rest associated with mind wandering and even pleasure. In other words, your brain has a whole network set up to help you unplug. Rest activities don't need to be "productive" or performative; they just help you refuel.

Refill

Refill is exactly what it sounds like: fun and fulfilling items like spending quality time with friends, family, or a partner; traveling; trying things outside of your comfort zone (like skydiving! Although I personally refuse to skydive—something about jumping out of a plane and trusting string and fabric to keep you alive doesn't sit right with me); or going to a concert. These are the pastimes that tend to light us up, engage us, and get us excited about our lives—the things that make life worth living. These types of activities tap into the emotion of awe, that feeling when something exceeds or defies our expectations—which also has the ability to calm us and make us healthier.

SELF-CONTROL AND SIESTAS

Doing activities in each of these categories, throughout the week, on the weekend, or during time off from work, is essential to creating balance. Ideally, you spread out the activities that fall under each category to span your workweek and time off. If you know Mondays are particularly stressful for you, perhaps don't make that the night you do all your chores; a better choice might be something from the rest category. If you're introverted and have meeting-heavy days, doing a maintenance task (like folding laundry while you watch a show you enjoy) might help you unwind from the day. The ways in which you act on these areas are up to you and your schedule; the important thing is that all of them make an appearance.

Many people who don't engage in balanced three-dimensional personal care accidentally overindulge in one category and neglect the others. Someone may spend the entire weekend cleaning out their garage (maintenance) and enter the week feeling unrelaxed or disappointed that they didn't get to do anything for themselves. Another person might spend the entire weekend binge-watching shows on Netflix (rest) or going out with friends (refill) and start the week feeling unprepared—with no groceries and a mountain of dirty laundry. These categories will help you plan your responsibilities and rest more thoughtfully.

If you're someone who rebels against structure and doesn't like being prescribed things to do, just think of these categories as training wheels. Once they become second nature to you, you can be less rigid about planning for them. You might also try having lists of tasks or activities for each category and then doing whatever you feel like doing at any given time, so it still feels like you have freedom.

This structure can also support you if you tend to struggle with self-control or moderation in the face of free time. You know how most working people just accept that the week between Christmas and New Year's Day is a free-for-all? People sleep different hours, indulge in holiday foods, veg on the couch, and justify inane purchases since their credit card bill is going to be crazy from the holidays anyway. Professionals who are so used to being on a busy, rigid schedule basically black out and revert to being short-term reward-driven teenagers trying to revel in every freedom they don't normally have. One of the reasons this lawless week occurs is that rest is often seen as a reward that we are allowed only at certain intervals (weekends, holidays, and vacations).

This lack of self-control when it comes to rest isn't a surprising result of the binge-restrict culture we live in. We binge Netflix shows; we restrict ourselves to diets and then go wild on cheat days. We work like madmen during the workweek and then try to binge rest on the weekend. Moderation isn't modeled for us as often as "work hard, play hard" is—at least not in the United States.

During my junior year of college, I studied abroad in Spain for six months. My American brain couldn't fathom how the country was still standing when everything was closed for siesta every afternoon and closed entirely on Sundays. I was accustomed to everything being open whenever you wanted it to be. Conversely, I couldn't believe that all the bars around my apartment building were full until two A.M. on *weekdays*. I was used to Monday through Friday being reserved for work, not intertwined with leisure. This culture shift challenged everything I had learned about work and rest. There was time for both during the week and on weekends; I just hadn't seen that modeled in my own life at home.

IT ISN'T ALL OR NOTHING

I once worked with a woman named Brooke who would turn on the TV after work and struggle to turn it off again until she needed to go to bed. Having mindless shows on and scrolling on her phone was how she decompressed. But once she found herself resting, she didn't want to turn the TV off and put the phone down to do anything more demanding. Unsurprisingly, this behavior prevented her from tending to things around the house or picking up a book she had left on her nightstand with the intention of reading. She *wanted* to engage in more well-rounded personal care in her evenings, but to her it felt like high stakes, as if she had to choose between resting, responsibilities, or engaging with a slightly more demanding interest.

As you'll recall from the mindset chapter, what Brooke was struggling with wasn't necessarily a lack of self-control; it was an all-or-nothing mindset. It felt like she could either rest and watch TV *or* take care of responsibilities. Once she figured out the kind of rest and maintenance she wanted to include on a weekly basis and how long they would realistically take (spoiler: far less time than she originally imagined), she was able to escape from her one-or-the-other mentality.

Now, when Brooke is faced with an afternoon when she wants to go grocery shopping *and* relax, she can curb those one-or-the-other thoughts by looking in the mirror and saying, *Grocery shopping will take an hour, maximum. If I go do it now, it will still only be 7 P.M. by the time I come home and if I don't go to bed until 11 P.M., that's four more hours of free time to eat, relax, and do something I enjoy. I can spare the hour to shop.* This framing helps us make decisions based on the reality of a situation rather than how things might *feel*.

Even though I eat, sleep, and breathe this material, I still sometimes find myself resisting to-do items, even when they're my nonnegotiables. For example, after a long day of work, I don't want to work out; I want to sit and rewatch *Gilmore Girls* for the fifth time. Just like Brooke, I have to remind myself of the reality of the situation. I can hop on the bike for thirty minutes, and it will still only be 6 P.M. by the time I'm done. I will still have *hours* to myself after doing the hard thing. Plus, usually I can bike *while* I watch TV. Being clear about what you are trying to accomplish and how long it will take helps deflate the feeling of being overwhelmed that paralyzes you into doing nothing.

So, what do you need to do in the maintenance, rest, and refill categories? At what frequency would you like to do them, and how can you carve out time in your schedule for them? Do you need a chore chart on the fridge? Or do you have to set reminders on your phone or calendar while you get used to a new practice? Can you reinforce your goals with your environment by keeping your book on your pillow and have your apps automatically shut down at 8 P.M.? How can you support yourself as you make these changes?

Get comfortable with your maintenance, rest, and refill *before* you begin your lifestyle design.

LIFESTYLE DESIGN

Lifestyle design is the sexy part of personal care.

Lifestyle Design
Business, Health, Personal, Social, Lifestyle

This is what people usually try to jump to before acknowledging that they miiiiight be lacking on the basics. It's not fun to acknowledge that you haven't been to the dentist in a year and should probably go. It is, however, very exciting to ask yourself what kind of vacation you want to take a year from now. The future is a fun, magical place without limits. Conversations about the future are *so* much fun because we usually ask "what" instead of "how." We think about *what* we want, paying no attention to *how* we will get it. **The what doesn't happen without the how,** so in this section we're going to help you define what kind of life you'd like to move toward and how exactly you're going to do so.

Lifestyle design is deciding what you want your life to look and feel like in five areas, and then building toward those things sustainably:

Business: What you do for a living and how you do it

Personal: Interests, personal development, hobbies, and spiritual life

Health: Physical, mental, and emotional well-being

Social: Friends, family, and romantic relationships

Lifestyle: Environments (like the spaces you work and live in) and experiences you want to have (traveling, fine dining, gardening, and so forth)

The purpose of lifestyle design is to know what your ideal looks like in each category so that you can make day-to-day choices that bring you closer to each of those goals. Lifestyle design is personal care because it ensures that you are respecting your limited resources and spending them on things that ultimately align with the life you'd like to live.

Perhaps in your best life you have a less stressful job, work 100 percent remote, or want to shift your hours so you work from 8 A.M. to 3 P.M. instead of 8 A.M. to 6 P.M. (business). Maybe you want to learn Italian (personal) and take that trip to Tuscany you've always dreamed of (lifestyle). Maybe you want to see friends once a month, call your mom more often, or actually sit down to have dinner with the people you live with each night (social). Maybe you finally get that nice gym membership so you can start swimming in the morning (health).

Before you begin your own lifestyle design, an important disclaimer: I've worked with too many people who think about these areas and immediately consider their limits—what a partner wants, what their family might think, sunk-cost bias about paths they've already started down, and how *other people* would feel about *their* priorities. Kindly, cut that out. For the sake of this exercise, imagine doing this as a person without obligations to others.

I know it seems counterintuitive to plan without permanent fixtures in mind like a partner or kids. But if you think about other factors in these exercises, you'll find an excuse for why you can't achieve something before you even try. It doesn't mean that you won't consider other people once you get further into the process; this is just a tactic to ensure that you are not sweeping your true needs or desires under the rug prematurely. Besides, if something like "backpack around Asia" isn't in the cards right now, you can always add it to a "when the kids are older" list so the dream isn't lost, just on hold.

When you're burned out, your first stab at lifestyle design might just look like returning to normalcy. And that's perfectly fine! Maybe your ideal work situation is just to get back to forty-hour workweeks, and your ideal personal life is dropping out of the book club you never have time to read the books for anyway. Or maybe right now you actually need to declare antisocial Sundays until you feel more recovered. You will reevaluate your vision for each of these areas throughout your life; this is just your first pass at it. Respect what your current phase of lifestyle design demands. Let's begin the process of designing your ideal lifestyle for this season.

HOW TO DESIGN YOUR LIFESTYLE

Here are the basic steps to designing your lifestyle, but remember that you shouldn't try to tackle them until you have solidified your non-negotiables, maintenance, rest, and refill. If your lifestyle design goals would add to-do items to your plate and you're already at capacity, wait until your plate isn't as full. It's better to tackle a few changes thoroughly at first than to incorporate too many, overwhelm yourself, and drop them all.

Step 1. Brain Dump: Write for about ten minutes, or as long as you need, about what you want—or don't want—in each of the five categories (business, personal, health, social, and lifestyle). Let this be messy and uncoordinated. Don't overthink or second-guess something before you put it down. Nobody will see this list but you. Just dump.

For example, my social brain dump might be: FaceTime my mom and dad once a week, go on one vacation per year with my friends, go to my book club once a month, refrain from socializing after 7 P.M. on weeknights, go on one date night a month, host dinner parties, tell friends and family I will not be taking calls during the workday anymore, check texts and DMs only for an hour each night, get to know my neighbors—anything I can think of socially even if there's no way I can do it all right away.

Step 2. Narrow the Scope: Once you've done a brain dump for each of the five areas, select your top three to five targets (total, not per category) that you want to focus on first. You

can choose based on whatever criteria align with your
circumstances—time sensitivity, what would make your life
better, what excites you the most, and so on. There is no
wrong way to do this. (Don't stress yourself out over this,
perfectionists, indecisive people, and overthinkers!) You will
eventually have time to get to everything, but it's important
that you start small and build in your first few selections before
worrying about including more.

Of all the social ideas I had, the one that would make the
biggest immediate difference is not socializing after 7 P.M. each
night. To put this into practice, I set my phone on Do Not
Disturb and let anyone who frequently reaches out at that time
know my new plan. As much as I would love to host dinner
parties, if I'm going through a busy season, I need extra time to
recover, so that's off the list for the time being. *Remember:
Because we're picking just three to five items total, I selected only
one goal from social—my other priorities would likely come from
other areas.* If three priorities feels like too little (I see you,
overachievers!), know that there's a method to this limit:
Research finds that if we don't meet a specific goal, we are less
motivated and confident about taking on new challenges. So
we're starting out with reasonable and achievable targets.

Step 3. Get Specific: What do you need to do to make that
goal happen from week to week? For example, if you want to
prioritize exercise, getting specific might mean setting a goal of
taking ten thousand steps per day or working out for forty-five
minutes every Monday, Wednesday, and Friday. If your goal is
to FaceTime your parents once a week, you might set a regular
time for the call so everyone knows you'll be having virtual
coffee together on Sunday morning at 10 A.M. Clarity around
action steps and accountability from an external source is
proven to increase your chances of hitting your target.

Step 4. Work It In: If you haven't done so already, answer the
question of how: *How exactly will you insert this new item into*

your life? Let's say you want to start going to sleep at 10:30 P.M. each night (health). You might set an alarm to go off at 9:45 to remind you to begin your nighttime routine, plug your phone in across the room, and read until you go to sleep.

Let's say your priority is to leave work on time. What might steps 3 and 4 look like for you? When *getting specific* about this goal, you conclude you would like to leave by 5 P.M. each day. In order to *work this in* to your day, you elect to set a 4:45 P.M. reminder to start wrapping up, add your business hours to your email signature so that people know when they can expect a response from you, and tell your team that you've gotten in the bad habit of staying late, so they need to bully you if they see you here after 5 P.M. (effectively conveying a new expectation in a lighthearted way).

There are many ways to get creative with your approach to lifestyle design. Again, "preparation isn't half the battle; it *is* the battle." Plenty of research finds that the more time you spend planning, the higher your chances of success. The more work you can do up front, the less work you have to do when it's time to execute the plan.

I once worked with a thirty-year-old woman named Olivia who hated getting ready in the morning but really wanted to look presentable every day for her Zoom meetings. She felt better when she took the time to ready herself, but she despised actually having to do it. To make it easier, she decided she would keep a mirror, makeup, jewelry, hair clips, and a nice blouse at the desk in her home office. Getting ready became something she could do while off-camera during her morning team meeting. This was far less intimidating and onerous than going around the house and doing those tasks separately; plus, she actually enjoyed having something to do with her hands during the meeting. She dedicated one of the drawers in her desk to products and even keeps makeup wipes and lotion in there so she can wipe it off after the workday instead of requiring a face wash routine later at night.

To reinforce her new habits, she made them as easy and obvious as possible. It is not a fluke that this method worked for her. James Clear, author of *Atomic Habits,* talks about the importance of making new habits "obvious, attractive, and easy." There is a reason his book has sold *millions* of copies; these methods of reinforcing a habit *work*. So, what steps can you take to ensure you're doing what the experts recommend and making your new habits as obvious, attractive, and easy as possible?

MAKING HABITS STICK

Why does it seem like some people are just better at doing things, as if they wake up and do all the tedious tasks on their plate without the overwhelming resistance, boredom, roadblocks, or breakdowns? After working with enough people, I've found that that air of effortlessness comes from excellent self-management. Many of these seemingly superhuman folks have systems, tricks, and tools that they may not have put into words but that make it easier for them to do what needs to be done.

The tools for getting things done will look different for neurodivergent individuals. If that's you, you know that personal management plays a large role in your day-to-day routine, and many traditional recommendations just don't stick. This is another place I want to empower you to modify tools until they suit you. If you see something that you'd like to try but an element of it doesn't work for you, adapt it and give it a chance.

Now, let's talk about how you might manage yourself in a way that makes doing the hard things easier.

SELF-MANAGEMENT TOOLS

The tools for self-management take many different forms. Some of them are listed below.

Minimums

Several years ago, a lawyer named Max asked me to help him find a better work-life balance. He told me that accountability makes him feel more guilty than motivated, particularly when a goal goes unaccomplished. The perspective shift I encouraged him to make—and that I encourage you to make as well—is instead of feeling a sense of shame for not having achieved what you set out to do, shift your thinking to *I didn't do it, so I'm doing the next best thing, which is* ___. Going forward, when I would text Max asking if he took his one-hour lunch break, he would say, "No, but I took twenty!"—a huge improvement from him not responding to me and skipping lunch altogether. When I asked if he had spent time on his hobby after work he'd say, "I haven't yet but I *will* make it happen tomorrow."

Committing to the next best thing is a powerful way to take some pressure off yourself and get comfortable rolling with the punches. A minimum is just the next best thing. It is a smaller version of what you wanted to do—something you can pivot to when the initial target is just not going to happen that day. **If we show up for ourselves only on the days when we have 100 percent to give, we won't show up very often.** Establish minimums to save yourself from this fate going forward. *I didn't have time for breakfast so instead of skipping it, I had a protein bar. I didn't have time to clean my house before the family gathering so I asked my sister to come over early to help me. I don't have time to chat on the phone but if you send me a voice memo, I can get back to you tonight.* There are a variety of ways we can do less and still meet our needs.

For each area of nonnegotiables, three-dimensional personal care, and lifestyle design, have a smaller version of your to-do items in mind so that the basic goal is still met when you don't have the energy or ability to accomplish its ideal version. Your minimum should be something that does not intimidate you or trigger a lot of resistance.

Here are some other ways to approach minimums:

- Keep microwavable meals, snacks, and shakes handy for when you do not have time to make food and the alternative is going hungry
- Check emails the night before work to mark items as "urgent" and save them for the following morning rather than doing them then

- Walk on the treadmill while watching a show when getting to the gym is just not in the cards
- Clean only large surfaces instead of the entire house each night
- Respond to texts with voice memos instead of messages

Should you ever find yourself deep in the grips of burnout, you can shift from the occasional minimum to what I call **bare minimum days.** A bare minimum day is a day when you scale back on everything you can and do only absolutely necessary work. This might look like quick and easy meals, ordering in, not responding to non-urgent texts or calls, and saving anything that can be done tomorrow for tomorrow. Is it ideal to be so exhausted that you have to rely on bare minimum days? Obviously not. However, if all you have in the tank is enough to get through a bare minimum day, then by all means, minimum away.

When I utilize a bare minimum day, I'm not checking out of my life. Rather, I am being realistic about what I can do today so that I can show up tomorrow. There is no sense in forcing productivity today at the expense of tomorrow's productivity. Know yourself well enough to know when you need a push and when you need to take your foot off the gas. It is *not* a character flaw to acknowledge that your energy level is low and take care of yourself. In fact, it shows self-compassion and practicality— you're taking the steps you need (and only you know what you really need) to soldier on. If you ever feel yourself heading toward a crash, show yourself some grace and empathy and try a bare minimum day.

A quick word about self-compassion: It may sound touchy-feely, but there are numerous studies showing that self-compassion is a powerful practice that can boost your resilience, your mood, and your motivation. It does this by activating our tend-and-befriend mode—that instinct to nurture and care for ourselves and others. Folks who score higher in self-compassion are healthier, less stressed, and even more likely to keep doctors' appointments according to researcher Kristin Neff, author of *Fierce Self-Compassion*. Acting from a place of kindness and empathy toward yourself is far more effective than bullying yourself into checking off your to-do list.

Romanticization

Romanticization is making a mundane or unpleasant experience pleasant. For instance, because Mondays are your hardest days, you wear your favorite outfit, buy yourself coffee before work, or plan to order dinner at 5 P.M. when you log off. These aren't revolutionary actions, I know—but I guarantee, they are small ways to make a rough day more bearable.

Many people have a horrendous habit of trying to lump bad things together to get them over with all at once, causing them to avoid or dread doing those tasks even more. I once worked with a woman named Tammy who would make herself listen to educational podcasts while she rode her exercise bike so she could kill two birds with one stone. Unsurprisingly, this made her want to bike even less because she associated the exercise with another activity that she felt resistance toward. With an easy switch to watching her favorite TV shows while she biked, exercising became easier and more pleasant.

Are there tedious things in your life that could use some romanticization? Could making dinner be paired with watching a fun new TV show and being in your pajamas? Could doing your laundry be accompanied by a latte and listening to a podcast you love? Don't underestimate how much your environment and a few mini luxuries can enhance your experience.

Next time you're feeling resistant to the task in front of you, take inventory of your five senses and decide if anything could be improved. Could you change into something more comfortable? Could you sip on a fun beverage or eat a snack while you work? Put on music or a YouTuber's vlog you love? Turn on the TV, do the activity outside, or change the lighting? Light a candle to upgrade the ambiance? The difference between doing laundry under fluorescent lights, in silence, while wearing your jeans, and doing laundry in a cozy pajama set, with dimmer lighting, your favorite show on, and a candle burning is astronomical—seriously.

Whenever I have extra work to do on a Saturday, I don't treat it with the same formality I do during the week. Instead, I take myself to a coffee shop in comfortable clothing and music in my headphones so that the experience feels chic instead of tragic. Small changes like this make a big difference in your overall experience.

Gamification

Gamification sounds a little sci-fi, but it's really just a way to use elements often found in games—such as setting timers and getting rewards—to prompt and improve your performance. It's a scientifically proven method to help motivate and engage you, and everyone from athletes to teachers to CEOs uses it to hit their targets.

When I'm faced with doing something cumbersome, my initial response is almost always *Ugh, I don't want to.* But when I apply gamification, my follow-up thought is *How can I make this feel more engaging?* For example, when I feel resistance to cleaning my home on the weekend, I tell myself I have just forty minutes (or until the end of a podcast episode) to do it and that once I'm done, I can walk to a coffee shop or read. With a renewed sense of urgency and in anticipation of a reward, I end up working much faster and more efficiently than I would have without gamification elements. If I have laundry to fold and dishes to do, I'll tell myself I have just one episode of *New Girl* to finish them. It's elementary, but that's why it works. Can you set new terms for yourself to manufacture engagement in cumbersome activities?

Reminders

Reminders are a tap on the shoulder to do something. They can take the form of alarms, calendar reminders, sticky notes, star charts on the fridge, or putting things in obvious places. I know reminders seem elementary, but they *work*. In a 2017 study from the Netherlands on the effectiveness of reminders, researchers found that participants who were battling insomnia and who received reminders—visual and auditory motivational cues via an app—to do relaxation exercises and use their sleep diary were more likely to adhere to their treatment and see improved sleep.

A man named Jeff whom I worked with was always tired. He'd wake up exhausted about five minutes before his first work meeting, pull his laptop onto his lap from the dresser next to him, and begin his workday. He would complete his workday and then hop online to play video games with his friends until the wee hours of the morning. Midnight? *The night is young.* 2 A.M.? *Probably time to get to sleep.* 4 A.M.? *Oh shit, not again.*

He would climb into bed, catch up on his social media and stare into the blue light until he was tired enough to fall asleep. After describing his routine to me, we just stared at each other for a while, because it was clear to both of us that his routine did not yield a well-rested person. Jeff might have been practicing the refill portion of personal care (video games with friends), but he was neglecting his need for less stimulating rest. The lack of real, rejuvenating rest in combination with his poor sleep schedule was causing him fatigue at work and during his personal time. After discussing his need for rest so that he could feel calmer and more in control of his day, he decided to implement a morning and evening routine. Going straight from sleep to work and from screens to sleep was not working. In order to cement this routine, he set himself about a dozen reminders and alarms to break him out of his old habits and prompt him into the new ones.

The key to a good morning and evening routine is that it should warm you up (in the morning) or cool you down (in the evening) both mentally and physically. Warming up mentally might be listening to music, journaling, meditating, reading, brain dumping, or listening to a podcast. Warming up physically might mean stretching, going on a short walk, having a coffee or smoothie, washing your face, or taking a shower. Cooling down mentally and physically can look much the same, except you might want to swap out your coffee routine for tea, and ideally the lighting is getting dimmer to signal to your body that you're winding down.

You wouldn't jump straight into a workout without warming up; if your body isn't primed for it, you're at risk of injury. Similarly, you shouldn't jump straight from REM sleep to being a professional either; give your brain and body a chance to warm up. Jeff decided that in the morning, he would set an alarm for half an hour earlier to give himself a chance to make coffee, watch the news, and stretch for a while before beginning work. In the evening, he would set an alarm to get himself in the habit of hopping off his video game at 11:30 P.M. and then transition to his nighttime routine and reading a book in bed until he fell asleep.

The hardest part of this routine (and most routines) was actually doing it when the time came. Even though he *chose* how he wanted to spend his morning and evening, it was a hard change to make when that morning alarm went off or his friends were asking him to play one more game. Without the reminders, he acknowledged that he probably wouldn't have tried to change his routine at all—his desire to do the most pleasurable thing would be his downfall. Keeping his phone across the room with a loud alarm set was the kind of prompting he needed to break out of the tunnel vision and go from one activity to the next. He also communicated to his friends that they needed to kick him off if he was on after 11:30 P.M. Obviously they still wanted him to stay on, but he needed reinforcement and accountability. So, like good friends, they obliged, his sleep improved, and he was rewarded with more energy each day.

Accountability

Accountability is the final piece of the puzzle. Many people struggle to perform without external expectations (and that is totally fine; know thyself). If that is you, let's explore how you can make accountability work for you. Accountability can come in many forms: going on a walk with someone else (if going by yourself is juuuust not happening); telling a friend that you'll have a personal project done by a certain date (so that you have a motivating deadline and someone who will give you some loving heat if you don't do it); committing to be somewhere with someone else (the movies, a coffee shop, the farmer's market); signing up for a class in advance, or you'll incur some kind of financial penalty (putting your money where your mouth is). This bit of accountability is the push many people need to do the thing they swear they want to do, but just need a little incentive to execute.

Here's how a client of mine, Mary, used accountability to wake up earlier. She wanted time to herself before the workday started. But Mary had a problem: She had always been an owl, not a lark, and she *hated* waking up in the morning. In order to motivate herself to make this change in behavior, we had to find something she hated even more. We realized there had to be money on the table or she wouldn't take the change seriously. Mary decided she would give her husband $500 to hold on to and if she didn't wake up at 6 A.M. Monday through Friday for a month straight, he would keep the money. Guess who started waking up at 6 A.M.? That's right, newly morning-person Mary. There is no motivation quite like having skin in the game.

Imagine that everyone has an internal cup of drive. Some people wake up with a full cup of drive and don't need any additional pressure to perform. Other people wake up with an empty cup and do need that additional pressure. Mary woke up with her natural cup of drive empty and needed the external pressure of money on the line to perform.

At the other end of the spectrum are people whose cups are so full that, should external pressure be added, they become overwhelmed. I personally wake up with a full cup of drive. I can do my morning routine, exercise, and finish my work without any external pressure. In fact, when there is too much external pressure, I struggle to perform. For example, if I have a list of chores to get through, I can power through them efficiently without a problem. But if someone tells me they're stopping by in twenty minutes and I have the added pressure that someone will be here to witness the result, that cleaning goes from leisurely while

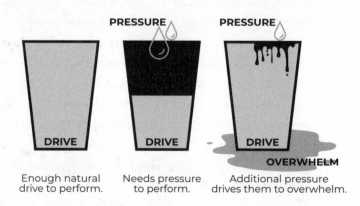

Enough natural drive to perform.   Needs pressure to perform.   Additional pressure drives them to overwhelm.

I enjoy a podcast to frantic. Conversely, I've worked with many people who *need* stakes and pressure in order to perform. Give them a tight deadline and they will make it happen. No deadline? Mmmm, must not be that important. This isn't a time to groan about what you need; it's encouragement to meet yourself wherever you are and be honest about how you perform best. The combination of self-awareness and preparation can make your personal care a thousand times easier.

By overcoming unhelpful mindsets about personal care (resting guilt, believing rest is a reward, treating rest like damage control), you can begin to mend your relationship with rest and recovery. Starting at the foundation, ensure that your nonnegotiables are consistently incorporated into your day. Then, experiment with different variations of three-dimensional personal care. Maintenance, rest, and refill will look different from week to week depending on any given week's demands; keep tweaking how you incorporate them until you find what works for you. Once nonnegotiables and three-dimensional personal care are settled, you can consider what your ideal lifestyle would be within the five main areas of business, personal, health, social, and lifestyle. Use what you learned about having minimums, romanticization, gamification, setting reminders, and creating accountability to reinforce the targets you are working toward. Personalize these suggestions to make your habits stick. Again, these are training wheels. Once you do them for long enough, they become your new default.

It's easy to put ourselves last and let ourselves down when it feels like our other to-do items need our attention more than we do. We might be accustomed to neglecting our needs in favor of the needs of others. In response, I want to gently remind you that taking care of yourself is also one of your responsibilities. As they say, you can't be everything for everyone else and nothing for yourself. You are responsible for you. **Prioritizing your own needs won't be the easiest thing you ever do, but it will be one of the most important.**

Personal care is not a luxury; it is a necessity. I'm asking you to be the type of person who does personal care, *even when it's inconvenient,* so that you don't wake up ten years from now wondering when the last time was that you did something for yourself.

CHAPTER FIVE

TIME MANAGEMENT

It's in the Eye of the Beholder

Are you ready to do some math? (What a horrible thing to do to you, I know. I promise there's a reason for it.) Give yourself one minute to score as many points as possible by completing the problems below.

(1 point): 29 + 17 =

(2 points): (45 × 9) – 31 =

(3 points): (54 + 957) × [62 × (17 / 3)] =

(4 points): (9 × 482) – (56 + 84) × [(89 – 32) – (45 + 17)] =

Now, what did you prioritize in that minute? Did you knock out the smaller problems first to rack up a few points in case the tougher problems took too much time? Did you opt for the problem worth the most points? Did you choose based on skill? Or did you start with the first one and move sequentially because that's how the problems are listed, and you assumed you'd get through them all in sixty seconds? When I've asked people to do this exercise, I've heard some say they did the easy problems for fun, points be damned. I've seen others not do anything during the exercise because they didn't think it was important enough to do.

I begin training sessions on time management with an exercise of this nature to illustrate how a group of individuals can look at the same four problems and decide to act on them in completely different ways when given a time limit. Similarly, in professional settings, we all manage our limited time uniquely with different motivations and justifica-tions. This math problem is a simple example. Our actual work gets more complex when you factor in demands from superiors, requests from colleagues, deadlines, interruptions, varying urgency and signifi-cance, and performance-based raises.

Time management determines your day-to-day experience, not only in your work life but for your mental health as well. People who have a good handle on how they spend their time report greater life satisfaction and less stress (along with better performance evaluations, to boot). Good time management—being self-aware and strategic about planning, prioritizing, and executing tasks—improves your pro-ductivity, reins in the chaos, and protects your downtime, all of which helps you prevent burnout. Poor time management—consistently mis-managing your time in a way that makes your work harder and bleed into other areas of your life—is unpleasant and makes you feel like you're always busy but never making progress. Losing track of your waking hours can result in a feeling of deep helplessness and the sense that your life is out of your control. And it is impossible to feel balanced when you feel no control over how you spend your precious time.

Struggling with time management is not always the result of having too much to do and trying to do it as effectively as possible. Some people grapple with "time blindness"—intentionally or unintentionally not considering or incorrectly estimating how long it will take to do something—which hinders their ability to keep track of time. People with time blindness might plan to wake up at 8 A.M. to get to the office around 9 A.M. without considering the various factors at play (traffic, weather, a fashion mishap) and just assume it will all go swimmingly. At work, these individuals might also find themselves agreeing to tasks without getting clarity on them first. "Sure, I can get that done." "I'd be happy to help with that." "Yep, I'll just add it to my list." But **igno-rance is not bliss; clarity is bliss.** When we accept tasks without con-sidering their scope and how they affect preexisting assignments, we are at risk of overextending ourselves and burning ourselves out. With clar-ity around how we're spending our time, we can more thoughtfully determine what we have time for.

For most of my life, my problem was the opposite of time blindness; I had a very tense and intimate relationship with time. When things got hard, I got structured. I planned my day down to the minute, leaving zero room for human error; if something went wrong, it was like watching dominoes crash. I booked myself solid and considered it good time management. I was praised for my efficiency but really, I was just an organized and reliable performer in a toxic relationship with my color-coded planner. My time management was very poor—I didn't discriminate when it came to requests others made of me; I just made room for them until I no longer had a life. I had zero sense of self-preservation and never prioritized recovery. If I had the time, it was up for grabs (and it was always grabbed by something or someone).

Time management is like a scale: On one side you have time blindness, and on the other, hyper-scheduling. You ideally want to live in the middle zone. Falling too close to either end is likely to result in burnout. A lack of awareness around time means you don't know when you're running low on it; too great a sense of control around time and you can get overconfident in your ability to manipulate it. If you manage your time too loosely, you risk burning out through overcommitment and lack of control. But if you manage your time too rigidly, you risk burning out through overcommitment and putting too much pressure on yourself. Remember, burnout is prolonged stress and exhaustion. How we fill our time and how we work through the items on our plate have a huge impact on our stress levels.

To build a thoughtful relationship with time, you need to be able to consider it clearly without letting it control you. Strong time management requires a few key skills: prioritization, condition management, and execution. You need all three skills to be as efficient as possible. Upon realizing the errors of my time management (I cried one too many times when the train got delayed), I started from scratch. I needed to take on less without sacrificing progress. I got better at prioritizing what truly moved the needle and said no to distractions disguised as opportunities. I figured out what working conditions allowed me to get more work done in less time. I made seemingly small changes to my time management that enhanced my productivity, improved my quality of work, and gave me time back to live my life.

The first order of business was determining what truly moved the needle. Let's discuss prioritization and how it can make or break your daily life.

PRIORITIZING IS A CONTACT SPORT

We have a daily "decision budget"—a limited supply of cognitive energy to make decisions each day—and once we've spent it, we experience cognitive fatigue.

DECISION BUDGET

We *need* to prioritize so that we are spending that decision budget on the most important priorities. Did you know that when President Obama was in office, he stuck to a capsule wardrobe of the same suits "because [he] had too many other decisions to make"? When we expend too much energy on trivial decisions, we eat into our decision budget and are more likely to max out before all our significant decisions are made. We stress out over what to eat for breakfast or what to wear to work, we wordsmith an email for fifteen minutes that was fine on its first draft, we answer non-urgent texts when there are more important thoughts to be had—we waste our decision budget before our workday even starts and find ourselves faced with decision fatigue by the afternoon. By quitting time, after a full day of intense work, we are usually too tired to do extra professional development or plan for the following day. We talk ourselves out of going to the gym, having that difficult conversation with a friend, or making that complicated dinner recipe. The alternative to this fatigue: knowing what our true priorities are so we can make sure to budget for them rather than force them on an empty tank.

Given the nature of my work, I get a lot of unofficial requests—people asking to "pick my brain," friends or family detailing a stressor and wondering what they should do in response. All these bids for my attention are different, but when they come in at the beginning of a busy workday, I have a choice to make. Do I start working on my true work priorities for the day, or do I engage with the various unanticipated requests? The answer is to do your paid work first, but when you're staring at a message from someone you care about asking for help, it's still hard to ignore and prioritize what you need to prioritize. If you do pick up that call or help your friend redraft an email to their boss a dozen times, you have wasted energy that should have been spent on your most valuable outputs. Don't get me wrong: There is a time to be as distractible and helpful as you'd like, but it is not when you're burned out, busy, and need to get a stronger handle on your priorities.

While it's often easy to discern distractions from priorities, it may not always be so straightforward to decide which of our priorities should come first. What do we do when we have an overwhelming number of *must*-do items?

Let's take as an example a woman I worked with named Holly. Holly is a go-getter who works as a project manager in addition to managing her team. When she called me, she was struggling to balance keeping her direct reports happy, keeping her clients happy, and keeping her managers happy. As you can imagine, each of those groups presented a different set of demands that felt equally important to Holly. Despite telling her managers that she and her team were at their capacity, her managers continued to increase her team's workload. In an effort to keep her direct reports from being overworked, she continued taking on the additional work herself. And because her work was client-facing, she didn't have the luxury of letting anything slip through the cracks. Work that went undone for clients would be noticed and rightfully criticized. Holly didn't want her clients' experience to be adversely impacted by her unsustainable workload, which resulted in her working overtime to ensure she didn't appear behind. Her job wasn't just a matter of prioritizing tasks; it was a matter of prioritizing competing priorities.

The challenge of prioritizing competing priorities is like sailing on a damaged boat. You need to get to a certain destination, but your sails are tattered and there is a hole in the hull. You would need to address the hole first, because there is no sense in having working sails if the boat has sunk. When you examine your priorities, you need to distinguish which priorities are holes versus tattered sails.

For Holly, the "hole in the boat" that would compromise any other work was that her superiors didn't believe her when she said her team's workload was unmanageable, so they kept piling on the assignments. She could have the perfect team and be as efficient as possible with her clients' projects (pristine sails), but it wouldn't matter if the volume continued to be unsustainable (hole in the hull). That made her priority—her *most* important and time-sensitive task—convincing her manager of her team's limits. We'll go into greater detail on how exactly she expressed these limits in the boundaries chapter, but the short and sweet preview is that she asserted her team's parameters more firmly than she had before and ensured her team got the help they needed to support their workload.

By prioritizing fixing the hole (the unmanageable workload), Holly managed to improve her team's daily workflow and their long-term experience. Once she had fixed the hole in the boat, she could proceed to fix the sails (ensure efficiency and cohesiveness among her team). Time management tools will help you optimize your performance, but you must be aware of this order of operations—holes before sails—as you determine priorities.

Let's take it a step further and discuss how you can actually prioritize the many competing demands in your day.

TOOLS FOR PRIORITIZATION

Dragging your feet to your desk at 8:59 A.M., you slump into your chair to the sound of incoming messages. You've got unanswered emails from yesterday with actions required; IMs that you dread opening because once you do, they become your problem; a couple of projects in process that you need to finish soon; and a smattering of meetings today that you haven't yet prepared for. With no plan, you decide to open the IMs first and sludge through your first hour of work. You proceed this way, choosing items based on seniority or persistence of the sender. You turn around and it's 3 P.M., only a couple of hours before you have to pick up your kids, or meet a friend for a drink, or go home to get started on dinner. What the hell did you even get done today besides the dozens of inbox fires you put out? We have *all* been there before—our priorities completely evade us because of the overwhelming, unpredictable, continuous demands on our time.

That's why I suggest you start every day with a "morning meeting." A **morning meeting** is a short meeting with yourself to sort out your thoughts before you "log on," or officially begin your workday. To avoid letting your inbox become your to-do list, write everything that you know needs to get done on a blank page and begin identifying your most important items for the day. This meeting doesn't need to last longer than one upbeat song (upbeat song not required but recommended—"Smooth," by Santana, is a classic). A morning meeting allows you to get your ducks in a row and respond with confidence when a colleague or manager inquires about your availability and priorities.

Once you have your list of tasks, you can utilize one of three prioritization systems to help trim the fat in your to-do list.

The Eisenhower Matrix

The **Eisenhower Matrix,** popularized by Stephen Covey in his bestselling book, *The 7 Habits of Highly Effective People,* is an extremely accessible method that can be applied to any area of your life. If you're a time management junkie, you've probably heard of this one. The grid categorizes items by urgency and importance.

EISENHOWER MATRIX

	URGENT	NOT URGENT
IMPORTANT	PRIORITIZE	PLAN
NOT IMPORTANT	DO DELEGATE SET TIME ASIDE SET EXPECTATIONS	AUTOMATE ELIMINATE DELEGATE OUTSOURCE

This matrix is like training wheels for prioritizing. It will help you get into the habit of hearing a request and quickly assessing how urgent and important it is so that you can decide how—and how immediately—to approach it.

Not every task is important and not every task is urgent. Believing that everything is important enough to do and urgent enough to prioritize is why so many of us burned-out folks find ourselves thinking *There is so much to do all the time.*

After using this matrix often enough, you'll find that spending your time on tasks that fall into the top half is ideal. You prioritize the urgent/important quadrant and plan in the important/non-urgent quadrant. Urgent and unimportant items will typically cause you the most distress because they derail the more important work you would prefer to be doing. To combat the sudden stress of urgent/not important tasks, you can *do* the task, *delegate* the task, *set time aside later* to do the task, and/or *set new expectations* so that this doesn't continue to happen. (If you are the victim of someone else's poor time management and find yourself frequently being asked to do last-minute urgent tasks, you may need to have a conversation with them about this habit because it impedes your ability to do the rest of your job well.) Do everything in your power *not* to spend time or energy on the non-urgent/non-important category—*automate, outsource, minimize, delegate, pause,* or *eliminate.* We will revisit these time management tools in the execution portion of this chapter.

If you don't have the luxury of minimizing the time you spend on non-urgent/non-important tasks—whether because of your rank in the corporate hierarchy or because completing these types of tasks is part of your job description—my next recommendation is to **contain, plan, and remind**.

Let's start with *contain:* Can the draining tasks be grouped together so that they feel less incessant? For example, if you hate scheduling meetings all day every day, schedule all meetings first thing in the morning instead. When a request for a new meeting comes up in the afternoon, make a note to yourself to schedule it the next morning. Make a *plan:* Can you create a predictable interval for recurring tasks to reduce their annoyance? For instance, respond to your emails and IMs at the top of each hour instead of the moment they pop up, which can help you reduce distraction and make unpredictable correspondence feel more predictable. Finally, *remind* yourself that you can be excellent at your job without internalizing the stressors that arise a thousand times a day and that this phase of intensely draining tasks is likely temporary.[*] Get creative about making this period endurable for you.

Time blocking

The second tool you can utilize for prioritization is **time blocking**— a visual tool that helps you to ensure that the way you spend your time

---

[*] If the bulk of this work makes you want to tear your hair out, and it's not temporary, this is a gentle nudge to read the chapter called "When to Walk Away" toward the end of this book.

aligns with the goals you want to prioritize. **If I had a printout of how you are spending the hours in your day, I should be able to tell what your priorities are.**

The tool is simple: Reflect on your priorities and block them into your schedule so that you can visualize exactly how you're spending your time.

TIME BLOCKING

Time blocking has been supporting leaders since long before Outlook calendars. In fact, the first known user of time blocks was Benjamin Franklin. Time blocking can be used as a follow-up step to the Eisenhower Matrix (just plug in the items from your quadrants as strategically as you can), or it can be used as an independent way to organize your day.

Time blocking has the added benefit of reducing anxious anticipation of your tasks. Have you ever woken up and immediately started thinking about everything you have to do? When you have a whole lot of responsibilities and you aren't sure when they will get done, it can be extremely overwhelming. A better alternative is to use your morning meeting to process everything you are thinking about, identify the priorities, and *block* them into your schedule. This way, when you start to anticipate something and worry about it, you can assure yourself that you have a nice chunk of time carved out to dedicate to it later. This is the mental equivalent of compartmentalizing a stressor and containing it to the time you have dedicated to dealing with it.

The questions that come up most often about time blocking are:

"What if my schedule is always changing?"

If the circumstances change, don't be afraid to change with them. I know it's frustrating when something doesn't go as planned, but rather than having an all-or-nothing mindset when your schedule changes and ditching the plans altogether, ask yourself the same question we asked when discussing minimums: *What is the next best thing?* If your schedule has changed and plan A isn't going to work out, shift to plan B.

"*What if other people don't respect my time blocks?*"

Reflect on why other people may not respect your calendar blocks. Do you keep allowing them to book over your blocks? If possible, create a boundary to better protect your block (we'll delve into this idea in the boundaries chapter). If that doesn't work, try getting creative about how to incorporate blocks, perhaps by scheduling them early in the morning or late in the day when it's less likely they'll be overridden. And if it's *still* an issue (and you're understandably incredibly frustrated by it), I hate to say it, but you might need to accept that your blocks will not be respected at your workplace. Decide if this kind of disregard is something that you can live with or if this will wear on you so much over time that it will burn you out.

"*What if I have trouble sticking to my blocks?*"

If you consistently need more time than you're giving yourself, either set longer blocks, or get comfortable pausing and resuming at a better time. When I run out of time during a block, I finish my thought and then make a note of where I am and what I need to do next. This way, when I return to the block, I remember what is going on without needing as much time to warm up to the work.

Try blocking out your time for a week. Build blocks into your schedule for meetings, projects, emails, and yes, even lunch, instead of knowing it all needs to get done and being unsure about when you'll do it.

This next tool is for my purists. My list people. This is the most adaptable system because when it comes to lists, you know yourself best and how the types of work you do can best be categorized.

Good old-fashioned lists

Email Jim back, unclog shower, submit project, and *call Mom* don't belong next to each other on a list. Mixing to-do items without regard for area of life or importance doesn't allow you to be as effective as possible. The organization of your lists matters. When you see these items next to each other, you may pick what to do first based on how you feel, what seems easiest, or the mere sequence of tasks as opposed to tackling the most important thing first. Break your work down into lists that reinforce your priorities.

To-Do List: Your *must do today* items. True priorities.

Shit List: Everything else that you still want or need to do but that isn't a must-do-ASAP task. This is a place to catch those distracting to-do items that threaten to derail us from our true priorities. Get back to that IM, upload that document you forgot about, return that package—these might be easier to check off or more fun, but they need to be approached thoughtfully.

When we aren't mindful or strategic about switching from a priority to a shit list task, we sabotage our "flow state." Working in flow state means being fully focused on a task (neuroscience has actually mapped what our brains look like in a state of "flow"). It is often described as being so focused that you "lose track of time." When we interrupt a flow state to do something menial, we are disrupting true productivity. The goal is to save shit list items for a more opportune moment. Remember the concept of a decision budget? If we only have so much energy to give, we want to make sure we are working from highest priority to lowest priority.

Shit list items should be organized in descending order from most important to least important *for when the time does come to get to them.* A study on the cost of interruptions while working found that after only twenty minutes of interrupted performance, people reported significantly higher stress, frustration, effort, and pressure. Interruptions—shit list or otherwise—make us less efficient and affect our working memory. That's because our working memory—which holds the relevant information needed for the task in front of us—gets overloaded when we pile things on, like pivoting to answer a colleague's question about how to fix the printer or having to "hop on a call really quick." (Have you heard of "mom brain"? It's a term used to describe lapses in working memory in mothers and is likely a by-product of the constant interruptions that come with parenthood.) Task switching and multitasking result in lost time (it takes us longer to refocus and do the thing we started on) and inaccuracy—people who task switch and multitask exhibit more errors, research shows. (Sorry, multitaskers.) Distractions severely hinder our output; they impact not only the speed and accuracy of our performance but also the quality of our experience. That's why priorities need to come first; shit list items come second.

Life List: These are personal to-do items that we want to prioritize. *Eat breakfast, step outside, work out, drink 64 oz. of water, make grocery list, call Dad back*—these are just as important as our professional to-dos. Where our to-do list and shit list reflect our quality of work, this list reflects our quality of life. Most of us assume we'll just remember to do the things on our life list and either don't write them down or put them on the same list as our professional priorities. By having a dedicated life list, we increase the likelihood we'll remember and prioritize these items. Often, these small tasks determine whether we get to the end of a day and feel like we took care of ourselves or not.

I also highly encourage having an **Eventually List.** Think of this list as a catchall for anything that does not actively need to get done *soon*. A task like cleaning the pantry can sit on your to-do list forever; the goal is to avoid exactly that. These lists should not be long and overwhelming. If a task has a "do-by" date, put a reminder on your calendar to revisit it then; don't let it sit on an active list and cause you unnecessary guilt in the meantime.

These prioritization methods are a great start for decluttering a full plate. Choose a combination of prioritization tools based on your current circumstances and workshop it from there.

Our next step is recognizing *how* you work best. All working conditions are not created equal, so let's figure out what kind of circumstances you need in order to perform. This is a no-judgment zone—I am open to hearing that you do your best work on a beach with a margarita in your hand.

CONDITIONS (AS IN "I CANNOT WORK UNDER THESE")

"I've spent the last two years taking calls from the bathroom so my husband can take his calls in the living room," said my friend Laura, a successful recruiter who lived in a beautiful loft apartment when Covid hit. She and her husband loved their space . . . *before* the pandemic, that is, and before they realized that a loft was a challenging layout for two people who were on calls for several hours a day. Their conversations quickly morphed into contentious battles over who commandeered the space and how one of them was distracting the other. They decided that Laura would take her calls from the bathroom because she had more of them and she wanted her husband to have the freedom to walk around when he wasn't on calls and she was. Unsurprisingly, that arrangement did not yield Laura's highest productivity.

The conditions in which you do your work impact the quality of your work. From environment to time of day, to what you're wearing or listening to, your conditions influence your productivity. It doesn't matter if you have a perfectly balanced to-do list if your working conditions are preventing you from doing what you need to do.

Where do you work best? What kind of environment preserves your focus and reduces distractions? Natural light, fresh air, normal temperatures—these factors have been proven to positively influence a person's work experience. But people's unique preferences for a work environment can have just as much of an effect on their performance. Do you work better while wearing comfortable clothes or professional clothing? Do you focus best with silence, music, or chatter in the background? Do you get more done when you are around other people who are also working, or do you prefer to work alone? Can you handle having your phone next to you or do you need to leave it in another room?

Have you ever heard that "dressing better makes you perform better" or been told to "dress for the job you want"? I have, and yet, I somehow perform miles better the closer my outfit resembles that of a starving college student. I do my best work at a coffee shop, wearing noise canceling headphones, in Costco sweatpants and a Costco sweatshirt—these are my ideal conditions for productivity. But it is someone else's worst nightmare.

The stark contrast in people's environmental preferences was first brought to my attention when there was a big push at one of my former workplaces to create "an excellent employee experience" by supporting employees however possible. Later that day, I put my headphones on so that I could focus on finishing a project, and someone on my team came up to my desk and jokingly asked me if wearing headphones created "an excellent employee experience." I said, "It does for me." We both laughed about it, but it illustrated that what creates an excellent experience for one person will not do the same for all.

Timing is everything

Beyond your preferences for work environment, you should also know what kind of work you do best during different times of day. Broadly speaking, there are four different types of work:

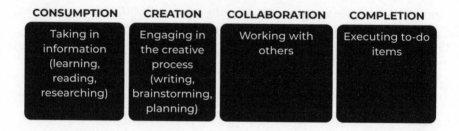

CONSUMPTION	CREATION	COLLABORATION	COMPLETION
Taking in information (learning, reading, researching)	Engaging in the creative process (writing, brainstorming, planning)	Working with others	Executing to-do items

I do my best creation and completion in the morning, over coffee, with upbeat music playing. I am useless from 1 P.M. to 3 P.M. I have tried to force completion or creation during those hours and it is always a fruitless, uphill battle. By contrast, I enjoy collaboration during the afternoon period. Meeting with people gets my energy back up and it is the best use of my time.

It is essential to understand when and how you do your best work so that you can set yourself up for success when the time comes to execute on that work. **It is better to work at 100 percent for one hour than at 30 percent for three hours.** Many of us wrongly believe that quantity outweighs quality in the world of time management. Being self-aware and strategic about how you approach various types of work will save time and improve your overall experience.

I often hear from clients that they do their best work during a certain window, but that the window is frequently interrupted. This is why it is *vital* to pay attention to when you do each type of work best so that you can preserve that time for that activity. (To the best of your ability.)

William, a member of a team I was helping to hone time management skills and curb burnout, explained to his colleagues that he does his best consumption and completion first thing in the morning. He worked in quality control, which required a lot of reading and writing reports—something he needed to do with a cup of coffee and a fresh mind. When he saved report reading and writing for too late in the day, he was notably slower and got distracted more easily. He also shared that he prefers to collaborate in the afternoon, once his reports are complete.

Communicating his best working hours reinforced the importance of respecting the time he and his colleagues blocked out on their calendars for "focused work." When possible, William's team agreed not to book over people's focused work blocks with a greater understanding that this was when the person was getting a certain type of work done. In turn, they respected that responses to emails and IMs might also be delayed until after the block. They also agreed not to have meetings before 10 A.M. and to have designated daily office hours for questions instead of fielding them all day, thus preserving their best working hours. Three months later, they reported having *much* more satisfying and productive workdays.

Break your workday down into the main types of work you do. You can use the four categories of work I have described, or you can create your own. What do you find yourself doing and when do you find it is done most efficiently? Under what conditions?

Next, think about what you need to do in order to make your workday align more closely with your preferences. Maybe you need to shift the hours of your workday (if possible) to suit your productive hours. Maybe you need to start admitting when your less productive hours are and focus on your shit list during that time instead, knowing that you are more likely to make progress on those tasks than on the ones you can't focus on.

And of course, it is wise to head off potential threats to your productivity upfront. Do you need to turn your phone on Do Not Disturb during certain hours or types of work? Do you need to tell common interrupters (you know, the colleagues who don't mind chatting in the middle of the workday) that you aren't available during certain times? Do you need to wear noise canceling headphones so that you can't hear your dog whimpering for attention outside the door? Try it for a month. Create the *perfect* conditions for yourself and see how your performance and experience are impacted.

LIGHTS, CAMERA, EXECUTION

You have a *ton* of work to do, so you take yourself to a quiet place with an overpriced latte. You lay out your planner, open your laptop, and pop your headphones on . . . only to scroll on your phone for thirty minutes before diving in. You've set yourself up for success, but now you're struggling to execute. We have *all* been there . . . maybe even as recently as this morning.

Executing even in ideal conditions can take some grit, but when we are experiencing burnout, that challenge increases exponentially. That's because burnout actually impairs areas of our brain involved in executing tasks. Research shows that someone experiencing burnout has thinning in the prefrontal cortex, the area of the brain that's responsible for complex decision-making. Wear and tear in these portions of the brain can lead to memory problems, difficulty with attention, and emotional distress. Put another way, burnout can cause even the highest of achievers to struggle to do basic things. (Don't worry—the changes can reverse once burnout lifts.)

This cognitive fatigue and emotional distress exacerbate our vulnerability to other threats to our execution, such as becoming overwhelmed, perfectionism, and task resistance, which tend to worsen under duress. The common factor in each of these three threats? Not wanting to face your to-do items because they feel *big*. Picture yourself sitting at that table in that quiet place again. The work is laid out in front of you, and you know that once you start, you have to finish it. It's easy to not want to begin at all.

One way to break down these big things so that they feel smaller is to **work in sprints.** A **sprint** is a fifteen- to fifty-minute period during which you have clear goals and complete focus, and after which you take a mini-break. People often underestimate what they can accomplish in a given amount of time. Maybe you imagined a piece of work would take you all day to do. When your manager suddenly says he needs it in two hours, all of a sudden you can get it done in two hours. When you think about sending those meeting reminder emails, you probably feel like they will be boring, tedious, and time consuming. Try setting a thirty-five-minute timer and telling yourself you *have* to send (or at least draft) *all* of them by the end of that sprint—I bet you can do it.

Imagine you tell someone that they need to run around a track for an hour. It doesn't matter how fast they run, they just need to stay moving for the hour. Naturally, they are going to run at a slow pace. Now imagine telling someone to run two laps. With a clear, short-term goal to hit, they will run at a faster pace. By framing a task in this way—specific and contained—you've increased clarity around what is expected and the urgency for completion. Without clarity and urgency, you get the leisurely completion rate of someone with an hour to stay moving around the track. **Clarity and urgency force us to *focus,* and focus is time management gold.**

While working in your sprints, minimize all potential distractions: Leave your phone across the room and have a shit list at hand to make note of any unrelated thoughts or tasks that come to mind. The sprint interval at which you choose to work will change depending on the demands of your day and how long you're finding you can focus. There is no shame in the interval length you choose; it is meant to support you. Many of the brightest individuals I've worked with get through their workday in twenty-five-minute chunks because sixteen small pieces feel a lot easier to move through than a single eight-hour block.

Now, this doesn't mean that whatever you produce in those twenty-five minutes is your final product; you just continue to work on that item in manageable chunks of time until it reaches your desired quality. You're not using sprints to cut corners, rather to create focus and urgency as you do the work you might otherwise have dragged your feet doing. By working in a sprint, you are ensuring you give 100 percent for the time you can, and you aren't forcing yourself to work for long stretches with lower efficiency.

Take scheduled breaks between sprint intervals that will actually rejuvenate you. Social media, for example, does not allow your mind to rest. Instead, spend that short two- to five-minute break stepping away from your desk, taking a deep breath, grabbing a cup of water, dancing to a song you love to get your energy back up, stretching, or stepping outside. Co-worker Tammy waltzing up to your desk unexpectedly to shoot the shit is not a break; that's an interruption. The difference between a break and an interruption is that **a break is a restful window you control,** and an interruption is typically out of our control and is not restful. It might seem like it would make your day less productive to take breaks every thirty to sixty minutes to regroup, but prolonged attention to a single task can reduce your efficiency, and mini-breaks improve focus when you return to the task. If the work is really depleting (intense, focused work), taking even longer breaks benefits your performance afterward.

Obviously, it is easier to do certain types of work in sprints than others. A social worker can't stop in the middle of a home visit because their sprint is up; they can, however, complete their reports in sprints. A therapist can't stop mid-session, but they can complete and send invoices in sprints. Do what you can, where you can.

Start ugly

Two common hurdles to execution are perfectionism and procrastination. On the one hand, perfectionism can be an asset—many perfectionists are naturally motivated and engaged. They do for the doing and don't often need carrots dangled to complete tasks (a manager's dream). But the desire for sky-high standards can also set you up for poor time management and burnout. In fact, people with "maladaptive perfectionism"—meaning their standards are so high they're unattainable, and they are driven by fear of criticism rather than the pleasure of success—have higher levels of burnout than non-perfectionists, research finds, in part because these folks spend extra time "perfecting" tasks while simultaneously not feeling satisfaction with the results—a stressful, emotional time suck. You don't even have to identify as a full-blown perfectionist to fall prey to its perils. I know I don't check all the boxes of a perfectionist, but I also do things like reread emails five times before sending them. (And I won't post a video if my nail polish is chipped, or take pictures in my space when it's cluttered, and I'll rerecord voice memos ten times if I feel like I'm rambling . . . you know what . . . maybe I am a perfectionist . . .)

It can be tempting to put things off that you know you need to do well out of desire for perfection. For this reason, procrastination is not uncommon for perfectionists. One can procrastinate in many ways, including by being productive in alternative areas instead of focusing on what needs to be done at present. This type of procrastination is so widespread that there is even a snazzy word for it: "procrastivity." This is when you pat yourself on the back for sweeping the floor and doing the laundry even though you were supposed to be preparing for your meeting tomorrow morning. You were definitely productive but at the cost of real progress toward what you probably *should* be doing.

Most perfectionists think that their first draft needs to be good enough to resemble their final draft; if this is you, take that pressure off yourself. Your first crack at anything can be sloppy. In fact, the less polished you expect your first couple of phases of progress to be, the easier it will be to get yourself to engage with that task. *Start ugly* and continue to improve the work from there.

Often, starting is the hardest part, so force yourself to start (even if you're starting small). An ugly first draft completed in a sprint will set you up for much greater success than continued procrastination and expectations of perfection when you begin. Now, I want to clarify that "starting ugly" is just a philosophy. It is counter to another popular philosophy: "Get it right the first time." Each can be true in different circumstances and for different people. If at the end of a long day you still have more work you want to get to, you have the choice between doing a quick start-ugly sprint to get your foot in the door and finishing it tomorrow, or just leaving it all for tomorrow. This decision will come down to what you believe would benefit you most in that moment. Will getting something started, as imperfect as it will be, make it easier for you to pick it back up the next day? Or would the result be better if you just start and finish the work in one fell swoop tomorrow?

Another important consideration is headspace. We've all been that person staring at the screen just knowing we are not mentally where we need to be in order to do the damn thing. If you have the flexibility, swap in a task that you can more easily complete in that moment (sending emails, organizing a different project, something from your shit list) and then take a break—a walk, power nap, mocha cappuccino, call with a friend—to transition into a different headspace before continuing. Here's the bottom line: Know thyself, listen to what your attention span is telling you it needs, and respect what your brain can do in the moment.

Now that you are armed to tackle prioritization, condition management, and execution, let's take a look at some additional time management tools that will help reduce burnout and improve efficiency.

TIME MANAGEMENT TOOL BELT

When Cara came to see me, she was like a pot about to boil over. She had a lucrative, rewarding job in tech, and her side hustle—selling collectible books—was booming. She was thrilled by its growth, except that now she was one person doing two jobs. She didn't want to give up either one, which meant she had to find ways to be extremely time efficient. Her nine-to-five was already a well-oiled machine, so she decided to test out various time management tools on her side business to maximize efficiency.

I pulled out my Swiss Army Knife of tools for Cara and we got to work. First, she *batched* her ordering/book-hunting days so that she was placing orders or out hunting one or two days a month rather than throughout the week. That helped contain her efforts and stress to certain times. Next, she *automated* the bidding process for her customers so they would be sent to a secondary page on her website that conducted auctions automatically, instead of Cara having to manually manage the bids. The automation saved her hours and effort. Then she decided to *delegate* mundane business tasks to an assistant she hired and *outsource* walking her dog to a professional dog walker to free up a little more time. Ultimately, Cara was able to manage the growth of her side business without allowing it to compromise her day job or her personal life. Plus, as an added bonus, these changes gave her enough of her time back that she could resume the pottery classes she had abandoned when she was in survival mode.

The beauty of these tools is that they are endlessly adaptable to any circumstances. Let's look at the tools one by one so you can understand why and how they work wonders.

> **TOOL: BATCHING**
>
> *Group similar to-do items together, because it takes fewer cognitive resources to complete like items than to go back and forth between dissimilar tasks and start from scratch each time. As we learned earlier, task switching can chip away at our attention little by little.*

At work, maybe you have to follow up on a variety of projects that are in progress. Rather than sending those follow-up emails sporadically, dedicate a specific time to send them all at once, while you're already in a flow of doing that work. At home, maybe you bought broccoli to eat for dinner each night this week. You could clean, chop, and cook the broccoli each night you eat it—or you could clean and chop it all at once and then just cook it the day you eat it. Sure, it's (a little) more work up front, but you're reducing time spent on the task overall.

It makes more sense to do like actions when we are already in the physical or mental space to do them. We don't realize the energy it takes to start and finish a task. By batching your tasks, you can reduce energy lost from stopping and starting, and instead you can complete what you need to while you are already in that headspace.

> **TOOL: DELEGATING OR OUTSOURCING**
>
> *Hire or ask someone else to do something that you would otherwise have to do yourself.*

Say you have an extremely busy week and don't want to have to think about cooking dinner at all. Plan to enlist help ahead of time—maybe your partner can meal plan and prep for the week, or maybe you subscribe to a meal kit company that does the work for you, or maybe you order your favorite takeout from the place down the street. Be honest with yourself when you need some help to make the most of your time, and don't be afraid to ask for it. You might believe it would just be more efficient if you did it yourself, but you should be spending your energy on things that truly need *you* doing them and outsource things that could be done by others.

> **TOOL: SCHEDULING**
>
> *Do something at a consistent time to reduce anxiety about when it will get done and avoid procrastinating indefinitely.*
>
> Maybe you don't like cleaning, but if you don't tidy your space regularly, you get overwhelmed. Instead of waiting until it gets "bad enough" (a personal low for me was being forced to eat salad with chopsticks because I had no clean forks left), you build a ten-minute pick-up into your schedule every night at 8 P.M., or, after dinner, everyone in the house knows it's ten-minute pick-up time. Build it in at a consistent, predictable interval instead of having to actively decide to do it every time.

> **TOOL: AUTOMATING**
>
> *Any time you say "every time" is a place for automation. "Every time someone asks this question..." or "Every time I have to order this*

product..." is a cue to make some type of shortcut: Create a template, add an FAQ to your email signature, compose a directory, develop a video training so that you don't have to explain the same thing again and again. Sign up for a subscription, set up auto-pay, and book in advance because you know it will need to get done later. Like batching, if you put in a little more effort upfront, you can put in less effort later.

I send the same twenty emails on a regular basis. *Thank you for your interest; thank you for hiring me; these are the next steps; attached are the requested forms; here is a link to the call.* No matter how brief the email, I have each of those templates saved to spare me the time it would take to frame the email again the next time. Not only does this automation save me time trying to wordsmith emails, but it reduces my resistance to answering those emails because I know each response is already 70 percent complete and all I need to do is edit the unique information. There is nothing too small to be automated.

TOOL: UNCLOGGING BOTTLENECKS
Make note of trouble spots that slow you down or compromise your work whenever you come across them.

On a freezing January day in 2017, my director brought a printed article with him into our team's morning meeting. The article was about "stopping the line." It spotlighted a factory where the quality of products was slipping. Upon closer inspection, it became clear that employees didn't feel they had the authority to stop the assembly line if an error was made. If something was done incorrectly in phase three, then phases four, five, six, seven, and onward would continue to build on the earlier error. The solution was to empower the workers to stop the line when something went wrong. Each phase in the assembly was given a button that, when pressed, would literally stop the assembly line from moving forward so that they could correct their mistake.

While some might worry that this stoppage would slow overall assembly, in reality the quality of products and employee experience improved. Our director read us this article to emphasize that he wanted us to take responsibility for our work. If we saw something that could be done better, we had his blessing to take action on it.

In your work, what problems do you frequently run into that could be corrected? Whose blessing do you need to stop the line and make a change? I encourage you to articulate improvements you'd like to see, as well as the person(s) affected in the process. You will likely share a goal with them of increased efficiency and quality.

For example, perhaps every time you initiate a project, you need to get approval from someone who is hard to get ahold of, so sometimes it takes weeks or even months to get the ball rolling. Instead of cursing Roger under your breath every time he takes two weeks to answer an email, ask him if he would be comfortable delegating approval to someone easier to reach. If that doesn't sound like it would land well in your work environment, alternatively, try batching your requests for approval in one email every week or requesting a regular meeting time with Roger to get these requests approved.

Ask for these changes on a temporary basis at first, because people are more likely to agree to temporary changes than permanent ones. During that time, collect data to support the benefits of the change: reduced back-and-forth, number of people (positively) affected, progress of projects, money made or saved—whatever would be most convincing in making the case that the new way works and should stay.

TOOL: WHO, WHEN, WHERE, HOW

Your what is the task, and the task isn't always flexible. Assuming your what drives you insane but isn't changing anytime soon, examine the who, when, where, and how to figure out if there is an alterna-

tive way to approach the "what." Can the people involved in that task change? Can the time you do it be altered? Can how you're doing the tasks be done differently?

Melanie, a coordinator for a large nonprofit, hated doing invoices, because they would pile up by the end of the month and then take hours to organize and process. She decided to make the simple shift of processing invoices every Friday morning instead of at the end of the month (scheduling/batching and effectively changing the when), setting a fifty-minute timer to get them all done to avoid getting distracted or bored (using a sprint and changing the how). Melanie rewarded herself by getting an iced coffee from her local coffee shop at the end of the fifty minutes (gamification/romanticization) and voilà, processing invoices was no longer the bane of her existence. Building small systems around unpleasant items to make them more enjoyable makes a big difference. Shaping tasks you hate into something you don't mind by getting creative about the who, when, where, and how is a skillset that will benefit you in and outside of the office.

Reflect on the tasks that cause you the most drain. Can any of these tools help improve your experience? Try writing the tools on a sticky note and keep it nearby so that next time you're struggling to manage your time, you can refer back to them.

ENERGY MANAGEMENT: TIME MANAGEMENT'S LONG-LOST SIBLING

"By the time I've gotten my kids ready and sent to school in the morning, half of my energy for the day is gone and my work hasn't even begun," Lucy, a mother of three, confided to me. What Lucy was lamenting was not actually an issue of time management but energy management. Lucy was already using tools like automation and batching to manage and maximize her time, but when she walked into her office every day, she was already emotionally drained from having to coach her kids through their morning routines. She found that even though she had the *time* to tackle her priorities, she was lacking the *energy* to get through everything.

Energy management is the observation and regulation of energy output as we move through our day. Energy is the cognitive, emotional, or physical effort we exert. If your day starts with an urgent email and you go straight from bed to frantically putting out that fire, you've started your day with a big energy drain.

Or if the last four hours of your workday are extremely stressful, then you might reach the end of the day and really regret having agreed to go to dinner with friends. Sure, the time is already blocked off in your calendar, but you do not have the energy.

Every responsibility or task demands different amounts of energy from us. You'll experience drain at a different rate when you're working with someone you love instead of someone you don't like or working on a project that is in your area of expertise rather than a project that requires skills outside of your comfort zone. Your burnout rate is higher when you do tasks you hate than when you do tasks you don't mind. When you have this awareness around how you're spending your time and energy, you can approximate what you have to give and your limits much more accurately.

Burnout is the result of depleting your energy consistently and not giving yourself enough time to recover it. To cure or prevent burnout, you must be cognizant of your energy management right alongside your time management. Energy is to time what the cheese packet is to macaroni. It doesn't matter if you cook the pasta perfectly; without the cheese, it will never be that delicious, satisfying macaroni and cheese. Whenever you show up with time and no energy, you are showing up as a bland noodle.

The clearer you are about what drains your energy or boosts it, the better you can prioritize, plan recovery, and avoid depleting yourself. In Lucy's case, she resolved that for as long as she had young children, she needed to do everything in her power to make the beginning of her workday calm. She needed an hour or two to recuperate energy and sip her coffee while answering emails in order to get her feet under her again. When you can't stop tasks that drain your energy, counter them with actions that replenish it. Oftentimes, energy management comes down to how we are managing ourselves; other times, our biggest energy drains will be *other* people. Or, as I like to call them: energy vampires.

ENERGY VAMPIRES WILL SUCK THE
B-POSITIVE RIGHT OUT OF YOU

I can see my colleague approaching out of the corner of my eye and wonder if it's too late for me to duck under my desk and pretend I'm not here. "How's it going?" I hear from Kent, my astoundingly social co-worker who has made it a habit to come over to catch up at some point each day. "Good," I say, smiling in his direction without turning my body away from my computer or removing my fingers from my keyboard, hoping he can sense that I'm too busy for this conversation. Kent proceeds to make small talk (whether he is choosing to ignore my body language or just doesn't take the hint, I'll never know). After telling me about what he had for lunch for way longer than I would have liked, he'll wander away to find his next victim. Once he leaves, I let out a big exhale and begin the uphill battle of getting my brain back into work mode. Not only have I lost the time I spent shooting the shit with Kent, but I have also lost my momentum, focus, and however long it takes to get back into flow.

Kent is one example of an energy vampire. You can imagine how severely a couple of encounters with energy vampires each day can derail your productivity, peace, and quality of work. Energy vampires might want emotional support for things causing them professional distress, a level of interpersonal contact that doesn't mesh with your working style, or maybe they're just . . . not your kind of person and spending time around them drains you. Whatever the reason these people drain you, you need to limit your exposure to them. The limits you set do not need to be about them as a person; instead, they concern the limited resources *you* have at work and your need to protect them. For example, instead of saying exactly what you're thinking ("stop loitering by my desk; you're draining me"), try something less blunt but still effective: "I hate to be boring, but I *have* to get something done so I can't talk right now. I'm sorry."

Let's say you've had your morning meeting, so you know what you want your day to look like. If you sense an energy vampire threat, have a strategy at hand to avoid getting sucked in. Perhaps one of your priorities for the day involves meeting with someone who is extremely chatty. Being proactive might mean starting your meeting by saying, "Hey! My schedule is pretty back-to-back, so is it all right if I guide us through the objectives of this meeting pretty quickly today?" Once they agree, you can get what you need from the meeting and then excuse yourself. If you get a lot of social calls or visits to your desk, try starting each of those interactions with, "Hi! What can I help you with?" instead of, "Hi! How are you?" That way, you're getting to the crux of the ask rather than starting a conversation. This might be a more direct approach than you are accustomed to, but if the alternative is an unnecessarily long interaction sucking your limited energy, being direct is often more favorable.

Now, there is something to be said about fostering and maintaining relationships with people at work. Networking is extremely beneficial. But for your own sanity, focus on distinguishing good times to connect with people from bad times. If your mind is going to be racing while you speak to your co-worker Cassie about the restaurant she went to last night and you are already late to your next agenda item, perhaps that is not the best time to hear her ranking of the best key lime pies in the city. (Important information, I agree, but nonetheless, there is a better time for it.)

This direct approach to colleagues and their distraction is particularly hard for extroverted people, but it is the best way to cut down on chitchat so that you can get your work done, manage your time, and cure your burnout. Hopefully, the other parties respond with what they need help with, and you can let them know that whatever it is, it's on your to-do list and you'll handle it soon. Remember, you aren't saying,

"I hate talking to you"; you're just kindly letting them know that you aren't available for more at that time.

Most tension is the result of unclear expectations—someone coming to chat your ear off when you don't have time because you haven't communicated that you're busy; staying at work until 7 P.M. because you're not sure of the office culture or what your manager expects; spending time in meetings you aren't sure you even need to be in. Seek clear expectations of every interaction or task, and then try to contain the energy you devote to that expectation.

Maybe your energy vampire is unnecessary meetings that sabotage your ability to work efficiently. There are several ways to make meetings more efficient: Creating a clear agenda, making direct asks, and using a ruthless facilitator who keeps time well are the most helpful. If you don't have control over those elements and can only control your presence, you can *contain* the ways a meeting might drain you by saying up front that you have a "hard stop," keeping your camera off (if this is a Zoom meeting and it's allowed), requesting that you present or ask your questions first, or asking the facilitator if your presence is truly needed or if you can have a team member you trust attend and take notes for you.

You may worry that some of these practices might come across as rude. But these approaches are just clear and firm. You can be clear and firm *while still being friendly!* I promise. You can even throw in a "so sorry" if that makes you more comfortable. Keep in mind that these practices to combat energy vampires will help you reduce the number of times you have to work late because other people or meetings stole the time you needed for your own tasks. You are prioritizing yourself—your energy, your time—over social bids and inefficiencies foisted upon you. You are ensuring you have the energy to do the job you were hired to do.

The clearer you are about your priorities and the conditions that suit you, the more efficiently you can execute on those priorities. Utilize time management tools to ensure that you're spending your limited time and energy as strategically as possible. ***This is your life, right now.*** **Not after your work is done, not once you reach a certain goal, not**

once you retire, right now. Optimizing how you manage your time and energy ensures that you spend the finite time you have as meaningfully and thoughtfully as possible. It would be a shame to reach the end of your life and feel like your time was never your own.

Now, you can't manage your time and energy effectively if you don't feel comfortable expressing when you've hit a limit. To get comfortable acknowledging and setting your limits, you must develop a strong, healthy relationship with boundaries.

CHAPTER SIX

Boundaries

They Really Should Have Taught This in School

Tina, a sales representative who was suffering at the hands of a workaholic manager, came to me on the verge of rage-quitting. She worked in an office of workaholics with "make it happen" attitudes and seemingly no personal lives. "Working hours" were an illusion—she received emails from her manager from 6 A.M. until he went to sleep. Even when she felt she could shut work down around 6 P.M., the anticipation of more time-sensitive work coming in kept her on edge. The stress had brought her nail-biting habit to new heights (her fingers were so shredded that it hurt to type); most of her interactions with her partner were exhausted bickering; and she couldn't remember the last time she'd eaten a proper lunch, instead opting to eat rolled-up slices of deli meat and cheese. She had almost no time for herself, and she spent the time she did have dreading work. The kicker was that Tina did not dislike her job. It was interesting and fast-paced, and she liked working with most of her clients, but the expectations of her manager and the culture of the workplace prevented her from enjoying her day-to-day.

The final straw? Tina, a non-smoker, thought about buying a vape pen to relieve stress. This led her to her "holy shit" moment: She was actually considering picking up a dangerous habit to survive a *job*. "How did I get here, and how do I get out?" she wondered. Tina was in a position many of us have found ourselves in—wondering if she should fight like hell to enforce boundaries where she was, or if she needed to find a new role, manager, team, or even company. She resolved to give the job three more months with firm boundaries and if her burnout didn't get any better, she would leave. (I know three months seems like a short time to the average person, but I assure you it's not when you're at a job that makes you want to throw yourself in front of a bus every day.)

Burnout persists when boundaries around its causes do not. Having no (or too few) boundaries with work or personal pressures ensures that these stressors get free rein. The link between a lack of boundaries and burnout became even more pronounced during the pandemic in 2020, when many people shifted to remote work, and lines between work life and personal life blurred. Interruptions accumulated: homeschooling between work meetings, your partner's Zoom calls from the other room breaking your attention, doing extra office work during and after dinner to catch up, solving your own tech issues during your lunch hour. Researchers have linked these types of interruptions, also known as "boundary violations," to increased rates of burnout. Even now that we have adjusted to the new work-from-home norm—or even returned to the office—so many of us continue to operate without the guardrails of strong boundaries to protect our time, energy, health, and sanity.

Because you do not have control over other people's boundaries (or a company's or a culture's), becoming skilled at and comfortable with setting boundaries of your own is essential. So why is something so critical to our well-being such a struggle to master? Well, a couple of reasons; setting boundaries has two parts:

1. Knowing, expressing, and holding your limits

2. Managing the experience, emotions, and perceptions of those involved

We wrestle with each of these parts for different reasons.

People often have trouble with the former because they haven't identified what their needs are, they struggle to express them, or they haven't built the confidence to hold limits. People struggle with the latter because they feel responsible for managing the experiences of other people—in other words, the fear of upsetting someone or being per-

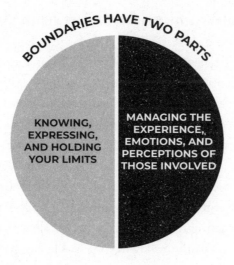

ceived in a negative light keeps them from setting boundaries. This fear may have been reinforced by experiences with people who have disregarded, criticized, or lashed out against boundaries they have set in the past.

Here's what you need to remember before you work through each of these parts: Boundaries are just limits. You have limits because you have limited resources to give, so you need to be able to regulate them. Time, energy, money, attention, tolerance—*everything* has a limit before you end up dipping into your reserves, become resentful, and feel like your life is out of your control. When you recognize that you have limited resources and that boundaries are your best effort at honoring your limits, they feel a lot less personal and easier to speak up for. The first step is understanding the limits on your resources and how you can express and hold them.

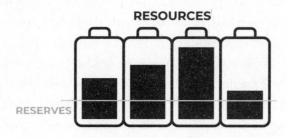

LEARNING AND HONORING YOUR LIMITS

Tina's bright red flag that she had hit her limit was when she began considering a nicotine addiction, but her yellow flags had been present and plentiful long before then. On our calls, she was visibly anxious, her eyes flitting to her phone every few minutes to make sure she hadn't missed a call, text, or email from her manager. When asked what she was doing after work, she would say things like, "I'm just going to monitor my emails while I watch a show." This behavior usually resulted in an unsatisfying combination of not really relaxing and not really making meaningful progress on work. When I asked if she was free to hop on a call the following week, she hedged while flipping through her calendar, before saying she could make time if she "moved some things around." These yellow flags aren't as egregious as forgetting a deadline or hoping you get sick so you can take a couple of days off of work, but they are indicators that it is time to set a boundary nonetheless.

There are three key steps to recognizing and honoring your limits:

1. **Be self-aware enough to know your limits.**

   We ask, "When should I set a boundary?" as though our minds, bodies, and calendars don't reflect our time and energy—or lack thereof—in real time. Tina was displaying signs that it was time for a boundary and she didn't even realize it. Knowing when to set a boundary isn't as ambiguous as you might think; you will have internal and external indicators that you're nearing a limit. *Internally,* the need for a boundary might feel like a physical stress response (an uptick in heart rate, rapid breathing, racing thoughts), dread or resentment when you receive a request, anxiety, wanting to flee, or freezing up. *Externally,* the need for a boundary might look like being double-booked, skipping events, making mistakes you wouldn't normally make, not having spare time during the day, or being told you seem distracted or busy. I know that when I have to control my facial expression because my ugh-I-do-not-have-time-to-do-that look is threatening to make an appearance, I need to set a boundary by saying no.

Once you notice these signs, ask yourself, "What *am* I available to do? What *do* I have the resources for?" When Tina initially recognized these signs, she attributed them to her workload and her manager. Upon further reflection, though, she realized that her workload was manageable, but the constant, unpredictable messages and requests she received from her manager were draining her time and energy more than anything else. In order to regain control, Tina needed to express her limits to her manager.

2. **Be able to express your resources and boundaries.**

Tina took an inventory of her workload and scheduled a meeting with her manager to establish some new work parameters. She said that she would be unavailable during certain working hours so she could get large chunks of work done; after 6 P.M. she wouldn't respond to non-urgent emails and messages; and she would express when she had no further capacity for new requests. She reinforced these changes by creating blocks on her calendar, and she created an automatic response for emails received after 6 P.M. that instructed the sender to call if it was an emergency, or else expect a response the following morning.

Tina's manager responded the way many workaholic managers do: by vehemently insisting that they would never expect their employees to try to keep up with their own workaholic habits. Whether or not a manager is being honest about these expectations and their respect of boundaries varies. In Tina's case, she took her manager's words at face value and enforced her new limits, and her circumstances improved enough that she lasted another six months. But eventually, she got tired of fighting the culture. The company valued go, go, go employees and she was ready to work somewhere that valued work-life balance more.

I once worked on a team that truly respected each other's boundaries and had a firm grasp on what kind of issue was worthy of interrupting someone's day off. When I first began with them, I had a question that could only be answered by someone who was on vacation. I reached out to them and they got back to me—probably to be polite because I was new—but when I asked a follow-up question, they didn't respond again. I was confused and embarrassed because the team I had worked on previously had not expressed any qualms about being contacted during their time off. (I'm sure they did have qualms, but everyone responded to requests regardless of whether they were technically working or not, so the requests never stopped.)

On my new team, I learned via an *active boundary* that the person I had reached out to did not work on vacation. **An *active boundary* is an action or behavior that reinforces a boundary. A *stated boundary* is the written or verbal expression of a boundary.**

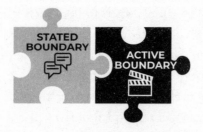

In this instance, when we hadn't discussed the boundary previously, an active demonstration of this boundary—not responding to my follow-up question while she was out of office—conveyed the unstated boundary. Stating a boundary without active reinforcement is often ineffective (this person would be considered a "pushover"). Conversely, action without a statement can seem passive-aggressive. It is important to get comfortable using both active and stated boundaries—together.

Let's say that you have gotten in the habit of working through lunch and it makes you resentful and snappish for the rest of the day. You might *state* your boundary by blocking a midday break into your calendar and letting your team know that you're determined to start taking your lunch hour. You might set an *active* boundary by declining or redirecting non-essential meetings booked over your lunch, stepping outside or into another room during that time, or walking to a nearby coffee shop to turn your brain off for a bit. For each boundary that you recognize needs to be set, brainstorm how you can state *and* reinforce it with action so it can be as strong as possible. (Stay tuned for some approachable scripts and tools later on!)

Now, all this stating and reinforcing means nothing if you don't:

3. **Have the confidence to hold this boundary.**

In order to set boundaries, you have to believe you have the right to do so. This is where a lot of people get in their own way. They might know where they need a boundary and how they would like to set it, but then they feel such a crushing sense of insecurity that they struggle to hold it.

Much of the hurdle is mindset. Many of us (particularly women) are encouraged to be the most obedient, accommodating version of ourselves for most of our lives. When we enter adulthood, nobody sits us down and tells us, "If you are accommodating others 100 percent of the time, you'll be eaten alive." But it's true! There is a lot to do and there is only one of you. You only have so many resources to give, so of course you're going to have to set and maintain boundaries. It's just good resource management.

If you, like most people, have a hard time setting and maintaining your boundaries, remember: Boundaries aren't as personal as we make them out to be, and the more we depersonalize them, the easier it is to keep them in place. Consider this analogy: You have ten chips, and you need three of them for yourself. Someone asks you for five chips; now there are just two left to dole out. Someone else comes along and asks you for three chips. But because there are only two left, your boundary is that you only have two chips left to give. You don't need to feel bad telling someone you only have two left—that limit is just the reality of the situation. You can even tell them to come by tomorrow when you'll have chips to spare again and you can give them one then.

People who don't feel confident that they have the right to express this boundary will sacrifice one of their personal chips so that the requester can have three immediately. (If this is you, no judgment, but you're going to need to change that.) If you get into the habit of giving away your personal chips, you will soon find that people will not stop asking for chips, whether you have three chips or zero chips to spare. We don't think of our resources as chips because it seems too simple, but this analogy demonstrates how cut-and-dried setting a boundary can be.

Consider your hours at work. If you have forty hours in a week and thirty-five of them are spoken for, when someone approaches you about a project that will take twenty hours, you have to say clearly that you unfortunately do not have twenty hours to give. It's simple math. It's not a proxy for how you feel about that person and it's not a reflection of your skills or passion. You have five spare hours this week; you can either talk to your manager and see if you can reprioritize your tasks to accommodate the new request, or you can let them know that the soonest you can finish the project is next week. But you don't just magically come upon twenty more hours. You don't want to blindly agree because you feel bad and then donate fifteen of your personal hours to the project.

The problem is that we all sometimes blindly agree. We say things like, "I'll find time," as if spare time is just hanging out under rocks at the park. If you are determined to cure your burnout, that kind of behavior needs to stop now. Instead, take inventory of your time and then thoughtfully decide whether you have that resource to give. Take stock of your limits as a person and as a professional, trust that they're reasonable, and feel confident holding them.

We gain confidence through experience because the more frequently we set boundaries, the more evidence we have that we can do it and all will be well. The more boundaries you set, the more comfortable you will feel setting them. Sure, it's intimidating to walk into your manager's office and tell them that you don't have twenty hours this week to complete that project. But having the confidence to do so should be rooted in your belief that you are making a reasonable request and managing your limited time as thoughtfully as possible. **You don't have to wait until things are *really bad* to feel justified setting and holding a boundary.** You don't have to have a dozen reasons why you can't work sixty hours this week (or any week, for that matter). And being someone who confidently asserts your boundaries isn't going to harm your career—it's more likely that it will accelerate your path toward success.

STOP MANAGING THE EXPERIENCE OF OTHERS

Does this sound familiar? *If I don't go to the party, their feelings will be hurt. If I don't say yes they'll think I'm lazy . . . If I don't ___, they'll say I'm ___.* These are just a few ways we, in effect, assume responsibility for the thoughts, feelings, and experiences of those around us to manage their perception of us or ensure that they never experience any discomfort or get upset.

This chapter is not meant to encourage you to be a raging asshole who doesn't care about anyone but yourself. But you can be considerate of the people around you and still have boundaries.

If you don't believe you can do these things simultaneously, you may be in the dangerous habit of tuning yourself out completely in favor of considering others' needs. People typically do this in order not to "rock the boat." You don't want to make anyone feel bad, you don't

CONSIDERATE & CONFIDENT

ASSHOLE   PUSHOVER

want to seem difficult, you don't want to start an argument—but that often means sacrificing your peace for others'.

Boundaries can feel like a horrifying social game. A yes feels like it brings us closer to people and a no feels like it builds walls. Our complicated relationship with boundaries begins early. Many of us were taught that obedience and being accommodating are equivalent to love and respect. When a child is disobedient, they are often labeled "difficult" and are punished with what feels like a loss of love or connection. (See: any child who was met with the silent treatment after doing something to upset a caregiver.) When a teenager is not accommodating, they're usually considered disrespectful as opposed to just figuring out where their needs begin and someone else's end. A lack of compliance is seen as a lack of respect in practically every space we occupy from childhood through early adulthood. When we're not accommodating, we are often met with messages of disdain or guilt: "I do so much for you . . . ," "If you cared enough . . . ," or "I'll remember this next time you want something. . . ."

Growing up this way leaves us out of touch with ourselves. Because accounting for the feelings of others has been ingrained in us from day one, we lose sight of our own desires, overestimate how responsible we are for other people's emotions, and underestimate the ability of others to regulate themselves. The idea that we are each in charge of our own emotions is called "emotional responsibility." When we take on responsibility for how others are feeling, however, it can lead to unfounded guilt and the false belief that it's on us to fix everything for everyone else. **It is not on you to flip through someone else's owner's manual in an attempt to troubleshoot.**

Sometimes, though, people do not set boundaries because they don't have faith in others. They don't believe that others are understanding enough to handle hearing no or not getting their way. In some cases, this may be true—that needy friend, that demanding manager, that difficult customer, that company where saying no might literally be met with a gasp of shock or worse because that's just the culture. But these are the exceptions, not the rule. Generally, people can understand your boundary without a dissertation from you about why you have dared to set it.

Once, when I was new to a role and needed to set a boundary with my team, I overexplained myself out of fear they wouldn't understand. One of my co-workers chuckled and said, "You don't have to explain it to me; I work here too." Like, duh! This person could see the situation herself; I didn't need to explain myself to death and over-apologize for setting a reasonable boundary. That conversation gave me faith that people could handle hearing a boundary, which in turn made them feel easier to set.

Where many people get caught up in the boundary-setting process is in the anticipated reception of their boundaries. Tina could have hesitated to set the boundaries she needed indefinitely, but she wanted an answer to the question *Is it possible to work here and maintain boundaries, or will my needs not be met here?* **It's natural to fear upsetting others, but that is not a good enough reason to suffer indefinitely.**

THE UNDERLYING FEAR: REJECTION AND IDENTITY LOSS

Fear of upsetting others and being rejected is as old as we are. As we discussed in the section on social burnout, we are social creatures who have a biological and physiological need for acceptance. *Please like me!* isn't just vanity—it can feel like life or death, and for good reason: Evolutionarily, we needed acceptance from others to have a community that ensured survival. So the emotions triggered by rejection and criticism—shame, jealousy, guilt, sadness, and embarrassment—are ingrained and not unusual responses. In fact, just imagining, anticipating, or remembering a past rejection can trigger a strong emotional response. Studying the impact of social rejection on the brain has even revealed that the emotional pain of being ignored or abandoned can be as painful as physical pain—and such instances light up the same regions in the brain. Therefore, if you have repeatedly experienced that setting boundaries results in rejection, it's going to take some time before you're comfortable with it, but it *is* possible. And it is absolutely worth the effort. **We don't wake up one day ready to upset people; rather, we wake up one day tired of upsetting ourselves.** We often ignore our lack of boundaries until the cost of not having them outweighs the benefits.

Perhaps always being flexible about work hours worked out well at the beginning of your career. It strengthened your reputation and made you "easy to work with" and a "team player." Now, years later, it has become the norm and you feel no sense of separation between work and life. You've moved past the "showing your worth" phase, and you are now in the miserable "this is costing me my peace" phase. And you're not alone! A recent study looking at mostly work-from-home professionals found that those without a firm distinction between work and personal life were less happy and more emotionally exhausted than those with stronger work-life boundaries. Perhaps always answering your boss's emails at 10 P.M. made you "reliable" and answering all your family's and friends' phone calls made you everyone's favorite confidant. You don't want to lose that status, but now instead of feeling pride when you see your phone light up, you feel anxiety because you don't want to be on your phone, you'd rather spend your time and energy on something else.

This is where one's boundaries and identity become intertwined. One of my close friends is the most giving person I know—she goes all-out for everyone's birthdays, picks people up from the airport, helps finish other people's work, and is always available for what anyone needs. As a member of her close friend group, I've seen how rewarding her giving nature is for her. She has so many rich relationships. But I have also seen the toll her generosity takes on her spirit and the disappointment that comes when other people don't treat her the same in return. When she had a minor social-burnout meltdown, I asked her why she didn't pull back and give less. She said, "It's what people know me for. If I don't keep it up, who knows what could happen." This is how she has always shown up in relationships. If she suddenly sets boundaries, will she lose those friends? Will people who depend on her suffer? Will people think less of her? What will she be known for then? The unknown struck fear in her people-loving but exhausted heart.

Much of the fear around setting boundaries is that they will result in weakened relationships, status, or perceived character. I can't make a blanket statement to comfort you about the chance of bad things like this happening. But what I can do is promise you that the people who love and respect you will trust that you're doing your best and that you have a good reason for drawing a line in the sand, especially if you communicate it kindly. **Reasonable people who see you as more than a basket of resources at their disposal will not have a problem with you setting limits that support you.** If they have your best interests in mind, personally or professionally, they *will* understand.

When we are burned out, we have to learn how to embrace "healthy selfishness"—a respect for our own needs, growth, joys, and freedoms. Healthy selfishness stands in stark contrast to "pathological altruism," a desire to please that always places others' needs above your own—when doing good actually becomes bad for you. Too much selflessness when you're already low on resources will hinder your quality of life and induce burnout faster. Being socially aware and reading the room is one thing; taking full responsibility for the room and how everyone in it feels is another.

READING THE ROOM

"Did you notice that Marge said 'That's fine' in a weird voice after I told her I wouldn't be here on Friday?" I cocked my head at my colleague as we walked back to our desks after our team meeting and asked, "What are you talking about?" She glanced around nervously and repeated, "She said 'That's fine' kind of snappy." In the most reassuring tone I could muster, I said, "I didn't catch that, but even if she did, she still said it's fine." With a large sigh and an unconvincing "I guess," my co-worker slumped back over to her desk. Knowing her, I suspected that she was going to worry about that interaction all day.

This is where reading the room goes from helpful to harmful. It's where one clipped word can derail your peace for the entire day. This pressure to anticipate others' needs and read the room is common in people who grew up in households where planning for other people's thoughts, feelings, and experiences is what kept them safe. If the need to determine someone's mood by the sound of their footsteps was your reality, I am sorry. You didn't deserve that. I'm sorry you had to learn this as a survival tool. I hope that you've built a new life for yourself full of people with whom you don't have to do this.

Setting boundaries becomes much easier when you aren't trying to anticipate a dozen realities (which is too tall an ask anyway because you're not psychic) and can instead comfortably ask yourself: *Am I honoring my limits and what I have to give?* I'm sure we've all had the experience of sitting in a team meeting while someone is talking about a new project idea, and then agonizing over the silence that follows "Can anyone take this on?" If you're like me, you begin feeling guilt and start storytelling immediately. *Everyone must be thinking I should volunteer, they're probably all busier than me so I should take it on, I feel so bad people are uncomfortable so I should take it just to end the awkward silence.* Guess what? The person who feels the guiltiest or is the most empathic does not need to take on every burden. Other people probably aren't thinking those things about you; they're probably thinking something similar about themselves and hoping they don't get stuck with it. Anticipating all those things is just extra mental work you don't need to do. Those unhelpful thoughts should not be the arbiter of whether you say yes or no.

The objective reality is that this is a project that will require three hours. Do you have three hours to spare? Does it make more sense for you to accept this project or keep that time available for work that more closely aligns with your job? It's easy to get lost in the interpersonal muddiness of boundaries—that is, how others may be feeling about themselves or you—but the more we can focus on the actual ask, the easier it is to set the boundary and not feel like you're snubbing anyone in the process. You have a limited amount of time and energy. **Boundaries are a reflection of your capacity, not your capability.**

BUT WHAT WILL THEY THINK?

As the saying goes, if we knew how often people thought of us, we wouldn't worry about what people thought of us. People are mostly concerned with themselves. If I tell someone, "I can't make it to a meeting at 6 P.M. because it's outside of my working hours," I suspect they might be peeved for the time it takes them to book the next available time, but then they'll go back to worrying about what they'll make for dinner. People aren't sitting around thinking about you for hours on end (and that should be liberating!). You can't live your life out of fear of how you're perceived.

Boundaries are meant to preserve your sanity, not hurt others. If preserving your sanity does hurt others, there is probably an imbalance of responsibility. Boundaries can still feel uncomfortable to set, particularly in the workplace (ironically, because that should be the most natural place to set transactional boundaries), so let's dive a little deeper.

PROFESSIONAL BOUNDARIES
(*CUE THE NERVOUS SWEATS*)

In the chapter on time management, we talked about my client Holly. She was struggling to regulate her workload as a result of her manager's committing to additional work on her behalf—work that she and her team couldn't reasonably handle. Despite her protests, her superiors didn't seem to believe that she or her direct reports had hit their limit. As the stress continued to mount and her workload grew, Holly knew that in addition to some cutthroat prioritization, she needed to set clear boundaries. As intimidating as it was, she scheduled a meeting to talk to her boss. Here's what Holly said:

"At this time, I am working eighty hours per week. My workload is

unsustainable, but my work is also visible enough to management and our clients that if I don't work overtime to get it all done, then it looks like I'm unprepared as opposed to overbooked. I've communicated this previously, and I don't want people to wait to take me seriously until things fall through the cracks. How can we reduce this workload? What is the timeline for that being done?"

Holly's clear request going into this conversation was "Things are not sustainable as they are. How and when is this situation going to change?" To help prevent that timeline from being pushed indefinitely, she made sure to schedule follow-up meetings. If that question couldn't be answered, then it was sadly fair to assume there were no plans for her workload to change any time soon.

While it's natural to worry that a conversation like this sounds like "I can't do my job," you need to believe that you are a reasonable person asking for a reasonable thing. You have only so much time and energy in a day. You are not expressing your boundary in order to be difficult; you are doing it because you respect yourself and want to do your job well and your current workload doesn't allow you to do those things.

In Holly's case, her managers decided to hire additional team members to account for her increased workload. The situation got worse before it got better because she suddenly had to make the time to train new employees, but over the following months, the pressure lessened and lessened until her role felt far more manageable. **Often, we have to choose between having a hard conversation or having a hard life.** Many people choose the hard life so they don't have to have the hard conversation. **Always, *always* choose the hard conversation.**

Most people aren't setting boundaries because they hate their job; instead, they are doing it because they *like* their job and want to make it work. The result of not protecting your job with boundaries is often resenting what your job turns into and needing to leave the role. If the options are having a hard conversation or forcing your company to backfill your role six months from now when you quit, I am pretty confident, based on the fact that hiring and training are extremely costly for organizations, that they would prefer you have the hard conversation.

YOUR TEARS-FREE GUIDE TO
SETTING WORKLOAD BOUNDARIES

How do you go about having a conversation about workload boundaries? Very objectively. First, break your work down into tangible pieces. Try creating an outline of what you're currently working on, how long everything takes, and how it's currently fitting into your schedule. Having a visual like this helps ground a conversation about workload in concrete resources as opposed to less measurable concepts such as capability or "bandwidth." The truth is, you're capable of practically anything, but that's a bad ruler to measure with.

Conversations about "bandwidth" are often ambiguous and misleading. "Do you have the bandwidth?" is a soft and fuzzy way to gauge capacity, and it's impossible to answer the question accurately until you translate it into a sharp, focused question. What it is really asking is "Do you have five hours this week to work on this project?" or "Are you willing to spend two hours per week for the next year being a go-to person for new hires?" or "Can you be a part of this committee that requires one hour per month after regular working hours?" The clearer we get about the request, the clearer we can be with the answer. And we can only give a proper answer if we have a good understanding of what is currently on our plate.

If you are actively drowning under your circumstances, outline your workload as described above, schedule this conversation, and present how you're spending the hours of your week and what changes you would ideally like to make. Include a requested timeline for implementing those changes so that you don't find yourself on the brink of burnout (and if you're already there, make sure to ask if there is anything that can be removed from your workload in the interim). You can even come prepared with a list of the items on your plate that don't align with your most important objectives and how you think they could otherwise be handled (e.g., pause, simplify, delegate, or automate). Rather than just coming to your manager with a problem, you've come to them with a problem *and* a solution. If you can't agree to a solution in the initial meeting, schedule a follow-up meeting so you know when it will come up again and you aren't living in a never-ending limbo.

LETTING BROKEN THINGS BREAK

Imagine you're an elementary school teacher and you notice that one of the crossing guards didn't show up one day. Out of the kindness of your heart you take up the duty, let the school know, and don't mind that you got home an hour later than usual. It feels like you did a good deed. The next day, you notice that the crossing guard has not been replaced. You fill the role again and reach out to the school administrators to let them know that they need to send someone else to step in. In return you get a vague response that they're looking for someone to fill the role, but they are extremely grateful to you for chipping in in the meantime. By day five of crossing guard duty, you feel resentful: This no longer feels like a good deed and instead feels like you are being taken advantage of.

This is a version of what we often experience at work. There are so many moving pieces, so many people, so much to do to keep things running that when a problem arises for which there is a convenient stopgap, a long-term solution is not prioritized because you are already managing the problem. One of the hardest lessons to learn and act on is that often **people don't believe something is broken until it breaks.**

Your company won't fix the software that your assistant Tom is torturing himself to manage manually because it's still getting done. They won't hire the extra employee the team desperately needs because all the work is still being completed (even if everyone is working overtime to do it). "If it ain't broke don't fix it" isn't just something to be said about your grandma's favorite recipe; it's also a living, breathing philosophy in many industries. But it *is* broke! It needs fixing! If they won't fix it until it truly breaks—and not just the threat of it breaking—it's time to step back, put your hands up, and let it actually break. (Within reason. Use your best judgment.)

Have you seen those videos of wives going on "strike" and not cleaning up the house in an effort to *show* their husbands the mess instead of telling them about it? This is the professional version of that. I have a friend who was so overworked that she got to a point where she simply didn't assign a batch of assignments that needed to be underway by a certain date. By dropping the ball, she received a "talking to," but she also finally got the support that she had been begging for.

Allowing natural consequences to take their course is difficult because it often requires letting someone or something fail. It's hard to watch something you've worked on and care about go south. There is also an added layer of fear that we will look bad by finally allowing something to fail. We don't want our name associated with things that break, but problems don't happen in a vacuum. Odds are you've brought this issue up before and were ignored, other people know it is a problem, your predecessors struggled with it, or it is on a long list of problems that "aren't solvable right now" and your organization is just seeing how long they can get away with not coming up with another solution. If your organization is relying on human effort to bridge gaps from point *A* to point *Z,* that is not an individual problem; it's a systemic and structural one.

It can be tempting to keep being a safety net, either because it feels like it provides job security or because you can't stand the thought of letting something go wrong. But you are being punished for someone else's problems. Imagine repeatedly telling someone the stove is hot. For one reason or another they don't believe you and continue reaching for it. You keep sticking your hand in between them and the stove to prevent them from burning themselves and you are getting burned in the process. By playing middleman, you are preventing them from learning. Once you've done your due diligence by warning them emphatically, they might just need to learn the hard way. Letting natural consequences take their course is not villainous. Those consequences would probably occur whether you were there or not; all you're doing is removing yourself from the equation long enough for them to experience the problem themselves.

Think about the colleague who waits until 4:30 P.M. to ask for your help with something. If every time this happens you get frustrated but then help them anyway, they're learning that they can keep doing this. (I'm trusting you know the difference between an accidental, infrequent request and someone who just won't learn and makes this sort of behavior a habit.) Consider saying, "I have obligations that begin at 5:30 P.M. each night; when I get requests late in the day, I often cannot get to them until the following morning." Or perhaps you need to say, "Would you mind letting me know if you'll need support by 3 P.M.? When requests come in after that, I can't guarantee I can prioritize them until the next day." Your colleague probably won't love hearing it, but the chances are much greater that the next time they need help they will send a request sooner or not expect it to be completed until the following day. To reinforce this stated boundary with action, you're going to have to put your money where your mouth is the next time they try to violate it. This isn't easy, but **people learn how to treat you based on how you allow yourself to be treated.** You might have to prove that you mean what you say a couple of times before they believe it.

Of course, the greater the hierarchical gap between you and the person you're setting the boundary with, the more frustration you may encounter. Someone five levels above you who doesn't know your name or what you do is an intimidating person to try to set a boundary with. You have to remember that no matter who you're talking to, boundaries are just about resources and what you are available for. Someone above you might not respect or like that you're setting a boundary, but they can't argue with how many hours are in a day. "The report you're asking for takes at least two hours to create" is an undeniable limit. "I am available to meet this Saturday; however, I am not available to meet perpetually on Saturdays" is also reasonable. Perhaps you have to give in to the ask the first few times to demonstrate you're a "team player," but if the troubling ask becomes a regular expectation, you'll need to find the words to express your parameters. If that prospect is horrifying to you, rest assured it doesn't have to be black and white. It's not "Yes, I will do exactly what you're asking" or "No, I won't do that at all." There is a middle ground that sounds something like, *I will do what they're asking in order to get a better idea of what they're asking for and from there try to come up with an alternative way for everyone's needs to be met that doesn't overextend me perpetually.* You're not trying to be difficult; you're still determined to do what needs to get done, you're just also respecting your limits, protecting your existing responsibilities, and trying to prevent burnout (and rage-quitting). It is unsustainable to disregard your limits and needs entirely. You will end up miserable, I promise.

The natural next step is learning how to actually set those boundaries, so let's explore some universal methods that can support you as you express your limits.

BOUNDARY TOOL KIT

Here are four easy tools to help in setting boundaries:

1. **Creating Space**

   Picture this: You're in a team meeting and as the meeting draws to a close, you're asked, "Are you coming to the team happy hour after work?" You look up to find your colleagues looking at you and feel that knee-jerk response of yes creeping in, even though you didn't know about the happy hour and had planned some much-needed rest after work. **Instead of saying yes to a request on the spot, get in the habit of creating space to consider it before committing.** In this case, you could easily respond with, "Oh, I didn't know about the happy hour. I need to check my calendar and will let you know."

   Rarely do we actually have to respond in the moment. Creating space is a great way to prevent accidental overcommitment. Another way to give yourself a moment to gather your thoughts is to ask a follow-up question. If someone requests that you join a new project, try asking, "What would your expectations be if I agree?" This gives you a moment to think and provides you with more information that can help you make a well-informed, strategic decision.

   A secondary benefit of creating space is giving yourself a

chance to emotionally regulate before responding. It is easy to mistake intensity for urgency or to get overwhelmed in the workplace. Being able to ask, *Can I take a moment to consider how this impacts my current deadlines?* and doing some deep breathing before responding can cut your stress in half.

When you receive a request and experience indicators that a boundary might be needed (feelings of dread, quickened breathing, needing to move things around on your calendar at the last minute), try to create space before responding. Think of it like retreating and regrouping. Creating space also doubles as boundary priming. While saying, "Can I check my calendar and get back to you?" doesn't explicitly set the boundary, it sets you up to follow up and say, "After checking my calendar, I don't have capacity to take on ___ at this time" or "After checking my calendar, the soonest I can complete this would be Thursday. Does that still work for you?" or "After checking my calendar, I can confirm I am available to support *A,* but I don't have capacity for *B* and *C.*"

This is not you being difficult. It is just a demonstration that you take your responsibilities seriously.

2. Using "I" Statements

Consider the statement "You micromanage me and you need to give me space to do my work." As you might imagine, people aren't very receptive to unsolicited negative feedback. Although the statement is clear (and probably true), we typically can't get away with this kind of bluntness in our professional or personal relationships.

A less abrasive way to suggest a change is to use an "I" statement—one where you are the focus rather than someone else. Instead of "you micromanage me," try "I work best when I have autonomy" or "I prefer to work for uninterrupted periods of time and respond to messages between those periods of time." When expressing a need, make *yourself* the focus, not the other person. Making yourself, your needs, or your changes the focus can help you have boundary conversations without feeling like you need to convince the other person of their behavior or to change it. Research has also found that people who use "I" statements more often than "you" statements are perceived as less hostile and as problem-solvers. **You don't set boundaries to change other people, but rather to change how you *interact* with them.**

Let's say you and a co-worker often chat in the middle of the day to touch base about different projects you're working on. You enjoy catching up with them, but you notice that the conversation always devolves into a vent session on their part, and you just don't have the energy to engage in venting during the workday. Using an "I" statement, creating a boundary might sound like, "I've noticed that at the end of our conversations we sometimes drift into venting, and I think it's impacting my attitude about work, so I'm going to try not to vent about work for a while and see if that helps." The next time it comes up, enforce your boundary in a lighthearted way: "Wait! I'm trying to get better about venting, new topic!" You aren't being rude, and you can say this with a smile. If they give you grief about it, then you can add, "I know it's boring but I seriously need to try this because my attitude about work is abysmal right now." Levity can help defuse tension in conversations that would otherwise be fraught and difficult. If they *still* push, you can get up and jovially tell them, "I have to walk away, I have to be strong, I'm sorry."

You can also use a conditional statement, or an "if-then" statement. "If *this* happens, then *that* happens." "*If* you yell at me, *then* I will excuse myself until you can have this conversation reasonably." "*If* you IM me during a meeting, *then* I will get back to you once I am out of it." "*If* you email me after 4 p.m., *then* the likelihood is higher that I won't be able to respond to it until the next day." Many boundaries can be framed in this way. In fact, research shows that if-then statements can be understood by kids as young as three years old. If a three-year-old can comprehend an if-then statement, I have faith the adults you're talking to can as well. (And if they genuinely can't, no verbal boundaries will save you from that person—you just have to create the physical boundary of space.)

"I" statements and if-then statements can support you outside the workplace, too. Maybe you crave quiet time to yourself after work but don't know how to lovingly tell your partner, "You rely on me for entertainment, and you need to leave me alone for an hour so I can decompress by myself." Instead, you might tell them, "I'm realizing I need more alone time to decompress so I'm going to start retreating to our bedroom to read for an hour each night. Can you help hold me to it?" You are the focus, and—added bonus!—by asking them to help hold you accountable, they will feel like they are helping support you instead of being deprived of something.

You might also use an if-then statement to head off intrusive personal questions at an upcoming family gathering. Instead of succumbing to fear and dread, decide that "if people ask me about ___, I'm going to say ___ and excuse myself." Boundaries preserve us. Without them, we can easily feel helpless in the face of stressors. By feeling confident about setting boundaries, we become less fearful about what might happen because we know that regardless of what happens we will be able to express ourselves and excuse ourselves if needed.

3. Stating the Obvious

Let's say every time you work with someone they wait until the last minute to send you the materials you need, forcing you to work outside of your normal hours to complete the project— and making you resentful. Stating the obvious to set a boundary might sound like, "Previously you've sent your materials over around 4 p.m. Going forward, could you please send the materials by noon?" No overexplaining, no beating around the bush, just using the obvious to frame your request. **Stating the obvi-**

ous eliminates the need to come up with an elaborate way to present a problem.

You don't need to find the perfect words to explain what has already happened. They were there, and they probably will not be surprised to hear you had to put in some overtime. You aren't laying it on thick and telling them that their submitting the materials late inconveniences you; you're letting the obvious speak for itself. While many people structure these boundaries as *the ask + the reason*, I suggest you **frame it as *the obvious + the ask* and let the obvious serve as the reason.**

This matter-of-fact approach is particularly helpful when it comes to setting boundaries around the way work is done. How often have you struggled to let co-workers know that you don't think their proposed strategy will work? The obvious is a great stand-in for difficult and unnecessary conversations that often detour away from finding a solution.

"Last time we did the project that way the result was _____. What can we do to ensure the result is different this time?"

"Based on how long this work took previously, it will most likely take until ___. Is that an acceptable timeline?"

"The best predictor of how things will go in the future is how they went in the past, and in the past _____. How can we ensure different results?"

Workshop these ideas to suit your circumstances. Personality, industry, and seniority will influence the leeway you have to state the obvious, but on a basic level, anyone can utilize this tool. Don't get me wrong: The obvious doesn't always make people *happy*, but stating it gives you a chance to reframe expectations and speak up for yourself without feeling like you have to explain your feelings about the experience. Whereas using an "I" statement makes *you* the focus, stating the obvious makes the *situation* the focus. Whether you are pointing out obvious factors in the current situation or from previous situations (time commitment, resource availability, timelines), this method will help you set a boundary without emotional baggage.

4. **Setting Expectations and Reaching Consensus**

This tool is particularly helpful for the type A people and type B people who are working together. Type A people are those who are aggressively on top of it, ensure everything is done ahead of time, and take responsibility for anyone associated with their work (in other words, they tend to expect others to meet their standards). Type B people tend to be more relaxed; for these folks, deadlines feel more like strong suggestions, and their pace is more leisurely than their type A counterparts'. One is not better than the other so long as the work gets done. However, when these two personality types work together, tensions often arise.

Type A people want to ensure type B people do what they need to do, and type B people want type A people to lay off. "I" statements and stating the obvious can sometimes work in these cases, but often, a more helpful strategy is to set clear expectations and reach consensus. For example, if you are type A and you are about to work on a project with a type B person who you don't totally trust will get the work done, you might say, "To save time and reduce back-and-forth, I just want to be clear that I'll need ___ by ___. Does that work for you?" Once they agree, send them an email restating the plan you agreed on. While that can still feel overbearing to a type B person, the clarity up front prevents micromanaging later (which a type B person would *really* dislike) and the anxiety or discord that would likely ensue without clear expectations.

The second part of this tool is equally as important as the first: You need agreement from the party to whom you are setting expectations. Setting expectations without having buy-in from all parties is just bossing people around. (Which I agree is much easier but unfortunately not always effective.) *Collaborating*, conversely, is actually seeing and hearing the person with whom you are working and ensuring they agree to the expectations so that the dynamic remains respectful.

BOUNDARIES FOR AT-RISK GROUPS

What if you feel hesitant about setting expectations? Junior employees, new hires, members of a marginalized group—for different reasons, these groups might feel an additional layer of fear when expressing themselves in the workplace. People in at-risk groups might not feel welcome creating boundaries or may have had negative experiences trying to do so previously. This fear is further heightened if your workplace doesn't have a culture that supports boundaries or inclusion.

Women, people of color, people with disabilities, women with children, plus-size individuals, and members of the LGBTQ+ community are more likely than other groups to experience microaggressions or even blatant discrimination in the workplace. As a result, it is helpful for these folks to feel confident setting boundaries so that they can protect themselves if need be. How often has a person of color been assigned to a diversity and inclusion committee without being asked if they want to or have time? How many examples have you heard of the only woman on a team being expected to take notes for the meetings? How often in job interviews have women been (illegally) asked whether they have children or plan to have children? But it's not always as easy as just communicating an expectation that you be treated equitably, is it?

For starters, previous experiences may have led you to believe that setting a boundary or an expectation will lead to a negative outcome, like being labeled as difficult or disruptive. A 2022 Deloitte Women @ Work global survey found that 16 percent of women, mostly ethnic minorities, did not report harassment or microaggressions because they feared it would have an adverse effect on their career. They were afraid of being seen as "troublemakers" when setting boundaries. Separately, although probably not unrelated, women of color are also more likely to experience burnout than non-minorities. And any gender-based discrimination is a risk factor for burnout, regardless of ethnicity.

It will take more than personal and professional boundaries to change these systems, but knowing your limits can protect you and benefit you nonetheless. When you are explicit about your expectations and boundaries, you aren't being abrasive; you're being clear about what is and isn't acceptable for you.

Erin L. Thomas, vice president of diversity, inclusion, and belonging at Upwork, told me one of her first pieces of advice for people from marginalized identity groups: Question whether you have internalized the roles that society has foisted on you, such as being the superhuman, always-supportive Black woman who *must* be resilient in the face of demands. She encourages people to "recalibrate yourself to a healthier baseline so you can find balance." This process can take a long, long time, but it is an important step for learning and honoring your boundaries.

Thomas shared two areas that are beneficial to be aware of when it comes to the need to set boundaries:

1. A lack of visibility, recognition, and/or access to opportunities

2. A lack of respect or safety

If these issues are compromising your professional experience, it is within your right to advocate for yourself. "When in doubt, share and speak up." You are your first line of defense. The big question is, How do you set a boundary in a way that feels safe and effective? "The calculus is different for everyone," Thomas says—the culture of the office, your style of communicating, whether you trust formal channels—but you can still consider the following options offered by Thomas. "People get fixated on just one approach, but there are a number of ways you can address a situation, from hunkering down and making a plan to handle it on your own, to being vocal, to enlisting informal support, to escalating it up the mandatory reporting chain."

- **Practice in private.** Practice setting boundaries so you're comfortable expressing yourself—either independently or with a trusted colleague or friend. That way, the next time you're interrupted and need to chime in with a "Pardon me, I'm going to finish my thought and then I'll throw it over to you," you're comfortable doing so.

- **Enlist support.** Ask trusted peers to vouch for you in meetings and help correct the record—"Amanda spent a lot of time fine-tuning the kickoff presentation"—so there is a more accurate sense of your contributions. Let's say you made a suggestion or completed a project that someone else took credit for. Those who are happy to advocate for you can always be at the ready to back you up or set the record straight in real time. "Great suggestion, Amanda; I like where you're going with that." "When Amanda presented that idea at the last meeting, I remember thinking it was innovative." "Amanda spearheaded that project so you can direct your thanks to her!"

  If you need to set a difficult boundary but aren't sure you carry enough weight for people to respect it, another tactic I recommend is knowing who in your corner is willing to be your "cc." Your cc is someone who's agreed to back you up and whom you can cc on emails if needed to make your point stronger. "Frank, cc'd here, wanted to be looped in so he could also take a look at the materials you're sending on Friday." If Friday felt negotiable to your recipient before, hopefully it doesn't now. Nobody wants to seem brown-nosey by looping others into in-teractions, but sometimes you need a witness and a little extra accountability. In these situations, the Franks are usually happy to do it too—it's like the easiest mentoring gig out there. Sup-port a rising employee for the small price of a cc'd email every once in a while? Helping in this way means little to no inconve-nience to Frank, but it means the world to the person who en-lists him. If you are a leader, you can also offer this service to members of your team in an act of solidarity.

- **Ask questions.** If you're asked to sit on a panel and you suspect it's a case of tokenism—just being there to give the illusion of diversity—ask for clarity. What exactly is my role on this panel? What am I expected to do in preparation for this?

How do I fit into this group? How does this benefit my team? Sometimes, just asking the questions is enough to get your point across. When your questions are answered, you can determine if there is a boundary to be set.

- **Consider formal channels.** Particularly when it comes to matters of respect and safety, don't overlook the option to take your experience to a trusted leader, HR, or a diversity officer if the company has one. One advantage of going this route is that it places the responsibility of the situation on the company. Thomas explains that many individuals waste energy determining whether incidents warrant boundaries or reporting. She instead insists that if you're having a subpar experience and a pattern of violated boundaries is hindering your performance, that's not just a "you" problem, that's a business problem. That makes it worth taking up with channels whose responsibility it is to come up with a solution. "It is not your job to figure out how to make a safer and more equitable workplace, it's HR or legal's job," says Thomas. "It's your job to share your experience." If you don't feel comfortable speaking to the channels available, you can go a more informal route and report your experience in an employee survey or lean into your social support and create a plan for how you will handle any instances that should follow.

- **Create a record.** No matter how you handle the situation in the moment, it's smart to keep records of your interactions and conversations.

People determine culture, so it is our collective responsibility to contribute to a safe, respectful, and inclusive work environment. Allyship—being an active support for a marginalized group that you are not a member of—can come in many forms: camaraderie, being an engaged member in employee resource groups, letting your team know that you are someone that they can come to for a cc. If you're in a leadership position, broadcast policies that lay the foundation of healthy work practices and boundaries. Creating this kind of social support helps buffer the emotional burden caused by discrimination and can make boundary setting less intimidating for members of marginalized groups.

WHEN YOU DON'T HAVE A CHOICE

The first time I heard a leader respond to "I could use support, my team is very busy" with "everyone is busy," my eyes nearly fell out of my head. Many industries and companies rely on employees overextending themselves to keep everything running. Stories are spun about "hard work" and "earning your stripes" that mask the ugly truth: It's too much. If it weren't too much, there wouldn't be nearly as many people making the same complaints.

How might we set boundaries in spaces that are not boundary-friendly?

1. Clarify for yourself what would need to change in order for you not to be burned out.

2. See if there is a timeline for these types of changes.

3. If there is a timeline, follow up when it is appropriate; if there is not, accept that this might be the role.

4. Assess how you feel about this role as it is: If you know it's not for you and you need to get out, begin taking steps to do so (more on this in the chapter about when to walk away). If you can't get out for the time being and boundaries are only providing so much relief, utilize the other burnout pillars—mindset, personal care, stress management, and time management—to endure The Suck in the meantime. You might not be able to turn it into your dream situation, but you can at least make it more bearable.

EMOTIONAL MANAGEMENT: PROTECTING YOURSELF

Rachel worked in the pharmaceutical industry and had a manager so turbulent he made Michael Scott—the fictional manager of NBC's *The Office*—seem reasonable: His moods were volatile, his actions unpredictable, and she frequently left meetings with him feeling like she needed to find a quiet room and sink into fetal position. All his direct reports would admit to each other that he caused them extremely high stress.

Rachel is a hardworking employee who wanted to make her manager happy, but his roller-coaster moods were making it difficult for her to keep her own emotions in check and to do her job. It didn't take long for Rachel to realize that she needed a way to create emotional boundaries with her manager, because absorbing his energy and going into meetings with him without mental armor on was leaving her fried. If you've ever worked with someone whose emotional regulation is so poor that it becomes everyone else's problem, this section is for you.

Rachel needed an emotional boundary to help create distance between her and her manager's feelings. Rather than taking his waves of irritation, anger, or negativity personally, she would repeat to herself before, during, and after their meetings *His feelings are not my feelings.*

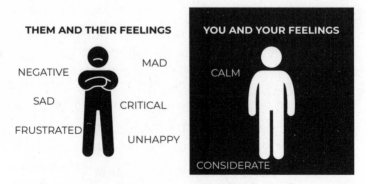

THEM AND THEIR FEELINGS

NEGATIVE
MAD
SAD
CRITICAL
FRUSTRATED
UNHAPPY

YOU AND YOUR FEELINGS

CALM

CONSIDERATE

"THEIR FEELINGS ARE NOT MY FEELINGS."

Rachel needed to remember that absorbing and trying to manage his feelings is not what makes her a good employee (nor is it in her job description); doing her job well is what makes her a good employee, and she is already doing that.

If you have colleagues who can't regulate their emotions or if you work with clients who demand a lot of emotional support and you tend to soak up the feelings of those around you, you are at risk of compassion fatigue. Compassion fatigue is caused by helping emotionally manage and care for others, and it can result in your own emotional and physical fatigue. It's common in industries where you are managing a spectrum of emotions and needs like nursing, teaching, and social work. But it can happen in any work situation where a sensitive person is in regular contact with someone who seems to demand more compassion, and, frankly, more energy. (Compassion fatigue is also more common in people who are experiencing burnout, because if you're already physically and psychologically spent, you have fewer resources from which to draw.) Compassion is a limited resource just like time, energy, or money. You can only do so much emotional management before you snap.

Like Rachel, you have to sit back and separate the logistical parts of your job from the emotional work you're doing. If you are internalizing and taking responsibility for every emotional stressor you come across, you are only doing yourself a disservice. Draining all your resources too quickly and becoming emotionally exhausted compromises your ability to show up in other areas in which your attention is needed. While it might seem altruistic to internalize others' emotions, doing so beyond your capacity actually stunts your ability to show up and help as many people as possible. Having compassion for yourself on the other hand is more likely to alleviate emotional exhaustion and reinforce that **other people's feelings are not your feelings.**

PERSONAL BOUNDARIES:
LIMITS IN YOUR PERSONAL LIFE

Quinn, the only daughter to a high-maintenance mother, was raised on conditional love. If she didn't do what her mother suggested—visit whenever she had a day off, dress the way her mother preferred, take on the extracurriculars her mom most respected—she would be met with disproportionate disappointment, anger, or sadness. Quinn's mother was a frequent user of guilt trips that sounded like "after everything I've done for you . . . you are so ungrateful . . . I guess I'm just the worst mother in the world. . . ." Growing up in this environment made Quinn into a people-pleasing adult who had trouble speaking up for her own needs and *definitely* resisted setting boundaries that could upset anyone. She attracted friends and partners who took advantage of her, criticized her, and generally shored up the belief that when she didn't do as they said, her value diminished. This mindset was hard on her mind, body, and spirit, but the alternative—potentially upsetting people—seemed out of the question. Personal boundaries are intimidating because people in your life can hurt you in ways you can't be hurt in the office. You can get a new job; you can't get a new mom.

"Making work your identity" is a commonly accepted concept that, as a culture, we've finally started to talk about and rebel against. But what's just as common is the practice of making relationships your identity. Some of us allow our relationships—how others perceive us and what others tell us about ourselves—to determine our self-worth. The development of our self-conception begins in childhood when we first start to receive feedback from others. When we bring treats into our classroom and get positive attention from our peers, or when we help the teacher and she tells us we're thoughtful, that feedback translates into believing that when we do things for others, we are thoughtful and are well liked. We can then start to believe that the opposite is also true: When we don't do things for others, we are not as likable. This is how our identity can begin to depend on what others think of us. Unchecked, this turns into a life of people pleasing and letting other people's needs, perception of us, and feelings dictate our lives.

How do you know if you need to set a personal boundary? Consider whether you're doing something because of positive or negative motivating factors. Positive motivating factors are love, excitement, and genuine desire. For example, *I want to finish this book because it's really good* or *I want to go to family dinner because I miss my family and want to spend time with them.* Negative motivating factors are guilt, fear, and disappointment. For example, *I should finish this book I don't like because I already bought it* or *I should go to family dinner; otherwise I'll get a guilt trip for not going.* By clarifying the motivation, you can differentiate between things you do to avoid feeling bad as opposed to things that themselves make you feel *good*.

There is also a difference between prioritizing others when you have an abundance of resources and prioritizing others at the expense of your few remaining resources. Periods of burnout are often some of the only times when people pleasers allow themselves to set boundaries. They decide that their situation has finally gotten "bad enough" that they have no choice but to set them: "I'm sorry, I don't mean to be rude, but I am genuinely so overwhelmed right now that I have to say no." Many struggle to justify setting and holding this boundary until they reach this point of desperation.

What many people pleasers learn once they get to this precarious place is that regardless of your resources, people won't stop asking for things. For instance, you may have told your partner that you want to watch your show by yourself with your favorite snack and walked into a different room with your snack in hand, but when they trail after you and start telling you about some conversation they had at work, you are going to need to restate your boundary: *"Would you mind if, after we finish this conversation, I watch my show? I want to hear about your day and then I really need to decompress." "I need to turn my brain off for a bit before I can give you my full attention. Can I come find you when I'm ready?"*

The question you are asking yourself is not *How much do I have to give?*; it's *How much do I have to give without compromising the things that are important to me?* You could technically move everything around in your weekend because your friend is moving and has sent out an SOS to the friend group for help, but it would also require you to forgo the slow Saturday morning that you look forward to all week, the peaceful walk to the farmer's market, or the lunch you had planned with your mom. There are many opportunities to show that you care for the people in your life. And I'm betting that you have shown up for practically all of them. Your love for them will not be called into question when you say the occasional no.

Feel confident enough to set personal boundaries by keeping in mind that boundaries strengthen relationships; they don't weaken them. **Boundaries aren't a rejection; they're an invitation to keep a relationship going without resentment.**

DIFFICULT PEOPLE (WE'VE ALL GOT THEM)

For many who struggle with social burnout, difficult people are the source of their drain. These people are often emotionally volatile, immature, or imposing. They also tend to hate when boundaries are set with them and will likely challenge them. When someone questions a boundary, it can feel like they're saying, "I know better than you" or "You should live your life in this way I recommend instead of how you are choosing to." For the most part, **the people who have a problem with your boundaries are those who benefit from your not having any.** When you are tempted to cave to these statements, remember: **People are the way they are because it has worked for them before.** Someone who hears a boundary and then pushes harder has probably had success wearing down people's boundaries before.

Even when a boundary has been violated, kind people often empathize their way out of reinforcing their boundaries: "They're only like that because ___." "They grew up ___ so it's not their fault." **Just because you know why someone is the way they are doesn't mean it's okay.** "They only call me crying and telling me I'm a disappointment because it's how their mom treated them and they're still outgrowing it." Okay . . . and you don't think they should improve? If you wouldn't let a friend be treated that way, you shouldn't subject yourself to being treated that way.

There are certain types of people in our lives who tend to necessitate boundaries:

- Needy: Consistently expect more from you than you are available to give
- Bully: Will push you if you aren't doing what they want
- Emotionally Unpredictable/Emotionally Abusive: Treat you unfairly and keep you on edge
- Entitled Takers: Make you feel like it's surprising you have the nerve to not be as available as they would like
- Guilt Inducers: Weaponize guilt to get what they want from you

I'm not saying these people can't be fine company or that they don't care about you in their own way. They just usually come with some serious emotional demands and a need for strong boundaries on your part. If you can't be ruthless with your boundaries and this is a voluntary relationship (like a friend or partner), I might gently suggest you find the nearest exit. If it's an involuntary relationship (like a relative or roommate), recognize when your boundaries are being violated and have some strategies to set those boundaries at the ready ("I" statements, if-then responses, stating the obvious, setting expectations).

"GO CHANGE OR I'LL GET A LECTURE FROM YOUR ABUELITA"

American culture is very individualistic. We pride ourselves on independent identities and oftentimes familial ties are loose. In collectivist cultures such as those in Asia, Africa, and South America, on the other hand, interpersonal relationships are paramount, and family members—especially children—are frequently expected to mirror cultural traditions and values from generations past; your individual identity and needs don't take precedence over the group, and instead are a piece of the whole. If you come from a collectivist culture, it is not uncommon to struggle with boundaries, especially in the context of your family.

I am from a Hispanic culture, and my family is *very* close. I don't think there is a single unit in our family tree who has not had other relatives living with them at some time. Need to borrow a car? *Sure.* You're coming over in five minutes? *Okay, let me stop what I'm doing and whip up some food.* I'm going abroad; do we know anyone in Spain? *Oh, we've got some distant cousins I've never met and they said we can stay with them for a week.* Someone disagrees with the length of your skirt or the cut of your neckline? You'll hear about it. Someone thinks you should have more kids or doesn't like what you posted on social media a month ago? They'll let you know—to your face and probably in front of a group.

This way of life is not without love—you know you will always be taken care of, and you know your network stretches far beyond you. But if you plan to make choices that the group has opinions about, arm yourself with some boundaries. It is difficult to begin setting boundaries with people you're close to if you haven't before, but it is essential to protect your mental health.

I once worked with a lovely young woman named Pamela, who was learning how to make her way post-college as an emergency room nurse. Pamela came from a collectivist culture like me. On top of adjusting to her stressful job, her parents had unrealistic expectations about how often she should be calling them. When she didn't answer their calls— usually because she was working—they would make her feel guilty the next time they spoke. Sometimes they'd "joke" that she didn't have time for them, but more often they would ask when they would see her next since she was *so* busy and share stories of their friends whose kids call and visit more frequently. Pamela was in desperate need of some boundaries to help set expectations.

After considering how often she would *like* to speak to her parents (a positive motivating factor, not a negative motivating factor like guilt), she ended up telling them that she would call them every Sunday morning so they could have virtual coffee together and visit them every other month. She also communicated that she loved them and wanted to share her life with them, but if they started to give her a hard time, she was going to point it out and change the subject. Again, boundaries are not about changing other people. They might still bring up things that she didn't like, but she knew that *if* they did, *then* she had a response that helped protect her. Over time, her stated and reaffirmed boundary was understood and the number of times she left their phone calls with a stomachache reduced significantly.

This was a scary choice for her to make; it felt like it could compromise her relationship with her parents. But if we're being honest with ourselves, **often the relationships we're afraid to compromise are already being compromised, just in a different way.**

BOUNDARY PHRASES AND TONES: CUSTOMER SERVICE VOICE VS. CEO VOICE

Consider how you would perceive two people who need to leave a meeting early. Person one confidently states, "Unfortunately, I'll need to excuse myself about fifteen minutes early. I'll make sure to review the meeting notes to ensure I didn't miss anything." Person two, visibly nervous, states, "I'm so sorry, would it by any chance be okay if I sneak away fifteen minutes early? I have another appointment and I tried to reschedule but couldn't. If it isn't okay, I'll try to move something else around. I'm so sorry for the inconvenience." The goal is to have the first person's confidence. **The way you assert your boundary does half the job of enforcing your words.**

Do you assert yourself in a customer service voice or a CEO voice? A customer service voice is high-pitched, makes everything sound like a question, and exudes accommodating and apologetic vibes. A CEO voice is pitched in a lower register, ends sentences with a downward inflection, and exudes authority and confidence.

Just by hearing someone's tone and word choice, you can tell whether or not they can be pushed around. You can hear how sorry they are for taking up space. Studies have found that vocal quality and tone make a greater impression than the content of what people say, that women who use uptalk (ending sentences like a question) are perceived as less credible, and the deeper a man's voice is, the more money he makes. (Wild, I know, but true.)

There is too much evidence to ignore that tone and delivery influence the credibility of your message. I struggled to speak up for myself for a long time. My spirit object used to be a doormat. But I grew a backbone when I went into business for myself. Previously, I could act small because I *was* small in the scheme of a company. I was low on the professional hierarchy, I could hide behind my manager, and I didn't have to stand up for myself often. Once I started my own business, it was baptism by fire. I alone represented myself, and so I was forced to stop being timid and start taking up space.

As we discussed at the beginning of this chapter, boundaries are both stated and active. I can suggest phrases you can use to state these boundaries, but you also need a backbone to reinforce them with your tone and actions. Here are some tools you can utilize when setting personal boundaries:

> **Redirection:** Shifting the request to something that you have capacity for.
>
> *"Unfortunately, I won't be able to make it to ___, but I would love to ___."*
>
> *"Sadly, I have to prioritize ___ at that time, but if you're free next Friday can we ___?"*
>
> It's not all or nothing; you can still satisfy the relationship even if it isn't with the original ask. This is a great way to deflect requests that drain you in favor of ones that better suit you. For example, if a friend is having a big party and you know that you hate big parties and would barely get to talk to her there anyway, you might ask if you can take her to coffee or drinks the following week. Perhaps there is a big family gathering you feel guilty not attending and there is no easy replacement for it. Instead, you might decide you're just going to go for the first hour. Pop in and give hugs, but then you excuse yourself before it drains you.
>
> **Blanket Explanation:** Expressing that for the foreseeable future you are going to be MIA for personal reasons. This one is helpful during busy seasons.

"Hi! I'm going through a busy season at work so I am in anti-social mode until ___. When I crawl out of the other side I would love to ___."

"Hi! I didn't want you to think I'm ignoring you so this is just a warning that I'll be MIA for approximately the next three months as I get through a busy season! Love you, see you on the other side <3"

"I am not available" does not equal "I hate you," and reasonable people know this! **If a relationship only works when you are available at their convenience, then the relationship will only ever be as full as your basket of resources is.** Setting expectations in your relationships like this can go a long way in reducing potential social stressors.

No is a complete sentence: As much as we love to have the perfectly worded reason, an explanation is not always necessary.

"Shoot. I'm not able to make it, but I hope you have fun!"

"Sadly, after checking my calendar I can't make it :("

And, of course, you can absolutely use the tools you learned previously to set personal boundaries (consider this your TL; DR*):

Creating Space: "Let me step away for a bit to consider this and then I can get back to you."

Using "I" Statements: "I won't be able to answer calls during the workday because it's hard for me to concentrate again afterward. If I miss your call, I'll ring you back as soon as I can :)"

Using If-Then Statements: Knowing that if Aunt Mandy brings up ___ I'm going to smile and say, "Oh, I'm actually not talking about that, will you excuse me?" and walk away.

---

* too long; didn't read

Stating the Obvious: "When we talk about ____ it always ends with an argument. To avoid arguing, let's avoid the topic."

Setting Expectations: "I'm honored you asked me to be your bridesmaid! When you get the chance, I would love to know what your expectations are for your bridesmaids so I have a better idea of scheduling and cost before I agree. I want to be sure I can commit to this properly before I do!"

Now, you know your personal indicators that a boundary is needed, feel confident about setting your reasonable boundary, are willing to let other people manage their own feelings, and have phrases and tools handy that you can use when limits are hit. **Boundaries are not an act of alienating people and being difficult; they are an olive branch you extend because you care enough not to just rage-quit and walk away.** They're your way of preserving yourself, your quality of work, and your quality of life so that you can keep showing up.

Boundaries are critical for preserving ourselves in the face of stressors. But we can't always boundary our way out of a stressful situation. To help extinguish the flame that fuels so much of burnout, we'll need to turn to the final pillar of burnout management: stress management.

CHAPTER SEVEN

Stress Management

When Fight-or-Flight Has Become Your Default

Bill came to me after being told by his doctor that if he didn't lower his stress he would end up in the hospital for chest pain . . . *again.* His blood pressure was through the roof, he constantly had anxiety, and he could barely sleep. Bill had started a successful investment firm and was managing millions of dollars. His business was booming, but the stress at work was having significant adverse effects on his body. He often woke up in a panic in the middle of the night to check his email, he had been working through the weekend for as long as he could remember, and he was experiencing marital strife with his husband as a result of his always-on lifestyle. Bill felt like he was dying a slow death.

As we've discussed, burnout is the result of prolonged stress. Bill was experiencing frequent stress without reprieve, and his body and mind were feeling the repercussions. When we perceive stress—anything that causes us to worry or that suddenly grabs our attention—our brain responds by sending our body adrenaline (or epinephrine, which primes our muscles, heart, and lungs to work harder), fat and sugar (glycogen, to give us fuel to respond to the stressor), and cortisol ("the stress hormone"), which keeps our body on alert until the threat has passed. This flood of hormones is often thought of as our "fight-or-flight" mode— our sympathetic nervous system's attempt to prepare us for the stressor in front of us.

When we encounter a stressor, our bodies seek a physical release for this extra energy so that we can return to our body's baseline. The problem is, we can't always respond to modern stressors in the ways our primitive fight-or-flight system may prime us to. When we get an over-whelming number of emails, we can't run from them. When a co-worker blames us for a mistake, we can't fight them. (I mean . . . we *can,* but we'll probably be escorted out by security shortly after.) Being full of cortisol and adrenaline without a way to burn through them can lead to feeling like we're "on edge," or "bursting at the seams," a moment away from turning into that guy who punches holes in walls.

Emotions such as fear and anger add fuel to the fire ("I'm going to get fired!" "I'm so pissed Craig messed our assignment up *again*!" "How will I get all this work done on time?!") and keep us in a full-body state of anxiety that is harder to switch off. And—no surprise here—when we're burned out, experiencing prolonged stress can have some serious long-term effects on our health. Chronic stress is a precursor for heart disease and immune disorders because prolonged exposure to it causes inflammation, disrupts our hormone balance, and wears our bodies down. The *worst* thing we can do is continually expose ourselves to stressors without any release.

So, how can you alleviate stress? We will discuss various tactics throughout this chapter, but in short, you need a) some sort of physical relief and b) reassurance that you are safe. Physical relief means doing something to burn through the excess energy—getting your blood pumping via exercise, putting some upbeat music on and dancing it out, having an ugly cry, or raging out for a minute and hitting your bed with a pillow. Physical actions help your body to work through the stress and convince your body that the threat has passed, explain Emily and Amelia Nagoski, authors of *Burnout: The Secret to Unlocking the Stress Cycle* (a great resource on stress). Reassurance that you're safe typically requires affirmation—via mental reasoning, support from others, or even a change in your environment—that there is not an immediate threat, and you can calm down. As humans, these are our *innate,* physiological stress responses. But our *conditioned* response to stress is to repress these stress-purge urges because we are taught that they're inconvenient or improper.

We see organic versions of a healthy stress-purge process in children all the time. For example, a child drops a toy that causes a bang (stressor);

the child gets scared (hormonal response to the stress); the child cries (an expression of their emotions that lowers the stress response); then the child picks up the toy and goes back to playing (recovery). The child's stress increased, they expressed it, and then their stress decreased.

As we get older, we are trained out of cycling through our natural responses in favor of responding in more socially acceptable ways. For instance, when we receive bad news in front of others, we are expected to bottle the feelings up so others don't sense our distress and then purge them on our own time. **Once we reach adolescence, having a stress response is treated as a choice instead of an inevitable human reaction.** Obviously, we don't want to cry regularly at work or every time we have a hard conversation with a friend, but these are natural physiological attempts to relieve stress.

Imagine you have a jug that accumulates stress throughout the day.

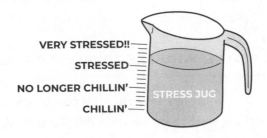

When you are cognizant of working through your stress, you empty the jug as the day goes on. By the end of the day, your stress jug is ideally close to empty. When you don't pay attention to the jug's accumulating stress, you will probably get to the end of the day and find your jug full. This can lead to feelings of being overwhelmed, extreme frustration, and anger that work stress is seeping into your personal time—because now you have to use time *after* work to decompress and empty the jug. Your goal should be to notice stress as you experience it and develop stress management strategies that help you to purge it in real time.

Anyone working in today's world knows that it's not a question of *if* you will experience stress; it's a matter of *when* and *how* you will handle it. It's important to learn how to manage three kinds of stress:

In the moment: A stressor that needs an immediate response

Short-term: A stressor with an end in sight

Long-term: A stressor without an end in sight

Stress comes our way with varying levels of urgency. Sometimes you need to deal with it immediately; other times it simmers in the background because you don't want or need to handle it right away (or you don't know how to). Often, stress is the result of fear that you don't have the resources to handle something—a hard conversation, a project looming in the future, a new job. This fear will stunt your growth. Conversely, when you're confident you can manage stress that arises, you are more willing to leave your comfort zone and grow in scary but important ways. In this chapter we will ensure that regardless of the situations you find yourself in, you can tackle stresses head-on.

STRESS STYLES: WHO ARE YOU UNDER PRESSURE?

"Don't bother him when he's stressed. He'll take it out on you." I had just started working with a new team and this was the word of warning I got about the team's manager. Naturally, people are more irritable when they are stressed; however, this manager had become known for being a "fighter" (in other words, his response to stress was to "fight"). When he was experiencing stress, anyone who got too close was at risk of receiving misdirected jabs. A few times a week, my colleagues and I would hear his raised voice from the hallway and take mercy on the poor sucker who was on the other end of the phone or who emerged from his office paler and sweatier than when they entered. Everyone had learned to endure this manager's behavior. But, knowing what I know now, I can't help but think that these incidents could have been avoided if he had been aware of his stress response, if he had cared about how it was affecting the staff (most people do not do their best in response to fear and intimidation), and if he had done the work to improve it.

The best indicator for how you will handle stress in the future is how you've handled it in the past. **Under stress we tend to do what we _know_ best rather than what would _be_ best.** The most common responses to stress are *fight, flight, freeze, mediate,* or *connect.* Familiarize yourself with these stress response types so that you can better understand your own go-to stress response and those of the people with whom you might regularly experience stressors.

Fight: You're ready to engage immediately and passionately with the stressor; you could benefit from taking a moment to breathe and collect your thoughts before responding.

Flight: Your instinct is to immediately create space between yourself and the stressor; you would benefit from asking for distance explicitly so that the other party understands your intentions, or self-soothing if you can't create space.

Freeze: You experience stress paralysis and have difficulty responding to a stressor in the moment; you would benefit from getting space from the stressor, expressing a need for more time before you respond, and self-soothing.

Mediate: You try to keep the peace and make others comfortable; you would benefit from reflecting on your own needs before jumping in to help others.

Connect: You seek social support in response to a stressor; you would benefit from self-soothing in case nobody is available.

I used to work on a small team of people with different stress response styles. My manager's style was fight, my co-worker's was freeze, and mine was flight. After a stressful meeting during which our team was delegated time-sensitive work, our manager was ready to dive into the action items immediately, my co-worker would sit quietly at his desk shaking, and I wanted to step outside to breathe and gather my thoughts before reopening the conversation. Fortunately, we recognized this pattern and had the wherewithal to discuss our stress styles.

Our solution was to take ten minutes to decompress after stressful meetings going forward. This adjustment allowed us to collaborate much more calmly and effectively, as well as better regulate our stress at work.

Your stress style is your natural response to stress, one you've been conditioned to have (maybe you grew up in a family of fighters or connectors) or that fits with your personality (perhaps you're an introvert and flight or freeze is your instinct). Once we know what kind of style we gravitate toward, we can think about how we might need to shift our response when future stressors arise.

Once I figured out that my style is flight, I became better equipped to manage stress when it arose. Now, if my husband and I ever bicker, my immediate thought is, *I need space, I want to go on a walk and then I can have our follow-up conversation more thoughtfully** rather than trying to have an important conversation while deep in my stress response. During very stressful seasons of work, I used to begin to look for a new job just so I could escape my stressors. Then, when the stressors weren't there anymore, I'd remember I liked my job and I didn't actually want to leave. Now, knowing my natural instinct is to flee, I can anticipate my need for space when stress occurs or find ways to self-soothe in another way if flight isn't the most appropriate response. When I receive hateful messages online, for example, my instinct used to be to delete everything and disappear. Now, I just take some time off of social media, which gives me the same sense of distance between myself and the stressor and allows me to regroup. Sometimes the proclivity toward flight *is* the best option in the moment. Other times I can benefit from alternative forms of stress relief before responding to the problem.

What is your stress style? How do you tend to behave when you're backed against a wall? Do you get confrontational? Look for an escape hatch? Freeze? Seek social support? What are the stress styles of those you spend the most time with—your partner, your manager, your par-

---

* Seeking space—to emotionally regulate and return with a thoughtful response—and stonewalling, cutting someone off and refusing to communicate or cooperate, are two different things.

ents? Next time you encounter a stressful situation with them, can you acknowledge the way your different stress responses may affect your dynamic? Better yet, can you have a proactive conversation about it before encountering the next stressor together?

When stress styles clash, relationships can suffer. A friend of mine shared with me that her instinct when having stressful conversations with her brother is to fight, while his is to freeze. As soon as a conversation starts to become stressful, her agitation grows, and he shuts down. The more she pushes, the more he withdraws. This results in a tense interaction that neither person leaves feeling satisfied.

For the most part, these conversations likely have a purpose, whether it's agreeing on where to host Thanksgiving, deciding what to get Mom for her birthday, or just "I need to express how I feel about ___ because we're in each other's lives and it's important to me." Each sibling's stress style will determine how they approach the conversation and how they hope to resolve the issue. My friend with a fight stress style is probably hoping for a quick resolution, especially if she already knows what her ideal outcome is. But for her brother with a freeze stress style, it can be debilitating to try to address the issue on the spot. He might not know what his goal is for the conversation beyond hoping it ends swiftly, which prevents him from responding effectively in the moment—*What if he answers prematurely or "incorrectly," which would then create more stress to address later?* In this instance, my fight-style friend might lower the stakes enough for her freeze-style brother to thoughtfully consider his options—in other words, present the situation and then give a timeframe to respond rather than expecting an answer on the spot. Is it annoying to have to create a plan for what could otherwise be a quick conversation? Maybe. But, if you want the best results, it helps to design the game in a way that people are comfortable playing.

This tension can occur between people of all stress response styles. Someone whose style is to mediate and who wants to smooth over any tension might get frustrated with a person whose style is flight and needs space before resolving. A person with a freeze stress style might get upset that their partner's stress style is to reach out for support because it feels like they're getting their army of friends on their side. And two people with fight stress styles are often prepared to verbally spar until someone finally storms off or shuts down.

Once you know your stress styles, you can have much more open conversations about your instincts and how you can better communicate while under stress in the future. The most important question to consider when confronting a stressor with someone else is *What are my hopes for this conversation?* Try saying out loud, "By the end of this conversation I'm hoping ___." Clarifying your goal—even if it feels silly—can help reduce the chances that the conversation derails unproductively. That blank could be anything from "find a resolution" to "land on a timeframe for your response" to "know how to address this when it comes up in the future."

When we notice our behaviors under stress, we are more likely to take a second, acknowledge what we might need, and then move forward with more compassion for ourselves and others, which in turn puts less pressure on the conversation. How might we notice that tensions are starting to rise and stress has entered the chat? By becoming *very* familiar with your stress tells.

CAN YOU STOP SHAKING YOUR LEG?

Most of us don't notice stress until we're in the red and doing damage control.

GREEN	YELLOW	RED
At peace	Beginning to display stress tells	Stress taking over, full fight-or-flight

In our chronically *on* culture, we are so used to operating at a baseline of stress that we hardly notice when we're beginning to display stress tells—or as I like to think of it, in the yellow. Have you ever been asked, "What's wrong?" or "Why are you stressed?" when you didn't really feel like you were stressed until being asked? Maybe you were shaking your leg, sighing loudly, or quiet all of a sudden. These are just a few examples of stress tells, indicators that you are in the yellow before you've hit the red.

Some common stress tells are:

- Biting your lip, mouth, or tongue

- Tensing your shoulders

- Clenching your jaw

- Wrinkling your eyebrows

- Fidgeting with things

- Breathing less or shallowly, or taking random deep breaths

- Sweating (palms, forehead, underarms)

- Experiencing an upset stomach or change in appetite

These are physical nods to your rising level of stress. I shake my leg, rub my neck or chest, and bite the inside of my mouth when I begin to feel unsettled. At a previous job, my desk was located between one co-worker who would click their pen when they were stressed and another who would sigh really loudly when they got emails from certain people. When we caught each other's stress tells, we would call each other out and laugh about it. (Feel free to play "name their stress tell" during your next team happy hour. With the right group it can be fun and enlightening.)

Our delayed awareness of our own stress can be traced to something called interoception—how we sense physiological signals like hunger or increased heart rate. In short, your brain often knows you are stressed before you do, and its job is to predict stressors out of an instinct for survival. So if you walk by your boss (or even see a picture of them), your brain might predict you are entering a stressful situation based on past experiences (even if you aren't consciously *feeling* stressed in that moment) and you start to breathe more shallowly or your heart beats faster. Much of the time, we override these signals—we would go nuts if we were totally aware of every time our heart beat faster. But when the situation gets more intense, we take note. Those little stress tells like shaking your leg are our body's way of starting to ramp up because it thinks we might need the extra energy to cope with impending stress.

Recognizing bodily sensations that indicate stress is one of the many ways we can become more self-aware. As author Hilary Tindle shared with me, "Awareness is key, because if you are not aware of what you are thinking or feeling it's hard to do anything about it." She recommends utilizing the triangle of awareness, a mindfulness tool for beginners and experts alike, to tune in to yourself if you are not in the habit of doing so.

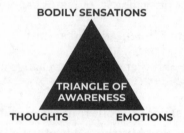

Each of the three points on this triangle (bodily sensations, thoughts, and emotions) is a point of entry to recognize whether you're experiencing stress. You might notice, for example, bodily sensations (displaying stress tells), emotions that you feel only when you're stressed (such as anger or resentment), or having thoughts that indicate your stress is rising (*I have so much to do. I wish there were two of me. Why can't anyone else around here do anything??*). Tindle underscores how "mindfulness helps us gain greater awareness of the full continuum of our moment-to-moment experience. It's not all about noticing only stress, it's about noticing. In practicing noticing, you may start to notice the beautiful, the curious, the unexpected." The triangle of awareness supports our quest toward increased self-awareness so that we can better understand and soothe ourselves in the face of stress.

Nowadays, more and more of us may be getting in touch with our stress, considering that levels of stress are higher than ever. Adults today are measurably more stressed than they have been historically. A recent

Gallup survey found that in 2021 people across the globe experienced the highest levels of worry, stress, and anger since 2006, when the organization started tracking these experiences. We need tools to manage stress because it's not going anywhere anytime soon. In order to live fruitful, peaceful lives, the best thing we can do is be prepared to handle stress when it arises. Because stress is inevitable and often predictable, we'll start by addressing how we can proactively manage it.

PROACTIVE STRESS MANAGEMENT: "I HAVE A BUSY SEASON COMING UP"

Paula was an accountant, and as tax season approached, she could anticipate her stress levels being sky-high. Every April, Paula's workdays were longer, she spent her personal time ruminating on work stress, and her usual personal care practices—like jogging and knitting—went out the window. Paula would wait until the busy season was over and then collapse and retroactively try to make up for months of being in fight-or-flight mode, ignored texts, and mountains of laundry. After several years of the same cycle, Paula wanted to find better ways to manage the inevitable stress. She needed tools to protect her well-being ahead of time instead of being sucked into the tornado like she always had been. She needed to implement regular proactive stress management.

The first thing she reflected on was her most predictable stressors and how she could manage them. For example, because explaining that she was busy to everyone who texted, called, and invited her to things caused her distress outside of work, she decided she needed to alert all her friends and family in advance that she wouldn't be getting back to texts or calls until tax season was over. Another substantial stressor for her was that work seeped into her weekends, making it feel like she *never* stopped working. In response, she resolved to leave the house at least once a day on weekends and spend time down at a local coffee shop, bookstore, or on walks to help maintain a boundary between work and leisure.

In order to take care of herself physically, she knew she needed to get eight hours of sleep no matter what and plan extremely easy meals or she just wouldn't eat (you may recall suggestions like this from the personal care chapter). Finally, she needed to prioritize time after work each day to decompress. Her favorite way to do this was by eating dinner in her backyard, reminding herself that there is a world beyond her laptop and that this busyness was temporary. Under normal circumstances, she could get away with not implementing these forms of stress management, but during tax season when work stress skyrocketed, they were necessary for preserving her physical, mental, and emotional well-being.

Some additional options for proactively managing stress are maintaining a morning and evening routine (our bodies love predictability and function better with a routine sleep schedule and meals); ensuring your nonnegotiables are being met; speaking to a therapist or mental health professional; and surrounding yourself with social support. If you're not sure what you need, start paying attention to what makes you feel more relaxed, regulated, and "safe" and what makes you feel more on edge and unsettled during times of stress. You might consider incorporating regular movement, practicing breathing exercises for relaxation, going on walks (nature calms our fear center and reduces stress), taking breaks during the day to avoid staring at your screen interminably, eating nutritious foods, and drinking enough water.

As I write this, I find myself in a very busy season. Because leaving the house makes a big difference for me during periods of stress, I know that when I am done with my work, I will go on a walk to the store down the street and grab myself a small treat (usually a sparkling water—the sweetened kind because I don't hate myself). To be honest, the treat is what incentivizes me to put my shoes on, not the walk itself, even though I know that the walk is the part that's good for me.

What do you need to do in order to proactively prepare for stress? Have the kids' clothes set aside for the upcoming week so you don't have to scramble to find them each day before school? Do all your chores on Sunday so the house is put together for the week? Avoid stressful conversations until the weekend? Many stressors can be prepared for.

It's not glamorous, but if you know a big project is your priority for the next two weeks, it's time to switch into personal care robot mode. This means not making daily decisions based on how you feel, but rather based on what you know you need. I'm sure you *feel* like scrolling on social media before bed, but unfortunately, you need sleep more. I'm sure you *feel* like having a drink after dinner, but that worsens the quality of your sleep and makes you foggier the next morning. I'm sure you *feel* like meeting up with a friend during the only free time you have this weekend, but you should probably spend that time actually resting. It *sucks* putting work over enjoying your life, but during crunch time, going back to the basics is your best energy-conserving bet. And when that feels unfair, remind yourself that this period is temporary.

This form of preparation doesn't magically make the work go more smoothly; it just ensures that you, the person doing the work, are doing everything you can not to add extra stress to your jug. When things get hard, we tend to revert to our bad habits and treat ourselves in small ways that end up costing us. Getting less sleep, consuming additional sugar, using substances to take the edge off, ruminating on our stress so every spare moment is still filled with work. Fight these urges and be the responsible parent you need in that moment who says you can't have a sleepover because you have a big test the next day.

Now, we can't always plan for stress. Sometimes it pops up unexpectedly and we have to respond to it without a plan. What do we do when we have to respond to a stressor in the heat of the moment?

STRESS IN THE MOMENT: WHEN THE ONLY WAY OUT IS THROUGH

I recently had an anxiety attack on a plane. My chest started to feel tight, hearing went out, vision became tunneled, and hands and feet started to tingle, but instead of succumbing to the panic (as I had in the past), I started doing a breathing exercise and forcing comforting thoughts. I'd breathe in for four seconds, hold for four seconds, breathe out for six seconds, hold for four seconds. I repeated this pattern until I felt calm again. (Try it now, it's a great tool.) I typically tap out the seconds with my fingers while repeating, "You're fine, nothing is wrong, it's just anxiety; if you keep breathing it will pass."

I am certain that without this stress management technique, I would have been waving down a flight attendant for a paper bag to breathe into. When I run into stressors like tech malfunctions during an important presentation, unconstructive criticism, or getting overwhelmed during huge projects outside of my comfort zone, I reach for these same tools: I focus my thoughts and slow down my breathing until I can determine the best next step. Some people I've worked with reach for social support; they prefer to problem solve with others. Others need to get up and move around to clear their head and determine the next best step. When we have the opportunity to ask for a moment to collect ourselves, stepping outside or away from the stressor to get some perspective can also help quell the pressure.

You can think of how you handle stress in the moment as a **stress Band-Aid,** something you can slap together really quickly to push through. When confronted with stress, sometimes we only have a moment before we need to respond. Being able to physically and mentally soothe yourself can make the difference between lashing out and responding calmly. You are probably familiar with the flutter of panic that can arise before you speak in a big meeting. To combat this panic, your stress Band-Aid might be taking deep breaths (physical soothing) and reminding yourself *They're just people; I can talk to people* (mental soothing).

Our breathing is one of the first things to change under duress, usually getting faster and shallower. When we get nervous and take quick breaths—or even hold our breath, depending on our body's MO—all our brain knows is that we are in a state of anxiety, which only fuels more anxiety and transmits stress hormones. So, instead, slow down and deepen your breathing to reassure your brain and body that it's fine. Fun fact: Deep breathing stimulates our vagus nerve, which runs from our diaphragm to our brain stem, and activating it turns on our calming system. It's why you immediately feel relieved after a deep inhale and a drawn-out exhale (the magic actually happens on the exhale).

Other mental tricks for reducing stress include listening to music, which changes your brain chemistry and relaxes you (any genre works as long as *you* find it peaceful or uplifting), journaling to brain dump (simply writing about how we're feeling is shown to help us feel better), reciting a comforting phrase, getting social support, or watching something funny or captivating to distract your mind from the stressor. Other physical tactics include stepping outside, stretching or jumping in place to stimulate some blood flow, taking a hot or cold shower, grabbing a glass of water, getting a tight hug from someone, or lying in a dark room under a weighted blanket.

Additionally, you can call upon what you learned in the boundaries chapter to address your stress. Let's say you're having a frustrating conversation and can feel the anxiety creeping in. You're getting angrier, teetering on the verge of tears, wanting to raise your voice, or freezing up. The next best step might be to create space by saying, "This is an important conversation and I want to make sure we have it right, so I'm going to step away for a couple of minutes to collect my thoughts and come back."

You could also try "stating the obvious" to allow people to see that you're moving through stress. At one of the first conferences I ever went to, one of the speakers walked to the front of the room and, surrounded by hundreds of eager faces, did something I didn't know speakers were allowed to do. She sat down on the stage and said, "I'm feeling a lot of nerves. I'd love it if you could take some deep breaths with me before I dive into what I get to share with you today." We did, she began her presentation still sitting on the floor, and as her stress dissipated, she rose to complete the remainder of her training while standing. There is value in going full steam ahead and bulldozing your fear, but there is also power in being open and vulnerable about what you are experiencing so that others can experience it with you.

Now, what do we do if a tense meeting with someone becomes a project that we need to work on with them for three months? That in-the-moment stressor has just turned into a short-term stressor.

SHORT-TERM STRESS: THAT'S SHOWBIZ, BABY

Short-term stressors loom over us. Upcoming projects, hard conversations, construction on a space in your home, planning a move or a wedding: These are all short-term stressors that have an end in sight. We are likely to ruminate on short-term stressors because we can see them on the horizon. When we know there is a storm coming, we tend to rehearse those troubles and wallow in anticipatory stress more than we need to. This anticipation of stress can actually worsen the stress of the event when it happens.

Our brains are primitive: They can't tell the difference between an imaginary stressor and a real one. Have you ever had a fake argument in the shower? (I'm pretty confident this is a universal human experience.) Think back to that moment—did you notice that you experienced real anger, your breathing changed, your heart rate accelerated? That's because your body doesn't know this argument is fake—the feelings are real.

When we repeatedly rehearse stress or envision upcoming stressors, we are essentially going through the physical stress of the event multiple times. Going through a performance review once is bad enough; why are you putting yourself through ten additional, imaginary performance reviews? Again, our brains are fixated on predicting things, and sometimes those things are negative, so we want to plan to either avoid or mitigate them. We tend to pay attention to and learn from negative things more than positive things—also called the negativity bias—and I'm sorry to say that evolution has hardwired us for it. There is, of course, something to be said about remembering what went wrong so we can avoid it in the future. But we need to counteract our natural inclination to dwell on what's negative. The good news is that we are more in charge than we think—we determine the lifespan and impact of many of our thoughts. That's why I recommend having a blasé, "that's showbiz, baby" attitude whenever possible. It keeps us moving and prevents the deep, dark wallowing that can occur when we take our stressors too seriously. This approach doesn't apply to true hardships, but it does work for many day-to-day hurdles. Bad performance review, traffic, forgotten lunch at home, rejection on a dating app—that's showbiz, baby.

One of the tools you can use to allay your negativity bias and manage short-term stress is **Fact, Feeling, Story.** This tool is utilized in many forms of therapy to break a situation into digestible pieces. The *facts* of a situation are just the cut-and-dried, observable pieces. They are not up for interpretation, they have no background story, they are just realities that could be captured by a camera. The next category is the *feelings* you are having about the situation. What do you feel in response to the facts? The final category is the *stories* you are telling yourself about the facts of the situation and the way you are feeling about it. When stressors arise, we can often get lost in our feelings and stories when the best solution is just a direct response to the facts.

Let's take as an example that your manager has called a meeting with you without explaining the reason for it. Your manager typically communicates a meeting goal when scheduling it, so there is a lot of room for storytelling about what this might mean. When you find yourself beginning to spiral into fear, break out the Fact, Feeling, Story tool to come up with a solution.

Facts of the situation: Upcoming meeting with your manager

Feelings about the situation: Fear, curiosity, anxiety

Stories you're telling yourself about the situation: *What if they want to fire me? Did I do something wrong? Maybe they noticed I've been coming in a little late and I'm going to be reprimanded. What if Tim from down the hall told them about that thing I struggled with on our last project?*

Your solution is a direct response to the facts—and *only* the facts. You have a meeting scheduled. All you have to do is attend the meeting. You won't know what it's about until you enter the room, and once you're there, you can nod until it's over and then take a beat before giving a thoughtful response. If the anticipation is really getting to you, you could probably just send your manager a preemptive message saying, "I'll be there! What will the meeting be about so that I can prepare accordingly?"

You can see how the feelings and story can overwhelm the true facts of a situation. Our brains love latching on to feelings and love telling stories. Stories are engaging. They help satisfy our curiosity and allow us to consider possible threats. Sometimes, we can accurately predict the threats, but most of the time, we're worrying for worrying's sake. Rehearsing stress in this way leads to unnecessary emotional labor—the management of our own and other people's feelings—which is itself a factor for burnout.

McKinsey's "Women in the Workplace" report determined that female employees undertake more emotional labor than do male employees. They found that female managers do things like check in on employees' well-being and provide emotional support more frequently than male managers. In an effort to be sensitive and make other people's lives easier, women in the workplace tend to pick up slack, whether by joining non-mandatory committees at work or attending events because they would feel bad if nobody attended. They also donate their time and energy—to customers, co-workers, clients—where men might not give a second thought.

On the one hand, this is not at all surprising. "Ever since the industrial revolution, white, wealthy men have structured society so that they would be the carriers of power outside the home as wage earners and political leaders. False ideas that defined women as people that were naturally better at caretaking and mothering—and who therefore preferred being in the home—supported this division," says Lisa C. Huebner Ruchti, a professor in the department of women and gender studies at West Chester University. Though social gender expectations have evolved, old habits die hard. Society still has us believing that women are kinder, more caring, and biologically better at regulating emotions . . . a belief that has been found by experts not to be true.

The first step in reducing this type of emotional brain drain is creating awareness when we are needlessly engaging in emotional labor. Stop overanalyzing a simple piece of feedback, spending thirty minutes after work making up stories about what Mark meant by "I'm not surprised you need extra time on that," and feeling guilty you didn't sign up to help plan the company potluck. Getting in the habit of separating the facts of a situation from the feelings and story will spare you a colossal amount of time.

You can also apply this tool to challenges in your personal life. Maybe someone invited you to an event this weekend and you've had to say no to the last few invites because you've been in the middle of moving apartments.

The facts: You were invited to an event this weekend. Objectively, you don't want to go and would rather prioritize your move and recovering from it.

Your feelings about the situation: Guilt and anxiety about saying no

The stories you're telling: *What if they take it personally? What if they think I don't care because I can't go? What if they talk about me when I'm not there? If I don't go, they'll think I'm a bad friend.*

Solution (direct response to the facts): Given the season of life you're in, you need to prioritize moving and rest this weekend. The people who have your best interests in mind instead of their own will understand. This boundary is just protecting your limited resources. And, as we learned, boundaries are only upsetting to those who benefit from your not having any.

The next tool I recommend for combating short-term stress is a **Tangible vs. Intangible List.** The tangible list holds explicit to-do items—tangible, resolvable items. The intangible list holds thoughts, feelings, stories, interpersonal stressors—anything you're thinking about that doesn't have an explicit action item to resolve it.

Let's say it's a Thursday night, you have a lot of work to do before the end of the day Friday, you're annoyed with a colleague, your house is a mess, and you're worried about a disgruntled client you have a meeting with next week. A tangible vs. intangible list allows you to separate logistical items from interpersonal, emotional items. When you're stressed and need a simple path forward, be clear on what is actually an actionable stressor versus a social or emotional stressor that doesn't require immediate action.

On the tangible side of that list (can be resolved), you would put the remaining work you have to do by the end of the next day and the household chores you want to get done. On the intangible side of that list (interpersonal, emotional) you would write down that your colleague is bothering you and that you have a stressful meeting next week (with no action required for it at this time). Neither of those intangible items is actionable. They are worthy of walking through Fact, Feeling, Story so that you can alleviate your anxiety about them, but there is nothing to do about them in this moment.

This tool also helps us acknowledge whether we truly plan to take action on a stressor. Say your colleague Charley annoys you every day. Are you going to set a boundary with him? Great, then put setting that boundary on the tangible list. If you're just annoyed and not going to say anything (because sometimes it's just not worth the trouble), then pop it on the intangible list. Once you're done expressing your irritation, don't let thoughts of Charley spoil your personal time outside of work. What a shame it would be if we let the most miserable people in our life determine the quality of our life.

When people say "protect your peace," they don't just mean from other people; they also mean from yourself, or from your tendency to pick at a stressor until it's a bloodier mess than you found it. *You are on your own team;* don't compromise your own peace. Many people are hooked on stress. It's all they've known, and as a result they might truly be addicted: Research shows that low-level, short-term stressors release dopamine, a feel-good chemical that also plays a role in clinical addictions.* "We all tend to desire the experience of scenarios that make us feel 'alive,' but we can mistake mild anxiety or other scenarios involving

---

* Over time, chronic stress eventually results in a depletion and dysregulation of dopamine during times of stress and anxiety.

heightened adrenaline for 'feeling alive,'" explains Hilary Tindle. If you have always fed your stress, it's going to take effort and intention to stop yourself in your tracks and choose a different response. **Protect your peace, especially from the part of you that might sabotage it because stress is all you've known.**

You can usually tell when you're about to go down the stress rabbit hole. Odds are you have repeated thought patterns or habits that start to suck you into the vortex. Perhaps every time you think about your manager, your mom, or that rude thing someone said to you in 2003 you end up chewing all the skin off your lip and you are in a bad mood for the rest of the day. Maybe most of your stressful thoughts start with "I should have . . . ," "I wish I . . . ," or "What if . . . ," and when you start to have them, you know you're about to feel really lousy. You know yourself. You are the only one living in your mind. What sends you down this spiral that you can catch and correct?

Cognitive reframing is the term for a tool used in cognitive behavioral therapy that allows us to catch and correct these unproductive thoughts. Essentially, you want to notice the unhelpful musing, pause, and replace it with something that feels better. For example, maybe you often think to yourself, *I should have responded by saying ___ during that argument,* and this pattern of thought typically results in a tight chest and raised blood pressure. Instead, guide your thoughts somewhere calmer: *I know you wish that, but no amount of thinking about this will change it. I'm not going to put my body through a stress response for something I can't change.* Maybe you have a strained relationship with your mom, and after you talk, you end up catastrophizing future interactions with her. Here you might notice yourself doing this and think, *You know what, I've gotten through every interaction with her so far, so I can figure out how to deal with whatever comes up in the future. I don't need to rehearse stress; I know what boundaries to set, and I can always walk away.*

I know that it can feel as if worrying about that thing is doing your due diligence—or maybe it's the way you repent for or learn from a mistake—so not worrying about it can feel as if you're being negligent in some way. You're not. You're just used to picking at the scab, and it's a lot more satisfying than putting a Band-Aid over it.

I think we all have memories of embarrassing things we've done or said (I'd share one of mine with you but then I'd have to kill you). Just thinking about them can make you want to face-palm and groan, *What the f*** was I thinking?!* Fixating on it doesn't change it and it doesn't help you. You accidentally insulted your co-worker, you sent a screenshot of something someone said *back* to the person themselves, you flashed people at the club—whatever it was, unless you plan to take some kind of action, let it go. It's out of your hands now and belongs to the past; stop dragging it into the future.

This brings us to the next tool for alleviating short-term stress: **compartmentalizing.** Focusing on one thing at a time can seem counterintuitive to someone who has a million things to do, but it allows you to turn your complete attention toward the task in front of you, without being distracted by other things going on in your life. Then, when you switch to your next task, you fully exit what you've just engaged in so you can enter the next one fresh and focused. Compartmentalizing is our heartiest tool against perpetual stress because it contains the stress. I *know* it's easier said than done but if you can master it, your life will feel a whole lot more manageable.

For example, if you have to work on a project with a colleague who stresses you out (let's call them Keith), that stress should be confined to the time you must spend with Keith on that project. Work stress begins to seep into your personal life when, instead of compartmentalizing, you leave your meeting with Keith and go vent to another co-worker about them, then you go home and rehash your problems with Keith to your partner or roommate, then you climb into bed and thoughts about stupid Keith are the last things you think before slipping into an angry slumber. All this does is exacerbate your stress.

Needlessly giving attention to a problem often enlarges it in our minds. Imagine each of your stressors is a flame and your thoughts are kindling. The more you think about a stressor, the more kindling you throw at that flame, and the bigger the fire grows. To limit stress, contain it to its designated compartment, give it your full attention in the time you've dedicated to handle it, and then do your best to leave it there and focus on what's in front of you next. The stressor will still be there when you come back to it (but in fact, its emotional impact on you may have shrunk because you haven't been feeding the fire), and if it's not something you can change, it's just something you have to endure. Don't torture yourself by carrying it around or making it worse.

Compartmentalizing also helps rein in "stress projection"—stress from one thing that you erroneously place on someone or something else. When a stressor persists, we can accidentally overlook its source and project how we're feeling onto something else—a partner, a friend, ourselves, our messy house. Have you ever been generally stressed and suddenly cleaning the house becomes urgent? We like to point the finger when stress rises because, theoretically, if we can resolve the source of our stress we'll feel better. But it's likely not because of your messy house that you're stressed; it was just the first tangible thing in sight to address.

One tool you can use to put into perspective the anxiety that comes with looming stress is looking back at the five areas of life we talked about in the personal care chapter: business, social, personal, health, and lifestyle. Reflect on whether there is something in any of these categories that needs to be resolved *immediately*, or if things could just be different or better. Sure, the dishes could be done. Yeah, that stressful conversation with your sister could have gone better. But they're not flashing red emergencies. Don't let your anxiety trick you into fixating on them and thinking they are 9-1-1–worthy. Be honest with yourself about the difference between something truly needing your immediate attention and something you're attributing your stress to that really could just be different or better.

When I was feeling really burned out, every Sunday I was one-thing-going-wrong away from having a toddler-style kicking and screaming meltdown. The result of my high anxiety was frantically cleaning, angrily meal prepping, and completing schoolwork I probably could have saved for later. I was focusing on various chores and nonurgent tasks to labor my way out of my feelings when nothing on my to-do list was truly on fire. Upon recognizing that I was erroneously projecting my anxiety onto my tasks, I could take my foot off the gas and instead concern myself with alleviating the stress moving through my body (via a jog, the hottest or coldest possible shower, making a comfort snack, or walking through the park).

A thoughtful combination of proactive, in-the-moment, and short-term stress management will make your relationship with stress so much healthier. Stress is an inevitable part of life, and the goal isn't to stop experiencing stress entirely (that's called being dead); it's about being confident you can manage it when it finds you.

LONG-TERM STRESS:
IS LIFE SUPPOSED TO BE THIS HARD?

Sometimes our stressors are long-term—without an end in sight or a clear escape route. Caring for a sick family member, dealing with a chronic illness, working in an industry that is stressful 24-7, experiencing financial insecurity—you might be thinking of one or two in your life that I've not mentioned. For long-term stressors, there is no clear action to take or a timeline; it can feel like a forever stress that you are simply enduring. When faced with this kind of stress, it is easy to adopt a variation of the self-victimizing mindset we discussed in the chapter on mindset—feeling helpless and discouraged about taking action to change your experience. To be fair, long-term stressors *suck,* so it's not that you aren't enduring something objectively unpleasant or downright cruel. You may very well be. But research shows that a positive outlook benefits you in even the darkest circumstances.

If your long-term stressor can be alleviated in part by some of the short-term stress solutions, wonderful. However, long-term stressors often require coming to terms with a certain lifestyle as opposed to solving one specific problem. If you work in a particularly demanding industry, you might need to accept that for as long as you want to be in this field, it is going to be this stressful. If you've chosen to have a baby, accepting that you're going to be sleep-deprived for a while will make your day-to-day reality a little more bearable. If you are experiencing a new chronic pain, creating new habits that suit your new reality will probably benefit you more than trying to make the old ones fit. If you have a sick family member, accepting that their health is out of your control but the time you spend with them is not will be a gentler way to cope.

Finding a way to accept a reality that you don't love is difficult. However, **if we are at war with our reality, it only makes the reality harder.** Instead, we need to acknowledge our situation and be creative about what circumstances around us can still be altered to buffer some of the inevitable stress.

The lowest-hanging fruit when it comes to reducing long-term stress is taking a look at your current load. I know we've been discussing the importance of assessing your capacity for a few chapters now, but seriously, if you haven't done so already, do it. Be honest with yourself about what is on your plate and whether you can make your life any easier. If someone you love is sick or you're a caretaker, is there any way you can reduce your caretaking, professional, or personal load? If you're working full-time and earning a degree at night, can you reduce personal obligations and automate as much of your life as possible? I've asked these questions before, but if you haven't already taken action, now is really the time to do so.

You don't have to "power through"; you can be gentle with yourself. Don't turn your resilience into a punishment. Yes, you're strong and determined, but that doesn't mean you have to choose the toughest path. Be kind to yourself when you're experiencing long-term stress.

This leads me to my next suggestion: getting support wherever possible. Do you have anyone in your life whom you could ask for help, or are there any services that you could hire that would prevent you from losing your mind? I hate to make suggestions about paying for help because it's already a *ridiculously* expensive time to be alive. However, if there is ever a time to justify asking or paying for help, it's when you're enduring long-term stress. It doesn't have to be forever—even a few weeks or months of help can make a difference. Let someone else lead the project, plan the bachelorette party, schedule the appointments, shop for the groceries, take care of the kids, clean up the space.

At a certain point, it may also be helpful to speak to a professional who knows the ins and outs of your particular circumstances, like a therapist or mental health counselor. Therapy has come a long way and there are services available through insurance as well as online and via apps. It's never convenient to carve out time to find a therapist, rehash the most stressful parts of your life, and be held accountable to making changes, but you aren't doing this out of convenience; you're doing it out of compassion and concern for yourself. Let yourself be seen and heard and supported.

If you work in a very specific industry that is contributing to your burnout, try to find a mentor who has endured what you are enduring. When you are seeking solutions to particular circumstances that only someone in your field can speak to, it can be frustrating to talk to someone who doesn't know what you're going through. Instead, search for industry-specific support or a counselor that specializes in your areas of concern, or seek mentorship from someone who has been there before.

In addition to mental health resources, some companies offer stress leave, family and medical leave (under the FMLA), sabbatical, or part-time options. If your burnout has put your mental and physical health at risk, you might need to consider a longer-term break. It can feel scary at first to consider this—our hustle culture doesn't encourage pressing pause (nor do our bills), but the people I've known who have taken a longer break did not regret it. In fact, they described it as "life changing" and "the best decision I ever made for my wellness." I know people who have moved in with family so they could take this break without worrying about finances; I've seen people go from a stressful six-figure job to working at a local coffee shop; I've heard of people spending their stress leave in Costa Rica and then never moving back. Where there's a will there is a way.

ANYONE UP FOR SOME BURNOUT JENGA?

When I am faced with a long-term stressor, I always visualize the pillars of burnout management like a game; I think of it as "Burnout Jenga." As in the game Jenga, we are always looking for the movable pieces. At any point in time, at least one of the burnout pillars can be shifted to improve your experience.

BURNOUT JENGA

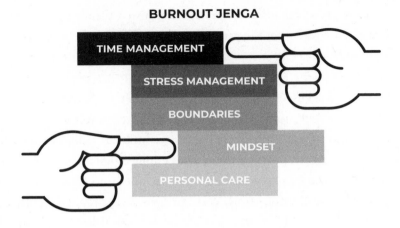

Let's walk through Burnout Jenga together by returning to Bill, whose health and personal life were collateral for his busy business. In order for Bill to get a handle on his stress, he had to make changes on multiple fronts, in big and small ways. The first Jenga piece he shifted was stress management. To empty his stress jug more regularly, he started ending his days with a tangible versus intangible list so he was clearer on what work needed to be done and didn't waste as much time ruminating on the intangible. The next piece he shifted was mindset: He had to stop taking stress at work so personally and having a strong emotional response to any small thing that went wrong. He also adjusted his boundaries, trusting his employees to do work without his micromanagement. And finally, to improve his time management, he had to confront the fact that he only had twenty-four hours in a day, so in order to free up his weekends, spend more time with his husband, and have time to take care of himself, he had to turn down new opportunities that, although they could make him money, would overload his business.

As a result of making these changes, he curbed many of the bad habits that were once his default. Once he was getting enough sleep, he didn't have to drink energy drinks every day and endure repeated energy spikes and crashes. Once he stopped micromanaging his employees, he didn't have to stay up late going over their work. Once he prioritized golfing one day each weekend with his husband, he had enough recovery time to decompress, lower his cortisol and blood pressure, and remember that life was worth living. There is no one-size-fits-all method of releasing stress; you have to explore the options available to you based on the Burnout Jenga pieces at your disposal.

Stress management isn't a set-it-and-forget-it tool—it's something that is determined moment by moment. You can master it in one season of life and then fumble the habits you've built the next time life gets busy. The goal is to practice these tools enough that they feel second nature when you are overwhelmed by stress.

If you can anticipate stress, you can proactively manage it. If you encounter stress suddenly, utilize your stress Band-Aids to give yourself a beat of recovery before responding. If you are enduring a short-term stressor, create space to acknowledge the facts, feelings, and story of the situation, correct thoughts that would exacerbate your stress, try to compartmentalize to contain the stress, and differentiate true emergencies from things that could just be done differently or better. If you're enduring long-term stress, consider whether you can lighten your load, seek external help, get support from a professional, or take a break, and think about which pieces of Burnout Jenga may be adjustable. Don't expect yourself to just remember all these things—make notes of tools and keep them at your desk or in your phone, tell people in your life about them so they can suggest them when your stress rises, and highlight and dog-ear these pages so you can refer back to them.

If there is ever a time to prioritize your recovery and take your stress management seriously, it's when you're burned out, or about to be. When you know that what's eating at you is not just some passing stressor, that it has the potential to compromise the quality of your health and life, it is paramount to address it head-on. You deserve to exist without constant stress weighing you down.

With a deeper knowledge of stress management, let's turn to what to do when your situation just isn't getting better. You've done everything you can to improve your mindset, personal care, time management, boundaries, and stress management, and you are still burned out and unhappy. It's time to determine whether you should double down or walk away.

PART III

MAKING LIFE LIVABLE AGAIN

CHAPTER EIGHT

When to Walk Away

When is it time to walk away from a job? When you have constant anxiety with no relief in sight? When thoughts about work keep you from sleeping through the night? When you have a certain amount of money saved up? When your manager's abusive behavior has hit a breaking point? When you have another opportunity lined up?

The question I ask people to gauge their readiness to leave is: Would any amount of change make this job bearable for you? And think only of feasible change—not things like suddenly getting a new manager, making significantly more money, or cutting your workload in half. Are there realistic changes that could be made to improve your experience? If there are, that's wonderful, and we're going to do our best to apply them. If not, then you might just be delaying your inevitable departure. If you do decide to stick it out for a little while longer because you aren't quite ready to jump ship, set a timeline for yourself. Six months from now, if you are still miserably burned out, resolve to look elsewhere. If you've made every change you can think of and your job still burns you out, the job is probably the culprit.

Don't be the perfect pirate on a sinking ship. There is no reward for being the perfect performer at a company that burns people out the way a juicer grinds the juice out of an orange and tosses the mangled peel to the side. It doesn't matter how much stress management and personal care you practice if you are regularly being verbally abused by your manager and you have a workload that's equivalent to that of three people. **You can't outwork a broken system,** and no amount of maintenance on your part can correct a company's practices.

If this sounds like you but you're starting to feel a pit in your stomach, I see you. Maybe you are already coming up with reasons to stay in the role a little longer: *I like my team, I don't want to change jobs while other aspects of my life are in flux, I don't have time to apply elsewhere, I'm in line for a promotion or raise, new leadership may offer an opportunity for growth.*

Let's unpack what might make a role "worth it." This is a particularly tricky question to answer if your industry is simply stressful by nature. Emergency medicine will probably always put you in fight-or-flight mode, disaster management crises will almost never come at a convenient time, and a night shift schedule is going to be difficult on your body and mind because we are not nocturnal beings. In order to differentiate between the standard stress of the job and the level of stress *you* can endure, ask yourself these two questions:

1. **Is the cost of this industry or role worth it to me?**

   Whether you work in healthcare, education, entertainment, law, or any number of other fields, are the sacrifices of working in that industry worth what you get in return? If the benefits outweigh the cost, remind yourself of those benefits whenever it gets stressful. If you realize that the cost is no longer worth the rewards, it is time to make a change.

2. **Am I doing what I can to detach from stressors?**

   Think back to the stress management chapter and our discussion about not feeding the flame of stress. Are you ruminating and venting about work in all your spare time? Are you storytelling and emotionally engaging with stressors that you could otherwise disregard or manage from an arm's length? Are you practicing regular stress management, personal care, monitoring your mindset, and setting boundaries to combat the challenges of the role? Sometimes we make a job more stressful than it is if we don't manage ourselves thoughtfully. Do what you can to detach from work stress whenever possible.

If your quality of life has taken a downward turn despite your efforts—and if leadership isn't supporting your requests for modifications—then move on to creating a timeline for an exit or a meaningful change. Sometimes you can improve your situation without leaving the organization, like switching teams, departments, managers, or roles or transitioning to part-time work. However, if you can't justify suffering in this role any longer and can't envision it realistically changing, it's time to institute an exit timeline.

YOUR EXIT TIMELINE: PREPARE FOR DEPARTURE

What does reaching the end of your rope look like? You might sound something like Jenny, who really needed to walk away from her job as an editor when I met her:

About two months in, I knew: This job was going to be the death of me. I was regularly working twelve-hour days (sometimes fourteen!) and several hours each weekend. And I was still falling behind. Crying at my desk between Zoom meetings was not how I pictured this role playing out. On paper it was a dream job: I could pivot my magazine skills into digital, I could work with industry professionals whom I greatly respected and could learn from, I had unlimited PTO, the job was remote, and I'd get a regular paycheck every two weeks—something I hadn't had in years as a freelancer. But in reality, the job was untenable. There simply was too much work for a team of three editors to accomplish.

I told myself it would get better after my learning curve—onboarding to new content management systems and software. I told myself it would get better after we hired another team member (whom I had to train in my "spare" time). I told myself it would get better after I shared my concerns with my manager, who was extremely sympathetic but admittedly burned out herself and not being heard by her own manager. She promised to take some work off my plate once certain projects were complete. But that never happened because there was no one to shift the work over to. The CEO refused to hire more staff until certain partnerships were in place, and those negotiations were taking months. In the meantime, the work continued to pile up.

After dozens of phone calls with close friends and my parents—who were becoming increasingly concerned about my physical and mental health and who hadn't seen me in months, despite the fact I'd moved across the country to be closer to them—I realized I just couldn't do it anymore. I wouldn't do it anymore. The uncertainty of the freelance life was much preferable to the certainty of this miserable existence, one in which I was losing my sense of self. I hadn't been able to exercise, socialize with friends, see my parents or niece or nephews. Who was I, even? I'd taken exactly one vacation day in five months (so much for unlimited PTO!). I'd gained weight, in part thanks to the unhealthy habit I'd developed of eating a carton of parmesan crisps every night to get me through my evening tasks, a small treat to power through the relentless editing and project management. At midnight, I'd close my laptop, drag myself to bed, scroll on IG for fifteen minutes, then go comatose. Eight A.M. came way too quickly, and then it began all over again. This was not a life.

The insult to injury was that despite devoting sixty-five+ hours a week to the job, I felt like I was failing. Praise came infrequently, and when it did, it was usually from the clients we served, rarely from management. I wasn't a praise hog by any means, but I needed to feel like sacrificing life and limb was appreciated. Apparently, though, it was just another day at the company. In lieu of real support, I got incessant Slack messages about keeping the pace up, reminders about deadlines, and a gazillion meeting invites about more work.

There wasn't an exact moment that I made up my mind to quit. Instead, there were many tiny moments of "I can't do this," "this is inhumane," "I hate this job," "how did I end up here?," "this is hell," and so on. The steady stream of negative thoughts culminated in a deep understanding that it was time to quit and save myself. Twenty years into my career, I'd had enough work experiences to know when a job was toxic, and this one definitely was.

Plus, I had a safety net of sorts: I knew that I could support myself freelancing because I'd done it before. Would there be a financially scary transition as I geared back up to be my own boss? Yes. Would I have to postpone my decision to buy a house? Yes. To get a pet? Yes. Still, I did not waver. I truly felt like I was rescuing myself from drowning, that this was not a matter of my not trying hard enough or waiting out a rough patch.

The conversation with my manager—whom I admired and trusted like a friend and who was the only reason I'd stayed beyond the one-month mark—was painful. I cried and she cried. But she got it (secretly I think she had the same thoughts herself) and I gave her a month's notice to transition someone else in, knowing how insane the pace was. I could handle another month knowing it was the last month.

I did not regret my decision for one second. It was hands-down a vote for thriving and a vote against a soul-sucking existence. But I also didn't look at having taken the job as a mistake. I was willing to take a risk and see how it played out. It was a ten-month experiment that left me exhausted and depleted but that taught me that the grass was not greener and that I had better options. I could also now add a batch of new skills to my resume.

It took me a good three months to recover. The first few weeks were like being a kid on summer break—freedom in the form of sleeping in, reconnecting with friends and family, staying up late watching reality TV, and getting back into my fitness routines and happy hours with neighbors. But I struggled with energy, with losing weight, with my finances, and with next steps. Going from having my days filled with nonstop tasks to full days with no set routine or agenda was disorienting.

But I figured it out. I reached out to my writing clients (a little bit chagrined but with full transparency) and reestablished relationships with editors. And little by little, my calendar filled up with projects. I took on small assignments at first, ones that were available as soon as possible and that didn't pay a lot, but I needed to stay busy and get my land legs back. And then things ramped up as I anticipated they would and I'm thriving. Is life perfect? Hell no! Is work stressful? Some days it is, some days it isn't. But I have the confidence that I can handle whatever comes

*up. I am also proud of myself for trusting my gut right away, for knowing
that my spirit was suffering and begging me to hit the escape button.*

Sometimes, the hardest part of making an exit timeline is deciding
to make an exit timeline. Quitting can be terrifying, even when you've
been fantasizing about it and know it's the right thing—the only
thing—to do. It requires jumping into the unknown and having some
faith. It is true that there is no guarantee that your next job will work
out. But think of it this way: What *is* guaranteed is that staying in your
current job means more suffering. That much you can count on. There
is no "good time" to quit. That might sound deflating at first, but it
should actually bring you relief. Because if there is no "good time" to
quit, then you are released from the burden of trying to figure out the
exact right time. I suspect that you may already know that you had
enough a long time ago, and the only thing left is to trust your inner
compass and steer toward the exit ramp.

If you are ready to learn how to create an exit plan, read on for the
tough love and encouragement you need.

1. **Acceptance**

    The first step is to accept that you want to quit. As soon as
    you acknowledge that you have one foot out the door, your en-
    tire demeanor will change: You will take less abuse because you
    aren't afraid of leaving, feel comforted on hard days by the
    thought that you'll only be there a little longer, and overall feel
    a sense of empowerment because you aren't "stuck." Knowing
    you're not afraid to walk away gives you an entirely new perspec-
    tive. Embrace the clarity of knowing what you want.

2. **Planning**

    How long a runway do you need for takeoff? If you have
    been deeply unhappy for a while, how much longer can you
    stand it? Imagine you are still in this job one year from now. If
    that makes you want to scream, then you can't stand it one more
    year. Tell yourself you have X months to create an exit plan.

Don't let yourself get overwhelmed by the process. You're going to take it one step at a time.

3. Reconnaissance

Start by researching the kinds of roles that sound interesting and reaching out to your network. Do *not* take on the pressure that the next role needs to be your lifelong career. Its only requirement is to be a productive stepping stone out of where you currently are. **Life is not that serious; a couple of detours won't catapult you into failure.**

4. Action

Once you have an idea of the kinds of jobs you might want to apply for and what openings are out there, rework your resume with an eye toward highlighting the skills that make you an appealing candidate. Then start applying to get your feet wet. Don't get discouraged if you have to apply to dozens of places before getting responses—it's just how the job market is nowadays. Remind yourself that *it only takes one yes*. Will there be days you feel like slamming your head into your desk? Yes. But it really is a numbers game: The more you network, the more people you reach out to, the more opportunities you apply for, the better chance you'll have. *Don't* overlook networking at this phase: Knowing the right person is the equivalent of getting a Disneyland FastPass into a new role.

FREQUENTLY ASKED QUESTIONS

How can you tell whether a job will burn you out before taking it?

Far too often I see people jumping from one burnout-inducing job straight into another. Out of desperation to escape, they don't ensure that their next role will offer them better circumstances. So, how can you protect yourself against future burnout? By determining whether an organization has a culture of burnout.

There are some universal indicators that a company has a culture of burnout: high turnover, untrained leadership, and dissatisfied employees. You can find much of this information online on websites like LinkedIn or Glassdoor. You can even take it a step further and reach out to employees at the organization for a quick informational interview, or progress through the formal interview process to get more insight into a team's culture. Ask the people you would be working with questions like: "Why is the role I am applying for vacant?," "How would you describe your own work-life balance?," and "Can you tell me a little bit about how your leaders model time management and boundaries for employees?" When you are speaking with people in leadership positions in particular—the people who set the tone and culture for a team—you will get a better idea of what kind of environment they foster.

How can you identify companies with great work-life balance?

Talk to people! Networking is the most surefire way to get your foot in the door *and* to learn about what working somewhere is really like. Spend time with people who love their jobs or workplaces and target organizations where employees seem to have a work-life balance that appeals to you. Not all company perks are created equal. Maybe you want to prioritize well-trained leadership, flexibility to work remotely, opportunities for development, great health insurance, or a certain number of vacation days—seek out whatever matters most for your next season of life.

How do you make time to network and apply to jobs when you're so burned out and busy that you can barely keep up with your current set of responsibilities?

Oftentimes, the biggest hurdle for applying to new jobs is the crushing workload of your current job. Ideally, you would take a step back from your current job (even if it's just for a short period of time) and reallocate some of your time and energy to apply to new jobs. If this is not a possibility for you, you might need to get creative about other options at your disposal. You could try recycling the "Who, When, Where, How" tool from the time management chapter. If you can't change the "what" (applying for new jobs), try changing the "who," "when," or "how":

> (*Who*) Can you pay someone (whether it's a relative, friend, or someone on a website like TaskRabbit or Fiverr) to find job openings that meet certain criteria, have them sent to you, and from there you can vet and apply for them?

> (*When*) Instead of working on applications right after work when you are already exhausted, could you dedicate two hours on Saturday mornings at a local coffee shop to work on applications? Or thirty minutes before work twice a week?

> (*How*) Instead of applying to jobs blindly, reach out to your friends, family, and fellow college alumni about what you are looking for and ask if they know of any openings. Let your network know you are looking for a new role.

When deciding what you want to do next, remember to consider your personality and preferences. If you are a social butterfly who loves working with others, that primarily independent project management role probably isn't for you. If you are an introvert who hates correspondence, recruiting probably isn't for you. If you know you need the energy and accountability of working in person, don't apply for fully remote roles. A job isn't just about the work itself; equally important are the day-to-day experience and lifestyle it offers.

I know applying for jobs is intimidating and can do a number on your spirit if you've sent out hundreds of applications to no avail. It's a tricky process. But you deserve a job that doesn't make you *miserable*. Polish your resume, *talk to people*, keep an open mind, and remember: It only takes one yes.

CHAPTER NINE

Road Map for Creating a Balanced Life
(Immediately!)

At this point, you may begin to feel your eyes crossing and your mouth forming the words, *What the hell am I supposed to do first?*

Now that you have a grasp on the five pillars of burnout management, you can begin the healing process and coach yourself out of your current situation and into a better one. These are your **Four Steps to Freedom.** (Okay, not total freedom, but Four Steps to Feeling Less Burned Out doesn't have the same ring to it.) You're going to start by getting an accurate picture of your current circumstances and then apply the burnout management concepts one at a time. By taking these steps, you can loosen the collar of burnout and improve your daily experience greatly.

Step 1: Track how you spend your time for at least three working days. I do this myself by carrying an obnoxious notebook with a pen attached to it throughout my day, but it can also be done digitally on your phone. You don't have to make a note of *everything* if certain tasks make more sense as a grouping (in other words, "get ready" is a fine substitute for doing your skin care, makeup, and hair routine, and getting dressed). Note when you wake up, how you spend your time at work, when you get distracted, when you take breaks, and what you do after work.

Once you have finished three days of tracking, reflect on what you have recorded. We are often so close to our schedules that we don't see patterns, or we are so used to believing we spend our time a certain

7:00 A.M.   Morning Routine (coffee, couch, podcast)
7:30 A.M.   Get ready for work (hair, makeup, clothing)
7:45 A.M.   Morning Meeting to organize the day
7:50 A.M.   Answer urgent emails
8:30 A.M.   Take a break for breakfast
9:00 A.M.   Work on project A
11:00 A.M. Lunch break

way we've lost sight of how we actually spend it. When it's written down in front of you, you can more easily observe your behavior as data. **You have to track it to hack it.** It's a lot easier to make improvements when you have a good understanding of the current state of your daily schedule.

Step 2: Review what you have recorded as though you're a stranger. If your best friend handed you these notes, what patterns would you notice? Perhaps upon closer examination, you find that you usually put off eating lunch until 2 P.M. each day, stay up past midnight every night, spend more time drafting and rereading emails than you thought, or lose hours of your day on social media between tasks. Be objective in your examination.

Step 3: Make a note of what you're already doing well and anything you might like to try doing differently. This is your chance to ask yourself, *What does the best version of my current situation look like?* This isn't you waving a magic wand to make all of your problems go away—this is you being realistic about what is possible *right now,* with the genuine intention of commitment to change.

We bend over backward to make things happen when requested by others; this change is something you are requesting of *yourself* and that you need to make happen with that same gumption. The change may be as simple as having a fifteen-minute lunch break instead of not having one at all, but those fifteen minutes might make the difference between having a mental breakdown in the afternoon or avoiding one.

What changes would improve your circumstances? Identify items you can change, pause/postpone, simplify, delegate/outsource, or quit. Let's take a look at a few examples:

CHANGE: Perhaps you want to change how you spend your morning because you currently wake up, immediately check your email on your phone, and go straight from your bed to your desk to begin work. Waking up and immediately diving into your potential stressors is no way to live. You are a person before you're a performer; give yourself a beat after you wake up to get your wits about you before you shift into work mode. Perhaps instead of reading emails within thirty seconds of opening your eyes, you'd like to start your day more gently, like by waking up, sitting in the backyard for fifteen minutes with a cup of coffee, getting ready, and then opening your laptop so that you feel like a human when you begin work. Slow things down to help mitigate your stressful mornings.

PAUSE/POSTPONE: You have a passion project you love but no longer have time for. You can *force* it into your schedule, but forcing it sucks all the passion out of it. You once loved this project (for example, volunteering at the local dog shelter, writing a personal blog, running an investment club with friends), but since you've been experiencing burnout, it has brought you more stress than joy; it feels like another chore because you would rather be resting during your downtime. Consider pausing or postponing this project until you can give it your full attention again. Putting something aside doesn't mean that you failed; know that it will still be there when you're ready to return to it with passion instead of guilt.

SIMPLIFY: Looking over your tracker, you see that you haven't gone to your pilates class once in the last three months. You tell yourself that you go a couple of times a week, but the data doesn't lie. What you *actually* do every day is make yourself feel guilty for not going. After considering what you want to prioritize during this season of life, you recognize that your real goal is just to move for a bit each day, and you are more likely to walk on your treadmill while watching TV each night than go to your pilates class. Cancel your membership and commit to walking for thirty minutes daily instead—a whole lot simpler, and a whole lot more achievable.

DELEGATE/OUTSOURCE: If you look at your tracker and find that walking the dog each day consumes an hour of your time that you would really like back, find a service to walk your dog. It's not forever; just to get through this busy season.

QUIT: You spend two hours a week on a committee that you hate being on. The PTA, a committee at work, a church group—regardless of what it is, you know in your heart you do not want to be on it anymore. It's time to put on your big-kid pants and set a boundary by letting them know that at this time you can't continue to hold your position. If it feels too hard to quit outright, let your group members know you need to step away for six months while you get through a busy season, and then after those six months, you can reconsider. You can always return to it when you aren't burned out. But right now, be honest with yourself about the time commitments that could be done differently or not at all.

Step 4: Write down what changes you'd like to make and *how* you can make them. Use this **Change Formula** to make the improvements stick:

1. **Change:** What change in behavior do you want to see in your-self?

2. **Action required:** What exactly do you need to do to make this change happen?

3. **Reinforcement:** How can you reinforce that action so that it requires less effort?

For example, if you said you want to drink more water, the change formula might look like this:

1. *Change:* The change you want to make is to drink more water.

2. *Action required:* To do this you need to remember to fill your water cup and drink your water throughout the day.

3. *Reinforcement:* To reinforce the desired actions you might buy yourself a 32-oz cup and set reminders that pop up on your computer to drink your water and to refill your water midday.

JENGA TIME

Once you've completed the Four Steps to Freedom, begin to implement the other tools and concepts that have resonated with you—the pages you dog-eared, the lines you highlighted. You may already have applied some of the most critical solutions out of sheer survival (which is amazing! The leap from information to action is an intimidating one and I'm proud of you for taking it!). Now you get to edit, evolve, and keep moving further away from burnout territory.

Let's go back to Burnout Jenga. Which of the pieces of burnout management are movable? What could be done differently or better in order to change your experience? What practices might you want to try from mindset, personal care, time management, boundaries, or stress management? In case you need a quick refresher, let's review what you might incorporate from the five pillars:

Mindset: Perhaps you know you would benefit from keeping reminders by your coffee machine or on the home screen of your laptop. These might look like:

- *A job is an exchange of service for money.*
- *I do not need to take myself or my life so seriously that I rob myself of actually living.*
- *My health is more important than my work.*
- *People respect my boundaries because I respect my boundaries.*
- *I have the authority to ask for things in my own life.*
- *I prioritize the things that are important to me.*

If this approach resonates, write these mantras down now. I recommend keeping them somewhere you frequent (the bathroom sink, your fridge, your phone's lock screen); it is easier to tack a change onto an existing habit than start one from scratch (this is called "habit stacking").

Personal Care: Take a look at your personal care pyramid. What nonnegotiables do you need every day? What kinds of maintenance, rest, and refill will boost your quality of life? What kind of predictable rest would provide the relief you require each day? After looking over your current schedule, where could you incorporate predictable rest, nonnegotiables, or maintenance, rest, and refill? Use the change formula to plug in the personal care that would be most impactful for you.

Time Management: Perhaps after reflecting on how you spend your time at work, you note times when energy vampires slow you down. You find yourself distracted by every email and Slack ping, tasks you thought took twenty minutes actually take an hour, and you tell yourself you work from 9:00 A.M. to 5:00 P.M., but it's consistently closer to 8:20 A.M. to 5:40 P.M. Commit to using tools like batching, delegating, and accountability to tighten the reins on your time management. Maybe you resolve to check Slack messages at the top of every hour instead of as soon as they come, you start time blocking so that tasks are realistically represented in your day, and you resolve to contain your workday to 9:00 A.M. to 5:00 P.M. for the next week to see how it goes.

Boundaries: What boundaries might help reinforce the changes you want to make? Do you need to express your availability to your colleague who continuously IMs you? If you want to start leaving the office at 5 P.M., maybe you need to tell your team and add your business hours to your email signature so that people know when to expect responses from you. To get some quiet time at night, announce to your household that you are having "quiet hour" from 8 P.M. to 9 P.M., during which you do not exist to them.

Stress Management: Many of these changes will help lower your stress, but you can also look at your daily outlines and see if there are predictable times of high stress. If you know that every Monday you're too overwhelmed to make dinner, make Monday pizza night and just bake or order your favorite pizza every Monday. Don't even think twice about it; just make that day easier for yourself. If you get calls from family members on weeknights that monopolize your time, set a clear boundary to reduce this stress by telling them you'd prefer to chat on weekends. If you notice that after meetings with Mike you can't get anything done for an hour because you're so stressed, try taking a short walk to a coffee shop down the street right afterward so you can leave the scene of the crime, get some fresh air, and remind yourself not to let Mike determine whether you have a good day or not.

Odds are you're going to have to try things more than once to get them to stick—and that's okay! You can even recruit someone you look up to or who you believe has strong work-life balance, show them your daily outlines, and solicit their opinion on how you can make improvements.

You are redesigning your relationships with your work and your life. You are reestablishing your priorities and what people can expect from you, and that's hard. When I made these changes in my own life, I spent a lot of time feeling bad for letting people down or letting opportunities go. But you only get one life, and it's not outrageous to want it to be pleasant.

Balance will always be a dance. Forward and backward, side to side, you will move based on your changing circumstances. It's not about having the perfect choreography. Instead, focus on learning a couple of different moves and getting comfortable enough with them that when the music changes, you can confidently shift along with it.

WHERE THE READING MEETS THE ROAD

Even when you master your mindset, personal care, time management, boundaries, and stress, burnout can still sneak up on you. Recently, I took on four large projects in addition to planning my wedding. Until a few years ago, this level of commitment and pressure would have resulted in me rocking back and forth on the floor of my shower. As it was, my schedule was uncomfortably packed and I was considering abandoning my wedding and eloping. Fortunately, I was able to continuously remind myself that this was a temporary busy season and I had survived every busy season before. I incorporated personal care that kept me sane—my slow morning routine, leaving the house at least once a day, reading before bed, eating off paper plates (because sometimes the sight of a sink full of dishes at the end of a grueling day can actually make you want to kill someone). I managed my time skillfully, getting the most important things done and being comfortable not prioritizing nonessential work items for this season. I dusted off my busy-season boundaries and reinforced antisocial weekends, rejected social calls during the workday, and relied on scripts for turning down opportunities that cropped up. I managed any impending stress with patience and heightened awareness around my stress tells, so I knew when to take a step back and get my wits about me. Using these five pillars, I have experienced firsthand that we can find freedom and balance even when we feel backed against a wall. **Burnout isn't a death sentence; it's a tap on the shoulder (okay, more like a shove) to pay attention to your life because something needs to change.**

Don't let this information die on the page. Keep tools from this book handy; put sticky notes in these pages; share what you've learned with your colleagues and friends so that they can help hold you accountable—there are myriad ways to keep these concepts alive and help them evolve with you.

Burnout management is not just done in crowded offices; it's done in the privacy of your home and your thoughts. Nobody can reach into your life and change it for you—this is up to you. You are only a couple of shifts away from a very different experience. This is the *only* life you get to live; it's worth making tough changes to feel like you actually get to *live* it. You can do this; I know you can. Wherever you are, I'm cheering for you.

ACKNOWLEDGMENTS

This book wouldn't exist without the help of some serious kismet and a lot of talented people.

To Noa Shapiro, my editor. You are not just an editor, you're an *EDITOR.* Every single sentence in this book is better because of you. Thank you for having undying faith in this book through all its evolutions. It would not be what it is without you.

To Katherine Hardigan, my agent, confidant, and champion. Thank you for being my go-to person as I experience a million "firsts" throughout this process. I needed no time at all after our initial meeting to know that we could do incredible things together, and that continues to be true today.

To Tula Karras, for lending me your guidance and talent as these chapters came together. Thank you for your willingness to go back and forth and back and forth and back and forth to make sure this book was as good as possible. It was an absolute joy working with you.

This book couldn't have come to life without the efforts of the Dial Press team: Andy Ward, Avideh Bashirrad, Raaga Rajogopala, Whitney Frick, Debbie Aroff, Michelle Jasmine, Vanessa Dejesus, Corina Diez, Benjamin Dreyer, Rebecca Berlant, Ted Allen, and David Goehring. You have done more than I know in order to get this book to the finish line, and I am sincerely grateful to each of you.

To Erin Thomas, Lisa Huebner, and Hilary Tindle, thank you for your time and expertise. This book is strengthened by what you have lent it and I appreciate your kindness and contribution.

Elana Seplow-Jolley, I must thank you for plucking me out of the ether. Before I even had a large social media following, you saw enough potential in my work to insist that I put my proposal together. Thank you for setting these plans into motion.

To my parents, there is no thank-you large enough for all you've done for me. I am who I am and where I am because of the support and love you've poured into me from the moment I was born. I have you to thank for the best parts of me.

To my younger sister, my "influencing" career didn't begin on social media, it began the day you were born. You are the most meaningful person I will ever influence and you have no idea how much you've influenced me in return.

To Navarre, my husband, my loudest cheerleader and warmest hug, who never once, not even when I was down to my last thousand dollars, made me feel like I needed to give up on my business and "go get a real job." Knowing without a doubt that you would catch me if I fell gave me the confidence to take the risks that have gotten me here today. I am better with you by my side. Thank you for loving me so well.

Finally, to my clients and every single member of my audience who has taken the time to connect with me, I couldn't do this without you. I would just be another person with an opinion had you not given me the opportunity to share with you, work with you, and learn from you. Your stories and support made this book worth writing, so thank you. Thank you, thank you, thank you. I appreciate you more than you'll ever know.

NOTES

INTRODUCTION: THE BREAKDOWN BEFORE THE BREAKTHROUGH

xvi One of the many adverse effects "State of the Global Workplace: 2021 Report," Gallup, 2021, https://bendchamber.org/wp-content/uploads/2021/12/state-of-the -global-workplace-2021-download.pdf.

xvi In 2021 and 2022 it spiked even higher "State of the Global Workplace: 2021 Report"; "State of the Global Workplace: 2023 Report," Gallup, 2023, https://www .gallup.com/workplace/349484/state-of-the-global-workplace.aspx.

xvi With 44 percent of workers reporting "State of the Global Workplace: 2021 Report"; "State of the Global Workplace: 2023 Report."

xvii The World Health Organization reported "Covid-19 Pandemic Triggers 25% Increase in Prevalence of Anxiety and Depression Worldwide," World Health Organization, March 2, 2022, https://www.who.int/news/item/02-03-2022-covid-19 -pandemic-triggers-25-increase-in-prevalence-of-anxiety-and-depression-worldwide.

xvii nearly two-thirds of professionals reported Kristy Threlkeld, "Employee Burnout Report: COVID-19's Impact and 3 Strategies to Curb It," Indeed.com, March 11, 2021, https://uk.indeed.com/lead/preventing-employee-burnout-report.

xvii The definitions of burnout 11th Revision of the International Classification of Diseases (ICD-11), World Health Organization, https://www.who.int/news /item/11-02-2022-icd-11-2022-release#:~:text=The%20International%20Classifi cation%20of%20Diseases,and%20is%20now%20entirely%20digital.

xviii Burnout has been linked to many health conditions Denise Albieri et al., "Physical, Psychological and Occupational Consequences of Job Burnout: A Systematic Review of Prospective Studies," *PLoS One* 12, no. 10 (October 4, 2017): e0185781, https://www.ncbi.nlm.nih.gov/pmc/articles/PMC5627926/.

xviii unhealthy changes in the brain Armita Golkar et al., "The Influence of Work-Related Chronic Stress on the Regulation of Emotion and on Functional Connectivity in the Brain," *PloS One* 9, no. 9 (September 3, 2014): e104550, https:// journals.plos.org/plosone/article?id=10.1371/journal.pone.0104550.

xviii burnout puts the body and mind under constant stress Tarani Chandola et al., "Work Stress and Coronary Heart Disease: What Are the Mechanisms?" *European*

Heart Journal 29, no. 5 (January 2008): 640–648, https://academic.oup.com /eurheartj/article/29/5/640/438125.

xviii **such as cortisol** "Cortisol," Cleveland Clinic, December 2021, https://my .clevelandclinic.org/health/articles/22187-cortisol.

xix **maintaining work-life balance results in higher productivity** Michiel Kompier and Cary Cooper, eds., *Preventing Stress, Improving Productivity: European Case Studies in the Workplace* (London: Routledge, 1999).

xix **worker satisfaction** N. Thevanes and T. Mangaleswaran, "Relationship Between Work-Life Balance and Job Performance of Employees," *IOSR Journal of Business and Management* 20, no. 5 (May 2018): 11–16, https://www.iosrjournals.org /iosr-jbm/papers/Vol20-issue5/Version-1/C2005011116.pdf.

xix **healthy relationships have a positive impact** David G. Myers, "Close Relationships and Quality of Life," in *Well-Being: Foundations of Hedonic Psychology,* ed. Daniel Kahneman, Ed Diener, and Norbert Schwarz (New York: Russell Sage Foundation, 2003), 374–391.

xix **found to alleviate burnout and increase** Andrea N. Leep Hunderfund et al., "Social Support, Social Isolation, and Burnout: Cross-Sectional Study of U.S. Residents Exploring Associations with Individual, Interpersonal, Program, and Work-Related Factors," *Academic Medicine* 97, no. 8 (July 2022): 1184–1194, https://pubmed .ncbi.nlm.nih.gov/35442910/.

xix **those struggling with exhaustion** Emma Seppälä and Marissa King, "Burnout at Work Isn't Just About Exhaustion. It's Also About Loneliness," *Harvard Business Review,* June 29, 2017, https://hbr.org/2017/06/burnout-at-work-isnt-just-about -exhaustion-its-also-about-loneliness.

CHAPTER 1: IDENTIFYING BURNOUT IN A WORLD ON FIRE

5 **a little stress is good for us** Wendy Suzuki, *Good Anxiety* (New York: Atria, 2021), 14.

5 **when we must endure it for too long** Marie-France Marin et al., "Chronic Stress, Cognitive Functioning and Mental Health," *Neurobiology of Learning and Memory* 96, no. 4 (November 2011): 583–595, https://pubmed.ncbi.nlm.nih.gov /21376129/.

6 **more of us than ever are reporting high amounts** "State of the Global Workplace: 2021 Report," Gallup, 2022, https://bendchamber.org/wp-content /uploads/2021/12/state-of-the-global-workplace-2021-download.pdf; Ashley Abramson, "Burnout and Stress Are Everywhere," *Monitor on Psychology* 53, no. 1 (January 1 2022): 72, https://www.apa.org/monitor/2022/01/special-burnout -stress; Kristy Threlkeld, "Employee Burnout Report: COVID-19's Impact and 3 Strategies to Curb It," Indeed.com, March 11, 2021, https://uk.indeed.com/lead /preventing-employee-burnout-report.

6 **Increased, prolonged stress means an increase in burnout** "Anatomy of Work, Global Index 2022," Asana, 2022, https://www.gend.co/hubfs/Anatomy%20of%20 Work%20Global%20Report.pdf.

6 **the Great Resignation** Juliana Kaplan, "The Psychologist Who Coined the Phrase 'Great Resignation' Reveals How He Saw It Coming and Where He Sees It Going,"

Insider, October 2, 2021, https://www.businessinsider.com/why-everyone-is -quitting-great-resignation-psychologist-pandemic-rethink-life-2021-10.

6 **the Great Reshuffling** Paul Krugman, "What Ever Happened to the Great Resigna- tion?" *The New York Times,* April 5, 2022, https://www.nytimes.com/2022/04/05 /opinion/great-resignation-employment.html.

6 **hitting a twenty-year high** "Number of Quits at All-Time High in November 2021," U.S. Bureau of Labor Statistics, The Economics Daily, January 6, 2022, https://www.bls.gov/opub/ted/2022/number-of-quits-at-all-time-high-in -november-2021.htm#:~:text=The%20number%20of%20quits%20 increased,first%20produced%20in%20December%202000.

6 **The main reasons workers left their jobs** Kim Parker and Juliana Menasce Horo- witz, "Majority of Workers Who Quit a Job in 2021 Cite Low Pay, No Opportuni- ties for Advancement, Feeling Disrespected," Pew Research Center, March 9, 2022, https://www.pewresearch.org/short-reads/2022/03/09/majority-of-workers-who -quit-a-job-in-2021-cite-low-pay-no-opportunities-for-advancement-feeling -disrespected/#:~:text=Majorities%20of%20workers%20who%20quit,major%20 reasons%20why%20they%20left.

7 **The quiet quitting trend** Matt Pearce, "Gen Z Didn't Coin 'Quiet Quitting'— Gen X Did," *Los Angeles Times,* August 27, 2022, https://www.latimes.com /entertainment-arts/story/2022-08-27/la-ent-quiet-quitting-origins.

8 **Some folks misdiagnose their burnout as anxiety** "Anxiety Disorders," National Institute of Mental Health, April 2023, https://www.nimh.nih.gov/health/topics /anxiety-disorders.

8 **or depression** "Depression," National Institute of Mental Health, April 2023, https://www.nimh.nih.gov/health/topics/depression.

9 **burnout is largely circumstantial** Arnold Bakker et al., "Using Equity Theory to Examine the Difference Between Burnout and Depression," *Anxiety, Stress & Coping* 13, no. 3 (April 2008): 247–268, https://www.tandfonline.com/doi/abs/10.1080 /10615800008549265.

9 **Experiences you might have as a result of burnout** Christina Maslach and Mi- chael P. Leiter, "Understanding the Burnout Experience: Recent Research and Its Implications for Psychiatry," *World Psychiatry* 15, no. 2 (June 2016): 103–111, https://www.ncbi.nlm.nih.gov/pmc/articles/PMC4911781/; Christina Maslach and Susan E. Jackson, "The Measurement of Experienced Burnout," *Journal of Organi- zational Behavior* 2, no. 2 (April 1982): 99–113, https://onlinelibrary.wiley .com/doi/10.1002/job.4030020205.

9 **Loss of motivation** Matararoria P. Lyndon et al., "Burnout, Quality of Life, Motiva- tion, and Academic Achievement Among Medical Students," *Perspectives on Medical Education* 6, no. 2 (April 2017): 108–114, https://www.ncbi.nlm.nih.gov/pmc /articles/PMC5383573/.

9 **Impaired concentration and attention** Hanna M. Gavelin et al., "Cognitive Func- tion in Clinical Burnout: A Systematic Review and Analysis," *Work and Stress* 36, no. 1 (December 2021): 86–104, https://www.tandfonline.com/doi/full/10.1080 /02678373.2021.2002972.

9 **Feeling ineffective** Taru Feldt et al., "The 9-Item Bergen Burnout Inventory: Facto- rial Validity Across Organizations and Measurements of Longitudinal Data," *Indus-*

trial Health 52, no. 2 (March 2014): 102–112, https://www.ncbi.nlm.nih.gov/pmc /articles/PMC4202758/.

9 Physical exhaustion Serge Brand et al., "Associations Between Satisfaction with Life, Burnout-Related Emotional and Physical Exhaustion, and Sleep Complaints," *The World Journal of Biological Psychiatry* 11, no. 5 (March 2010): 744–754, https://www .researchgate.net/publication/42439860_Associations_between_satisfaction_with _life_burnout-related_emotional_and_physical_exhaustion_and_sleep_complaints.

9 Insomnia Brand, "Associations Between Satisfaction with Life."

9 Forgetfulness Gavelin, "Cognitive Function in Clinical Burnout."

9 Escapism Michael P. Leiter, "Coping Patterns as Predictors of Burnout: The Function of Control and Escapist Coping Patterns," *Journal of Organizational Behavior* 12, no. 2 (March 1991): 123–144, https://onlinelibrary.wiley.com/doi/abs/10.1002 /job.4030120205.

10 Procrastination Murat Balkis, "The Relationship Between Academic Procrastination and Students' Burnout," *Hacettepe University Journal of Education* 28, no. 1 (August 2013): 68–78, https://www.researchgate.net/publication/256627310 _THE_RELATIONSHIP_BETWEEN_ACADEMIC_PROCRASTINATION _AND_STUDENTS'_BURNOUT.

10 Change in food/drug/alcohol use Michael R. Oreskovich et al., "Prevalence of Alcohol Use Disorders Among American Surgeons," *JAMA Surgery* 147, no. 2 (February 2012): 168–174, https://pubmed.ncbi.nlm.nih.gov/22351913/.

10 Persistent physical pain Galit Armon et al., "Elevated Burnout Predicts the Onset of Musculoskeletal Pain Among Apparently Healthy Employees," *Journal of Occupational Health Psychology* 15, no. 4 (October 2010): 399–408, https://pubmed.ncbi .nlm.nih.gov/21058854/.

11 Compulsive shopping Thomas J. Moore, Joseph Glenmullen, and Donald R. Mattison, "Reports of Pathological Gambling, Hypersexuality, and Compuslive Shopping Associated with Dopamine Receptor Agonist Drugs," *JAMA Internal Medicine* 174, no. 12 (October 2013): 1930–1933, https://jamanetwork.com/journals /jamainternalmedicine/fullarticle/1916909.

CHAPTER 2: THE THREE TYPES OF BURNOUT

21 In 1930, economist John Maynard Keynes John Maynard Keynes, "Economic Possibilities for Our Grandchildren," in *Essays in Persuasion* (New York: W.W. Norton, 1963).

21 A 2018 Pew Research Center survey Patrick Van Kessel, "How Americans Feel About the Satisfactions and Stresses of Modern Life," Pew Research Center, February 2020, https://www.pewresearch.org/short-reads/2020/02/05/how-americans-feel -about-the-satisfactions-and-stresses-of-modern-life/.

25 mental fatigue can set in Sointu Leikas, "Sociable Behavior Is Related to Later Fatigue: Moment-to-Moment Patterns of Behavior and Tiredness," *Heliyon* 6, no. 5 (May 2020): e04033, https://pubmed.ncbi.nlm.nih.gov/32490243/.

29 In a recent study from Finland Markus A Penttinen et al., "The Associations Between Healthy Diet and Burnout Symptoms Among Finnish Municipal Employees," *Nutrients* 13, no. 7 (July 2021): 2393, https://www.ncbi.nlm.nih.gov/pmc /articles/PMC8308766/.

29 people who show signs of burnout Jennifer R. Brubaker and Elizabeth A. Beverly, "Burnout, Perceived Stress, Sleep Quality, and Smartphone Use: A Survey of Osteo- pathic Medical Students," *The Journal of the American Osteopathic Association* 120, no. 1 (January 2020): 6–17, https://pubmed.ncbi.nlm.nih.gov/31904778/.

29 Maslow's hierarchy of needs Douglas T. Kenrick et al., "Renovating the Pyramid of Needs: Contemporary Extensions Built upon Ancient Foundations," *Perspectives on Psychological Science* 5, no. 3 (August 2011): 292–314, https://www.ncbi.nlm .nih.gov/pmc/articles/PMC3161123/.

30 scientists have studied FOMO Mayank Gupta and Aditya Sharma, "Fear of Miss- ing Out: A Brief Overview of Origin, Theoretical Underpinnings and Relationship with Mental Health," *World Journal of Clinical Cases* 9, no. 19 (July 2021): 4881– 4889, https://www.ncbi.nlm.nih.gov/pmc/articles/PMC8283615/.

30 You may also feel ostracized Kipling D. Williams, "Ostracism," *Annual Review of Psychology* 58 (January 2007): 425–452, https://www.annualreviews.org/doi /abs/10.1146/annurev.psych.58.110405.085641.

30 feelings of rejection arise Williams, "Ostracism."

33 Inspirational speaker Iyanla Vanzant Iyanla Vanzant (@iyanlavanzant), "When the time comes for you to make a change or to grow, the universe will make you so uncomfortable you will eventually have no choice," Twitter, August 21, 2013, 7:00 a.m., https://twitter.com/IyanlaVanzant/status/370153411678715905.

33 Our brains need novelty Leyla Bagheri and Marina Milyavskaya, "Novelty-Variety as a Candidate Basic Psychological Need: New Evidence Across Three Studies," *Mo- tivation and Emotion* 44 (October 2018): 32–53, https://link.springer.com/article /10.1007/s11031-019-09807-4.

33 In a 2015 study from Johns Hopkins Aimee E. Stahl and Lisa Feigenson, "Observ- ing the Unexpected Enhances Infants' Learning and Exploration," *Science* 348, no. 6230 (April 2015): 91–94, https://www.science.org/doi/10.1126/science .aaa3799?url_ver=Z39.88-2003&rfr_id=ori:rid:crossref.org&rfr_dat=cr_pub%20 %200pubmed.

33 A part of our brain called the hippocampus Daniela Fenker and Harmut Schütze, "Learning by Surprise," *Scientific American*, December 17, 2008, https://www .scientificamerican.com/article/learning-by-surprise/.

34 repetition leads to lower levels of task engagement Natália Lelis-Torres et al., "Task Engagement and Mental Workload Involved in Variation and Repetition of a Motor Skill," *Scientific Reports* 7 (May 11, 2021): 14764, https://www.nature.com /articles/s41598-017-15343-3.

34 This is one of the reasons burnout Sylvie Droit-Volet et al., "Time and Covid-19 Stress in the Lockdown Situation. Time-Free, Dying of Boredom and Sadness," *PLoS One* 15, no. 8 (August 2020): 0236465, https://journals.plos.org/plosone /article?id=10.1371/journal.pone.0236465.

35 Boredom in short bursts James Danckert et al., "Boredom: What Is It Good For?" in *The Function of Emotions*, ed. Heather C. Lench (Cham, Switzerland: Springer, 2018), 93–119, https://link.springer.com/chapter/10.1007/978-3-319-77619-4_6.

36 busy people are more motivated Keith Wilcox et al., "How Being Busy Can Increase Motivation and Reduce Task Completion Time," *Journal of Personality and Social Psychology* 110, no. 3 (March 2016): 371–384, https://pubmed.ncbi.nlm.nih .gov/26963764/.

36 Positive challenge is a balanced combination Betsy Ng, "The Neuroscience of Growth Mindset and Intrinsic Motivation," *Brain Sciences* 8, no. 2 (January 2018): 20, https://www.ncbi.nlm.nih.gov/pmc/articles/PMC5836039/.

36 In their book *First, Break All the Rules* Marcus Buckingham and Curt Coffman, *First, Break All the Rules: What the World's Greatest Managers Do Differently* (New York: Simon and Schuster, 1999).

CHAPTER 3: MINDSET

44 our brain's neuroplasticity Richard J. Davidson and Bruce S. McEwen, "Social Influences on Neuroplasticity: Stress and Interventions to Promote Well-Being," *Nature Neuroscience* 15, no. 5 (April 2012): 689–695, https://www.ncbi.nlm.nih .gov/pmc/articles/PMC3491815/.

44 hardwiring your brain for happiness Rick Hanson, *Hardwiring Happiness: The New Brain Science of Contentment, Calm, and Confidence* (New York: Harmony, 2013).

44 optimistic individuals have lower rates of burnout James B. Fowler et al., "The Correlation of Burnout and Optimism Among Medical Residents," *Cureus* 12, no. 2 (February 2020): https://pubmed.ncbi.nlm.nih.gov/32181095/.

44 have lower levels of stress hormones Joelle Jobin, Carsten Wrosch, and Michael F. Scheier, "Associations Between Dispositional Optimism and Diurnal Cortisol in a Community Sample: When Stress Is Perceived as Higher Than Normal," *Health Psychology* 33, no. 4 (April 2014): https://www.ncbi.nlm.nih.gov/pmc/articles /PMC4151978/.

44 better immune functioning Suzanne C. Segerstrom and Sandra E. Sephton, "Optimistic Expectancies and Cell-Mediated Immunity: The Role of Positive Affect," *Psychological Science* 21, no. 3 (March 2010): 448–455, https://pubmed.ncbi.nlm .nih.gov/20424083/.

44 reduced threats of diabetes Sara Puig-Perez et al., "Optimism Moderates Psychophysiological Responses to Stress in Older People with Type 2 Diabetes," *Psychophysiology* 54, no. 4 (December 2016): 536–543, https://onlinelibrary.wiley.com /doi/10.1111/psyp.12806.

44 and stroke Hilary Tindle, *Up: How Positive Outlook Can Transform our Health and Aging* (New York: Avery, 2013), 6–10.

45 one-quarter to one-half of our outlook is genetic Thomas J. Bouchard, Jr., "Genes, Environment and Personality," *Science* 264, no. 5166 (June 1994): 1700–1701, https://www.science.org/doi/10.1126/science.8209250.

46 Research by Sian Leah Beilock Gerardo Ramirez et al., "Math Anxiety, Working Memory, and Math Achievement in Early Elementary School," *Journal of Cognition and Development* 14, no. 2 (May 2013): 187–202, https://psycnet.apa.org /record/2013-16742-002; Andrew Mattarella-Micke et al., "Choke or Thrive? The

Relation Between Salivary Cortisol and Math Performance Depends on Individual Differences in Working Memory and Math Anxiety," *Emotion* 11, no. 4 (August 2011): 1000—1005, https://pubmed.ncbi.nlm.nih.gov/21707166/.

46 **kinder self-talk** Christina N. Armenta, Megan M. Fritz, and Sonja Lyubomirsky, "Functions of Positive Emotions: Gratitude as a Motivator of Self Improvement and Positive Change," *Emotion Review* 9, no. 3 (July 2016), https://journals.sagepub .com/doi/10.1177/1754073916669596.

47 **High achievers tend to be system- and planning-oriented** "Characteristics of High and Low Achievers," Perspectives and Resources, Iris Center, Peabody College Vanderbilt University, https://iris.peabody.vanderbilt.edu/module/ss1/cresource /q1/p01/.

47 **can find team-based, collaborative learning challenging** Hye-Jung Lee, Hyekyung Kim, and Hyunjung Byun, "Are High Achievers Successful in Collaborative Learning? An Explorative Study of College Students' Learning Approaches in Team Project-Based Learning," *Innovations in Education and Teaching International* 54, no. 5 (November 2015): 418–427, https://eric.ed.gov/?id=EJ1157285.

49 **We exhibit this cooperative behavior** Daniel B. M. Haun, Yvonne Rekers, and Michael Tomasello, "Children Conform to the Behavior of Peers; Other Great Apes Stick with What They Know," *Psychological Science* 25, no. 12 (October 2014), https://journals.sagepub.com/doi/10.1177/0956797614553235.

50 **Glennon Doyle writes** Glennon Doyle, *Untamed* (New York: Random House, 2020), 173.

52 **view external factors as barriers** Scott Barry Kaufman, "Unraveling the Mindset of Victimhood," *Scientific American,* June 29, 2020, https://www.scientificamerican .com/article/unraveling-the-mindset-of-victimhood/.

54 **might make a person feel safe** Kaufman, "Unraveling the Mindset of Victimhood."

57 **has a powerful impact on an organization's outcomes** Ralph H. Kilmann, Mary J. Saxton, and Roy Serpa, "Issues in Understanding and Changing Culture," *California Management Review* 28, no. 2 (Winter 1986): 87–94, https://kilmanndiagnostics .com/wp-content/uploads/2018/04/Kilmann_Issues-Culture.pdf.

57 **"culture" often meant** Áine Cain, "The Progression of Office Culture from the 50s to Today," Insider.com, October 2018, https://www.businessinsider.com/office -culture-then-and-now-2018-5.

58 **Portugal passed a labor law** "Portugal: A New Law on Remote Work Prohibits Contact with Employees After Working Hours," *Industrial Relations and Labour Law Newsletter*, International Organisation of Employers, December 2021, https:// industrialrelationsnews.ioe-emp.org/industrial-relations-and-labour-law-december -2021/news/article/portugal-a-new-law-on-remote-work-prohibits-contact-with -employees-after-working-hours.

58 **In Britain** "Statutory Maternity Pay and Leave: Employer Guide," www.gov.uk /employers-maternity-pay-leave.

58 **Australians are entitled to** "Annual Leave," Australian Government, Fair Work Ombudsman, https://www.fairwork.gov.au/leave/annual-leave.

58 **no mandated paid leave for new mothers** "Family and Medical Leave (FMLA)," U.S. Department of Labor, https://www.dol.gov/general/topic/benefits-leave/fmla.

58 **no mandatory paid time off** "Vacation Leave," U.S. Department of Labor, https://www.dol.gov/general/topic/workhours/vacation_leave.

58 **no protection for employees** "Employee Overtime: Hours, Pay and Who Is Covered," OSHA Education Center, https://www.oshaeducationcenter.com/articles/employee-overtime/.

60 **we adapt to an initial set of conditions** J. Bruce Overmier and Martin E. Seligman, "Effects of Inescapable Shock upon Subsequent Escape and Avoidance Responding," *Journal of Comparative and Physiological Psychology* 63, no. 1 (1967): 28–33, https://psycnet.apa.org/record/1967-04314-001.

60 **adverse feelings and memories remain** K. N. Ochsner, "Are Affective Events Richly Recollected or Simply Familiar? The Experience and Process of Recognizing Feelings Past," *Journal of Experimental Psychology: General* 129, no. 2 (June 2000): 242–261, https://pubmed.ncbi.nlm.nih.gov/10868336/; L. Cahill and J. L. McGaugh, "A Novel Demonstration of Enhanced Memory Associated with Emotional Arousal," *Consciousness and Cognition* 4, no. 4 (December 1995): 410–421, https://pubmed.ncbi.nlm.nih.gov/8750416/.

68 **busy all the time is a form of** Silvia Bellezza, Neeru Paharia, and Anat Keinan, "Conspicuous Consumption of Time: When Busyness and Lack of Leisure Time Become a Status Symbol," *Journal of Consumer Research* 44, no. 1 (June 2017): 118–138, https://academic.oup.com/jcr/article-abstract/44/1/118/2736404?redirectedFrom=fulltext.

68 **the more ambitious and competent you seem** Bellezza, "Conspicuous Consumption of Time."

70 **number one contributor to happiness and health** McKinsey & Company Author Talks, interview with Robert Waldinger, author of *The Good Life: Lessons from the World's Longest Scientific Study of Happiness* (New York: Simon and Schuster, 2023), https://www.mckinsey.com/featured-insights/mckinsey-on-books/author-talks-the-worlds-longest-study-of-adult-development-finds-the-key-to-happy-living. See also "Welcome to the Harvard Study of Adult Development," Massachusetts General Hospital and Harvard Medical School, https://www.adultdevelopmentstudy.org/.

70 **shown to boost your happiness quotient** Sarah D. Pressman et al., "Association of Enjoyable Leisure Activities with Psychological and Physical Well-Being," *Psychosomatic Medicine* 71, no. 7 (September 2009): 725–732, https://pubmed.ncbi.nlm.nih.gov/19592515/.

71 **the emotion of amusement** David R. Herring et al., "Coherent with Laughter: Subjective Experience, Behavior, and Physiological Responses During Amusement and Joy," *International Journal of Psychophysiology* 79, no. 2 (October 2010): 211–218, https://www.researchgate.net/publication/47633505_Coherent_with_laughter_Subjective_experience_behavior_and_physiological_responses_during_amusement_and_joy.

71 **tamps down negative feelings** Nicole R. Giuliani, Kateri McRae, and James J. Gross, "The Up- and Down-Regulation of Amusement: Experiential, Behavioral, and Autonomic Consequences," *Emotion* 8, no. 5 (October 2008): 714–719, https://pubmed.ncbi.nlm.nih.gov/18837622/.

71 **our body's natural self-soothing mechanism** Yan Wu et al., "How Do Amusement, Anger and Fear Influence Heart Rate and Heart Rate Variability?" *Frontiers in*

Neuroscience 13 (October 2019), https://www.frontiersin.org/articles/10.3389 /fnins.2019.01131/full.

CHAPTER 4: PERSONAL CARE

74 **shame—the painful feeling** June Price Tangney, Jeff Stuewig, and Debra J. Mashek, "Moral Emotions and Moral Behavior," *Annual Review of Psychology* 58 (April 2011): 345–372, https://www.ncbi.nlm.nih.gov/pmc/articles/PMC3083636/.

74 **Zeigarnik effect** Colin M. MacLeod, "Zeigarnik and von Restorff: The Memory Effects and the Stories Behind Them," *Memory and Cognition* 48 (April 2020): 1073–1088, https://link.springer.com/article/10.3758/s13421-020-01033-5.

74 **guilt can be beneficial** June P. Tangney, Jeffrey Stuewig, and Andres J. Martinez, "Two Faces of Shame: Understanding Shame and Guilt in the Prediction of Jail In-mates' Recidivism," *Psychological Science* 25, no. 3 (March 2014): 799–805, https:// www.ncbi.nlm.nih.gov/pmc/articles/PMC4105017/.

77 **Americans who worked full-time in the workplace** "American Time Use Survey— 2021 Results," U.S. Bureau of Labor Statistics, June 2022, https://www.bls .gov/news.release/pdf/atus.pdf; "American Time Use Survey—2012 Results," U.S. Bureau of Labor Statistics, June 2013, https://www.bls.gov/news.release/archives /atus_06202013.pdf.

77 **fifteen-minute power nap** Charlotte Fritz et al., "Embracing Work Breaks: Recovering from Work Stress," *Organizational Dynamics* 42, no. 4 (October 2013): 274–280, https://www.researchgate.net/publication/259095808_Embracing_work _breaksz_Recovering_from_work_stress.

77 **better at remembering new things** Sara C. Mednick et al., "Comparing the Bene-fits of Caffeine, Naps and Placebo on Verbal, Motor and Perceptual Memory," *Be-havioral Brain Research* 193, no. 1 (November 2008): 70–86, https://pubmed.ncbi .nlm.nih.gov/18554731/.

78 **allowing you to process new experiences** Victoria Jaggard, "Naps Clear Brain's Inbox, Improve Learning, *National Geographic*, February 23, 2010, https://www .nationalgeographic.com/science/article/100222-sleep-naps-brain-memories.

78 **boost memory performance by nearly 43 percent** Sara C. Mednick et al., "Sleep and Rest Facilitate Implicit Memory in a Visual Search Task," *Vision Research* 49, no. 21 (October 2009): 2557–2565, https://www.ncbi.nlm.nih.gov/pmc/articles /PMC2764830/; Graelyn B. Humiston and Erin J. Wamsley, "A Brief Period of Eyes-Closed Rest Enhances Motor Skill Consolidation," *Neurobiology of Learning and Memory* 155 (November 2018): 1–6, https://pubmed.ncbi.nlm.nih.gov/29883710/.

78 **A study in the journal** *Psychosomatic Medicine* Sarah D. Pressman et al., "Asso-ciation of Enjoyable Leisure Activities with Psychological and Physical Well-Being," *Psychosomatic Medicine* 71, no. 7 (September 2009): 725–732, https://pubmed .ncbi.nlm.nih.gov/19592515/.

78 **help prevent prolonged fatigue** Gerhard W. Blasche, Anna Arlinghaus, and Thomas Ernst Dorner, "Leisure Opportunities and Fatigue in Employees: A Large Cross-Sectional Study," *Leisure Sciences* 36, no. 3 (May 2014): 235–250, https:// www.researchgate.net/publication/262582748_Leisure_Opportunities_and _Fatigue_in_Employees_A_Large_Cross-Sectional_Study.

78 **mini-vacations persist for hours** Matthew J. Zawadzki, Joshua M. Smyth, and Heather J. Costigan, "Real-Time Associations Between Engaging in Leisure and Daily Health and Well-Being," *Annals of Behavioral Medicine* 49, no. 4 (February 2015): 605–615, https://academic.oup.com/abm/article/49/4/605/4562699.

79 **even *Forbes* called hustle culture toxic** Julia Ball, "Hustle Culture Can Be Toxic—Here's How to Navigate it Successfully," *Forbes,* March 21, 2022, https://www.forbes.com/sites/forbesbusinesscouncil/2022/03/31/hustle-culture-can-be-toxic-heres-how-to-navigate-it-successfully/?sh=3407c65444e1.

80 **Charles Darwin reported working only** William Waring Johnston, *The Ill Health of Charles Darwin: Its Nature and Its Relation to His Work* (New York: Wiley, 1901), 153.

80 **work was done seasonally, based on demand** James E. Thorold Rogers, *Six Centuries of Work and Wages: The History of English Labor* (Kitchener, Ontario: Batoche Books, 2001).

80 **according to the International Labour Organization** "Statistics on Working Time," International Labour Organization, ILOSTAT, https://ilostat.ilo.org/topics/working-time/.

80 **768 *million* vacation days in the United States went unused** "Study: A Record 768 Million U.S. Vacation Days Went Unused in '18, Opportunity Cost in the Billions," Ipsos/Oxford Economics/ U.S. Travel Association study, 2019, https://www.ustravel.org/press/study-record-768-million-us-vacation-days-went-unused-18-opportunity-cost-billions.

80 **Hispanic women earned just 57 cents** "Census Data Show Historic Investments in Social Safety Net Alleviated Poverty in 2020," Center for American Progress, September 2021, https://www.americanprogress.org/article/census-data-show-historic-investments-social-safety-net-alleviated-poverty-2020/.

81 **Our need to pace ourselves** "Hardwired for Laziness? Tests Show the Human Brain Must Work Hard to Avoid Sloth," *ScienceDaily,* September 2018, https://www.sciencedaily.com/releases/2018/09/180918090849.htm.

84 **"Being prepared isn't half the battle"** Autumn Calabrese (@autumncalabrese), "Being prepared isn't half the battle, it is the battle," Instagram, March 10, 2019, https://www.instagram.com/p/Bu1WTlIAwUK/?hl=en.

86 **"default mode network,"** Michael D. Greicius et al., "Functional Connectivity in the Resting Brain: A Network Analysis of the Default Mode Hypothesis," *Proceedings of the National Academy of Sciences of the United States of America* 100, no. 1 (January 2003): 253–258, https://www.pnas.org/doi/10.1073/pnas.0135058100.

86 **has the ability to calm us** Jennifer E. Stellar et al. "Positive Affect and Markers of Inflammation: Discrete Positive Emotions Predict Lower Levels of Inflammatory Cytokines," *Emotion* 15, no. 2 (April 2015): 129–133, https://pubmed.ncbi.nlm.nih.gov/25603133/.

93 **if we don't meet a specific goal** Jessica Höpfner and Nina Keith, "Goal Missed, Self Hit: Goal-Setting, Goal-Failure, and Their Affective, Motivational and Behavioral Consequences," *Frontiers in Psychology* 12 (September 2021), https://www.frontiersin.org/articles/10.3389/fpsyg.2021.704790/full.

93 **Clarity around action steps** Sarah Gardner and Dave Albee, "Study Focuses on Strategies for Achieving Goals, Resolutions," *Dominican Scholar,* Dominican Uni-

versity of California, press release, 2015, https://scholar.dominican.edu/news-releases/266/.

94 **the more time you spend planning** Peter M. Gollwitzer, Kentaro Fujita, and Gabriele Oettingen, "Planning and the Implementation of Goals," in *Handbook of Self Regulation: Research, Theory, and Applications,* ed. R. F. Baumeister and K. D. Vohs (New York: Guilford Press, 2004), 211–228.

94 **James Clear** James Clear, *Atomic Habits* (New York: Avery, 2018).

97 **can boost your resilience** Kristin Neff, "The Five Myths of Self-Compassion," *Greater Good Magazine,* September 30, 2015, https://greatergood.berkeley.edu/article/item/the_five_myths_of_self_compassion.

97 **activating our tend-and-befriend mode** Shelley E. Taylor et al., "Biobehavioral Responses to Stress in Females: Tend and Befriend, Not Fight-or-Flight," *Psychological Review* 107, no. 3 (July 2000): 411–429, https://pubmed.ncbi.nlm.nih.gov/10941275/.

99 **scientifically proven method to help motivate** Karl M. Kapp, *The Gamification of Learning and Instruction* (San Francisco: Pfeiffer, 2012).

99 **study from the Netherlands on the effectiveness of reminders** Corine Horsch et al., "Reminders Make People Adhere Better to a Self-Help Sleep Intervention," *Health and Technology* 7, no. 2 (December 2016): 173–188, https://www.ncbi.nlm.nih.gov/pmc/articles/PMC5686282/.

CHAPTER 5: TIME MANAGEMENT

111 **The Eisenhower Matrix** Stephen Covey, *The 7 Habits of Highly Effective People* (New York: Free Press, 1989).

113 **Benjamin Franklin** Chris Good, "Picture of the Day: Benjamin Franklin's Daily Schedule," *The Atlantic,* April 20, 2011, https://www.theatlantic.com/politics/archive/2011/04/picture-of-the-day-benjamin-franklins-daily-schedule/237615/.

115 **neuroscience has actually mapped** Dimitri van der Linden, Mattie Tops, and Arnold B. Bakker, "The Neuroscience of the Flow State: Involvement of the Locus Coeruleus Norepinephrine System," *Frontiers in Psychology* 12 (April 2021), https://www.frontiersin.org/articles/10.3389/fpsyg.2021.645498/full.

115 **study on the cost of interruptions** Gloria Mark, Daniela Gudith, and Ulrich Klocke, "The Cost of Interrupted Work: More Speed and Stress," *Proceedings of the 2008 Conference on Human Factors in Computing Systems* (April 2008): 107–110, https://www.researchgate.net/publication/221518077_The_cost_of_interrupted_work_More_speed_and_stress.

115 **less efficient and affect our working memory** Wesley C. Clapp, Michael T. Rubins, and Adam Gazzaley, "Mechanisms of Working Memory Disruption by External Interference," *Cerebral Cortex* 20, no. 4 (July 2009): 859–872, https://pubmed.ncbi.nlm.nih.gov/19648173/.

115 **Task switching and multitasking** "Multitasking: Switching Costs," American Psychological Association, March 2006, https://www.apa.org/topics/research/multitasking.

120 **thinning in the prefrontal cortex** Armita Golkar et al., "The Influence of Work-

Related Chronic Stress on the Regulation of Emotion and on Functional Connectivity in the Brain," *PloS One* 9, no. 9 (September 2014): e104550, https://journals .plos.org/plosone/article?id=10.1371/journal.pone.0104550; Alexandra Michel, "Burnout and the Brain," *Observer*, January 29, 2016, https://www.psychological science.org/observer/burnout-and-the-brain.

122 **mini-breaks improve focus** Atsunori Ariga and Alejandro Lleras, "Brief and Rare Mental 'Breaks' Keep You Focused: Deactivation and Reactivation of Task Goals Preempt Vigilance Decrements," *Cognition* 118, no. 3 (March 2011): 439–443, https://pubmed.ncbi.nlm.nih.gov/21211793/.

122 **longer breaks benefits your performance afterward** Patricia Albulescu et al., " 'Give Me a Break!' A Systematic Review and Meta-Analysis on the Efficacy of Micro-Breaks for Increasing Well-Being and Performance," *PLoS One* (August 2022), 0272460, https://journals.plos.org/plosone/article?id=10.1371/journal .pone.0272460.

122 **many perfectionists are naturally motivated** Joachim Stoeber, Charlotte R. Davis, and Jessica Townley, "Perfectionism and Workaholism in Employers: The Role of Work," *Personality and Individual Differences* 55, no. 7 (October 2013): 733–738, https://www.sciencedirect.com/science/article/abs/pii/S0191886913002432.

122 **people with "maladaptive perfectionism"** Randall M. Moate et al., "Stress and Burnout Among Counselor Educators: Differences Between Adaptive Perfectionists, Maladaptive Perfectionists, and Nonperfectionists," *Journal of Counseling & Development* 94, no. 2 (March 2016): 161–171, https://www.researchgate.net /publication/297650229_Stress_and_Burnout_Among_Counselor_Educators _Differences_Between_Adaptive_Perfectionists_Maladaptive_Perfectionists_and _Nonperfectionists; Andrew P. Hill and Thomas Curran, "Multidimensional Perfectionism and Burnout: A Meta-Analysis," *Personality and Social Psychology Review* 20, no. 3 (July 2015): 269–288, https://pubmed.ncbi.nlm.nih.gov/26231736/.

123 **procrastination is not uncommon for perfectionists** Fatemeh Jadid, Shahram Mohammadkhani, and Komeil Zahedi Tajrishi, "Perfectionism and Academic Procrastination," *Procedia—Social and Behavioral Sciences* 30 (2011): 534–537, https:// www.sciencedirect.com/science/article/pii/S187704281101929X.

CHAPTER 6: BOUNDARIES

136 **Researchers have linked these types of interruptions** Vânia Sofia Carvalho et al., "Please, Do Not Interrupt Me: Work-Family Balance and Segmentation Behavior as Mediators of Boundary Violations and Teleworkers' Burnout and Flourishing," *Sustainability* 13, no. 13 (June 2021): 7339, https://www.mdpi.com/2071-1050/13 /13/7339.

144 **it can lead to unfounded guilt** June Price Tangney, Jeff Stuewig, and Debra J. Mashek, "Moral Emotions and Moral Behavior," *Annual Review of Psychology* 58 (April 2011): 345–372, https://www.ncbi.nlm.nih.gov/pmc/articles/PMC3083636/.

145 **emotions triggered by rejection and criticism** Mark R. Leary, "Emotional Responses to Interpersonal Rejection," *Dialogues in Clinical Neuroscience* 17, no. 4 (December 2015): 435–441, https://www.ncbi.nlm.nih.gov/pmc/articles/PMC 4734881/.

145 **can trigger a strong emotional response** Leary, "Emotional Responses to Interpersonal Rejection."

146 **light up the same regions in the brain** Kirsten Weir, "The Pain of Social Rejection," *Monitor on Psychology* 43, no. 4 (April 2012): 50, https://www.apa.org/monitor/2012/04/rejection.

146 **but it *is* possible** Ben Knight, "Understanding and Reframing the Fear of Rejection," NeuroscienceNews.com, June 22, 2022, https://neurosciencenews.com/rejection-fear-20892/.

147 **"healthy selfishness"** Scott Barry Kaufman and Emanuel Jauk, "Healthy Selfishness and Pathological Altruism: Measuring Two Paradoxical Forms of Selfishness," *Frontiers in Psychology* 11 (May 2020), https://www.frontiersin.org/articles/10.3389/fpsyg.2020.01006/full.

150 **training are extremely costly for organizations** Lorri Freifeld, ed., "2021 Training Industry Report," *Training* magazine, November 19, 2021, https://trainingmag.com/2021-training-industry-report/.

157 **are perceived as less hostile** Shane L. Rogers, Jill Howieson, and Casey Neame, "I Understand You Feel That Way, But I Feel This Way: The Benefits of I-Language and Communicating Perspective During Conflict," *PeerJ* 6 (May 2018): e4831, https://peerj.com/articles/4831/.

157 **and as problem-solvers** Rachel A. Simmons et al., "Pronouns in Marital Interaction: What Do 'You' and 'I' Say About Marital Health?," *Psychological Science* 16, no. 12 (December 2005): 932–936, https://journals.sagepub.com/doi/10.1111/j.1467-9280.2005.01639.x.

161 **experience microaggressions** "Women in the Workplace Study 2021," McKinsey & Company and LeanIn.Org, September 2021, https://www.mckinsey.com/-/media/mckinsey/featured%20insights/diversity%20and%20inclusion/women%20in%20the%20workplace%202021/women-in-the-workplace-2021.pdf.

161 **16 percent of women** "Women @ Work 2022: A Global Outlook," Deloitte, 2022, https://www2.deloitte.com/content/dam/insights/articles/glob-175228_global-women-%40-work/DI_Global-Women-%40-Work.pdf.

161 **afraid of being seen as "troublemakers"** Kami Rieck, "Women and People of Color Can't Afford to 'Quiet Quit,'" *The Washington Post,* September 6, 2022, https://www.washingtonpost.com/business/women-and-people-of-color-cant-afford-to-quiet-quit/2022/09/05/1707431e-2d28-11ed-bcc6-0874b26ae296_story.html.

161 **more likely to experience burnout than non-minorities** Rieck, "Women and People of Color."

161 **any gender-based discrimination is a risk factor** Linda J. Wang et al., "Gender-Based Discrimination Is Prevalent in the Integrated Vascular Trainee Experience and Serves as a Predictor of Burnout," *Journal of Vascular Surgery* 71, no. 1 (January 2020): 220–227, https://www.jvascsurg.org/article/S0741-5214(19)31029-8/fulltext.

167 **Compassion fatigue is caused** Jeremy Adam Smith, "What Happens When Compassion Hurts?" *Greater Good Magazine,* May 8, 2009, https://greatergood.berkeley.edu/article/item/what_happens_when_compassion_hurts.

167 **like nursing, teaching, and social work** Fiona Cocker and Nerida Joss, "Compas-

sion Fatigue Among Healthcare, Emergency and Community Service Workers: A Systematic Review," *International Journal of Environmental Research and Public Health* 13, no. 6 (June 2016): 618, https://www.ncbi.nlm.nih.gov/pmc/articles /PMC4924075/; Françoise Mathieu, "Running on Empty: Compassion Fatigue in Health Professionals," *Rehab and Community Care Medicine* (Spring 2007), https:// www.semanticscholar.org/paper/Running-on-Empty%3A-Compassion-Fatigue-in -Health-Mathieu-Cameron/dbf9e4f776b1a9544e9eeda93fd8f219b072df01.

167 **more common in people who are experiencing burnout** Cocker and Joss, "Compassion Fatigue Among Healthcare, Emergency and Community Service Workers."

171 **American culture is very individualistic** Abigail Marsh, "Everyone Thinks Americans Are Selfish. They're Wrong," *The New York Times,* May 26, 2021, https://www .nytimes.com/2021/05/26/opinion/individualism-united-states-altruism.html.

171 **needs don't take precedence over the group** Yuriy Gorodnichenko and Gérard Roland, "Understanding the Individualism-Collectivism Cleavage and Its Effects: Lessons from Cultural Psychology," in *Institutions and Comparative Economic Development,* ed. M. Aoki, G. Roland, and Timur Kuran (London: Palgrave Macmillan, 2012), 213–236.

173 **vocal quality and tone** Sue Shellenbarger, "Is This How You Really Talk?" *The Wall Street Journal,* April 23, 2013, https://www.wsj.com/articles/SB100014241278873 23735604578440851083674898.

173 **women who use uptalk** John Baldoni, "Will 'Upspeak' Hurt Your Career?" *Forbes,* July 30, 2015, https://www.forbes.com/sites/johnbaldoni/2015/07/30/will-upspeak -hurt-your-career/?sh=67a2de134edc.

173 **the deeper a man's voice is** William J. Mayew, Christopher A. Parsons, and Mohan Venkatachalam, "Voice Pitch and the Labor Market Success of Male Chief Executive Officers," *Evolution and Human Behavior* 34, no. 4 (July 2013): 243–248, https:// www.sciencedirect.com/science/article/abs/pii/S1090513813000238.

CHAPTER 7: STRESS MANAGEMENT

177 **epinephrine** "Epinephrine (Adrenaline)," Cleveland Clinic, March 2022, https:// my.clevelandclinic.org/health/articles/22611-epinephrine-adrenaline.

177 **glycogen** "Understanding the Stress Response," Harvard Medical School, Harvard Health Publishing, July 2020, https://www.health.harvard.edu/staying-healthy /understanding-the-stress-response.

177 **on alert until the threat has passed** James C. Root, Oliver Tuescher, and Amy Cunningham-Bussel, "Frontolimbic Function and Cortisol Reactivity in Response to Emotional Stimuli," *NeuroReport* 20, no. 4 (March 2009): 429–434, https:// www.researchgate.net/publication/24023395_Frontolimbic_function_and_cortisol _reactivity_in_response_to_emotional_stimuli.

178 **wears our bodies down** Agnese Mariotti, "The Effects of Chronic Stress on Health: New Insights into the Molecular Mechanisms of Brain-Body Communication," *Future Science OA* 1, no. 3 (November 2015): FSO23, https://www.ncbi.nlm.nih.gov /pmc/articles/PMC5137920/.

178 **Physical actions help your body to work** Emily Nagoski and Amelia Nagoski, *Burnout: The Secret to Unlocking the Stress Cycle* (New York: Ballantine, 2019).

185 **interoception—how we sense** Kim Armstrong, "Interoception: How We Understand Our Body's Inner Sensations," *Observer,* September 2019, https://www .psychologicalscience.org/observer/interoception-how-we-understand-our-bodys -inner-sensations; Melissa Barker, Rebecca Brewer, and Jennifer Murphy, "What Is Interoception and Why Is It Important?" *Frontiers for Young Minds,* June 30, 2021, https://kids.frontiersin.org/articles/10.3389/frym.2021.558246.

186 **we override these signals** Lisa Feldman Barrett, *How Emotions Are Made: The Secret Life of the Brain* (New York: Mariner, 2018), 67.

186–87 **A recent Gallup survey** Julie Ray, "World Unhappier, More Stressed Out Than Ever," Gallup News, 2022 Global Emotions Report, June 28, 2022, https://news .gallup.com/poll/394025/world-unhappier-stressed-ever.aspx.

188 **function better with a routine sleep schedule** Tianyi Huange, Sara Mariani, and Susan Redline, "Sleep Irregularity and Risk of Cardiovascular Events: The Multi-Ethnic Study of Atherosclerosis," *Journal of the American College of Cardiology* 75, no. 9 (March 2020): 991–999, https://pubmed.ncbi.nlm.nih.gov/32138974/.

188 **and meals** Emily N. C. Manoogian, Amandine Chaix, and Satchidananda Panda, "When to Eat: The Importance of Eating Patterns in Health and Disease," *Journal of Biological Rhythms* 34, no. 6 (December 2019): 579–581, https://journals .sagepub.com/doi/10.1177/0748730419892105.

188 **nature calms our fear center** Sonja Sudimac, Vera Sale, and Simone Kühn, "How Nature Nurtures: Amygdala Activity Decreases as the Result of a One-Hour Walk in Nature," *Molecular Psychiatry* 27 (September 2022): 4446–4452, https://www .nature.com/articles/s41380-022-01720-6.

191 **changes your brain chemistry** Shuai-Ting Lin et al., "Mental Health Implications of Music: Insight from Neuroscientific and Clinical Studies," *Harvard Review of Psychiatry* 19, no. 1 (January-February 2011): 34–46, https://pubmed.ncbi.nlm .nih.gov/21250895/.

191 **relaxes you** Darcy DeLoach Walworth, "The Effect of Preferred Music Genre Selection Versus Preferred Song Selection on Experimentally Induced Anxiety Levels," *Journal of Music Therapy* 40, no. 1 (Spring 2003): 2–14, https://pubmed.ncbi.nlm .nih.gov/17590964/.

191 **simply writing about how we're feeling** Joshua M. Smyth et al., "Online Positive Affect Journaling in the Improvement of Mental Distress and Well-Being in General Medical Patients with Elevated Anxiety Symptoms: A Preliminary Randomized Controlled Trial," *JMIR Mental Health* 5, no. 4 (October-December 2018): e11290, https://www.ncbi.nlm.nih.gov/pmc/articles/PMC6305886/.

192 **our brains are fixated on predicting things** Lisa Feldman Barrett, "What Do You Consider the Most Interesting Recent [Scientific] News? What Makes It Important?" Edge.Org, 2016, https://www.edge.org/response-detail/26707.

192 **evolution has hardwired us for it** Amrisha Vaish, Tobias Grossmann, and Amanda Woodward, "Not All Emotions Are Created Equal: The Negativity Bias in Social-Emotional Development," *Psychological Bulletin* 134, no. 3 (May 2008): 383–403, https://www.ncbi.nlm.nih.gov/pmc/articles/PMC3652533/.

194 **Rehearsing stress in this way** Da-Yee Jeung, Changsoo Kim, and Sei-Jin Chang, "Emotional Labor and Burnout: A Review of the Literature," *Yonsei Medical Journal* 59, no. 2 (March 2018): 187–193, https://www.ncbi.nlm.nih.gov/pmc/articles /PMC5823819/.

194 **McKinsey's "Women in the Workplace" report** "Women in the Workplace 2022," McKinsey & Company and LeanIn.Org, October 2022, https://www.mckinsey .com/-/media/mckinsey/featured%20insights/diversity%20and%20inclusion /women%20in%20the%20workplace%202022/women-in-the-workplace-2022 .pdf.

194 **"Ever since the industrial revolution"** Huebner Ruchti, Lisa C. Interview. Conducted by Emily Ballesteros and Tula Karras. May 18, 2023.

196 **short-term stressors release dopamine** "Chronic Stress Dampens Dopamine Production," MRC London Institute of Medical Sciences, News, November 12, 2019, https://lms.mrc.ac.uk/chronic-stress-dampens-dopamine-production/; Michael A. P. Bloomfield et al., "The Effects of Psychosocial Stress on Dopaminergic Function and the Acute Stress Response," *eLife* 8 (November 2019): e46797, https://elifesciences .org/articles/46797.

196 **also plays a role in clinical addictions** "The Neurobiology of Substance Use, Misuse, and Addiction," Surgeon General's Report, 2016, https://addiction.surgeongeneral .gov/executive-summary/report/neurobiology-substance-use-misuse-and-addiction; Mark A. Ungless, Emanuela Argilli, and Antonello Bonci, "Effects of Stress and Aversion on Dopamine Neurons: Implications for Addiction," *Neuroscience & Biobehavioral Reviews* 35, no. 2 (November 2010): 151–156, https://pubmed.ncbi.nlm.nih .gov/20438754/.

196 **Over time, chronic stress** Bloomfield, "The Effects of Psychosocial Stress."

197 **Cognitive reframing** James Crum, "Understanding Mental Health and Cognitive Restructuring with Ecological Neuroscience," *Frontiers in Psychiatry* 12 (June 2018), https://www.frontiersin.org/articles/10.3389/fpsyt.2021.697095/full; "Positive Reframing and Examining the Evidence," Harvard University Stress and Development Lab, https://sdlab.fas.harvard.edu/cognitive-reappraisal/positive-reframing-and -examining-evidence.

200 **research shows that a positive outlook** Hilary Tindle, *Up: How Positive Outlook Can Transform Our Health and Aging* (New York: Avery, 2013),197–199, 209–211.

EMILY BALLESTEROS holds a master's degree in industrial-organizational psychology and worked in corporate training and development before launching her burnout management coaching business. In addition to being featured in media such as *The Wall Street Journal, CNBC, Today .com,* and *BuzzFeed,* she regularly provides burnout training for corporations such as PepsiCo, Thermo Fisher, Salesforce, and Nickelodeon, among others.

Instagram: @Emilybruth
TikTok: @Emilybruth

This book was set in Garamond, a typeface originally designed by the Parisian type cutter Claude Garamond (c. 1500–61). This version of Garamond was modeled on a 1592 specimen sheet from the Egenolff-Berner foundry, which was produced from types assumed to have been brought to Frankfurt by the punch cutter Jacques Sabon (c. 1520–80).

Claude Garamond's distinguished romans and italics first appeared in *Opera Ciceronis* in 1543–44. The Garamond types are clear, open, and elegant.